PEARSON BACCALAUREATE

Theory of Knowledge

CHRISTIAN BRYAN • GEOFFREY THOMAS
SERIES EDITOR: CHRISTIAN BRYAN

Supporting every learner across the IB continuum

Pearson Education Limited,
80 Strand, London WC2R 0RL.

www.pearsonglobalschools.com

Text © Pearson Education Limited 2016

Edited by Penelope Lyons
Proofread by Karen Williams and Helen Sutherland
Typeset and project managed by
Ken Vail Graphic Design Limited

The right of Christian Bryan and Geoffrey Thomas to be identified as authors of this work has been asserted by them in accordance with the Copyright, Designs and Patents Act 1988.

First published 2016

19 18 17 16

IMP 10 9 8 7 6 5 4 3 2 1

British Library Cataloguing in Publication Data
A catalogue record for this book is available from the British Library

ISBN 9781447990703
eBook only ISBN 9781447990710

Printed in Slovakia by Neografia

Acknowledgements

The authors and publisher would like to thank Becky Hall, Ruth Ripoll and Ric Sims for their help with and feedback on this title.

We are grateful to the following for permission to reproduce copyright material:

Text, tables and figures

Quote on page 10 from *Memories, Dreams, Reflections*, Collins (Jung, C. G., & Jaffe A 1962) p.256, reprinted by permission of HarperCollins Publishers Ltd and © 1962 , Jung C.G & Jaffe, A; Table and text extract on page 11 reprinted from Reconstruction of Automobile Destruction: An Example of the Interaction Between Language and Memory' *JOURNAL OF VERBAL LEARNING AND VERBAL BEHAVIOR 13, 585-589 13*

(ELIZABETH F. LOFTUS AND JOHN C. PALMER 1974) Copyright 1974, with permission from Elsevier; Quote on page 90 from Winston Churchill The May 1940 War Cabinet Crisis meeting, from the works of Winston S. Churchill reproduced with permission of Curtis Brown, London on behalf of the Estate of Winston S. Churchill Copyright © The Estate of Winston S. Churchill; Text extract on page 122 from The Universal Declaration of Human Rights, © United Nations http://www.un.org/en/documents/udhr/index.shtml. Reprinted with the permission of the United Nations. Figure 11.1 from *Handbook for Culturally Responsive Science Curriculum*, Fairbanks: Alaska Native Knowledge Network (Stephens, S 2000), Alaska Native Knowledge Network with permission.

Text extracts relating to the IB syllabus and assessment have been reproduced from IBO documents. Our thanks go to the International Baccalaureate for permission to reproduce its intellectual copyright. This material has been developed independently by the publisher and the content is no way connected with or endorsed by the International Baccalaureate (IB). International Baccalaureate ® is a registered trademark of the International Baccalaureate Organization.

Photographs (Key: b-bottom; c-centre; l-left; r-right; t-top)

123RF.com: Photo 2.1, 8.1; **Alamy Images:** Photo 8.2 © Heritage Image Partnership Ltd / Alamy stock photo, Photo 10.1 © Universal Images Group Ltd / Alamy stock photo; **Mary Evans Picture Library:** Photo 10.4 INTERFOTO / Sammlung Rauch / Mary Evans; **Pearson Education Ltd:** Photo 10.3 Gareth Dewar; **Shutterstock.com:** Photo 4.1 Maksim Toome, Photo 6.1 ntstudio, Photo 10.2 Lane V. Erickson, Photo 10.5 Stewart Smith Photography. All other images © Pearson Education.

Websites

Pearson Education Limited is not responsible for the content of any external internet sites. It is essential for tutors to preview each website before using it in class so as to ensure that the URL is still accurate, relevant and appropriate. We suggest that tutors bookmark useful websites and consider enabling students to access them through the school/college intranet.

Dedications

Christian Bryan:

Mne hotelos' bi posvetit' etu rabotu moim lyubimim mal'chikam, Fyodoru y Charlie. Ya nadeyus' chto v odin prekrasniy den' vi poymete kak ya vas lyublyu y kak ya gorzhus' bit' vashem otcom.

Geoffrey Thomas:

Catalina emlékének

Contents

eBook System requirements

System requirements supported are listed below:

Windows	Macintosh	iPad	Android
• Windows 7, Windows 8 • Intel® Pentium® II 450 MHz or faster processor (or equivalent) • 128 MB available RAM (256 MB or higher recommended) • 20 MB hard drive space • Supported browsers: IE 9.0, IE 10, IE 11 (Desktop Version), Chrome 25.0 or higher, and Firefox 19.0 or higher	• OS X version 10.6.x, 10.7.x, 10.8.x, 10.9.x • Intel Processor • 256 MB or higher RAM • 20 MB hard drive space • Supported browsers: Safari 5.1, Safari 6, and Firefox 19.0 or higher, Chrome 25 or higher * One-finger and two-finger swipe gestures are not supported	• iPad1, iPad2, iPad3, iPad4 or iPad mini • iOS 5, iOS 6, iOS 7 or higher * One-finger and two-finger swipe gestures are not supported	• Android 7" and 10" tablets • OS v4.0.x (Ice Cream Sandwich), v4.1 (Jelly Bean), v4.4 (Kit Kat) or higher • Accessible via Google Play only

Other requirements:

- Adobe Flash Player 11.2 or higher
- Javascript enabled in your browser to view and use the online Help
- Screen resolution: Minimum 1024 pixels wide x 768 pixels high
- Internet connection: Broadband cable, high-speed DSL, or other equivalent is recommended.

Welcome to your Essentials Guide to Theory of Knowledge (TOK). This book has been designed to solve the key problems of many IB Diploma students. It will:

- make the IB TOK Guide accessible
- relate material to the IB TOK Guide
- show how to write IB TOK essays
- show how to complete IB TOK presentations, and provide examples and potential knowledge questions.

Who should use Essentials Guides?

Essentials Guides serve as highly effective summaries and have been carefully designed with all International Baccalaureate (IB) students in mind.

However, the Guides also deal with the particular interests of IB students whose first language is not English, and who would like further support. As a result, the content in all Essentials Guides has been edited by an EAL (English as an additional language) expert to make sure that:

- the language used is clear and accessible
- key terms are explained
- essential vocabulary is defined and reinforced.

Key features of an Essentials Guide

Reduced content

Essentials Guides are not intended to be comprehensive textbooks – they contain the essential information you need in order to understand and respond to the stimulus questions for the ways of knowing (WOKs), and knowledge framework for the areas of knowledge (AOKs) in the IB TOK Guide. This allows you to understand material quickly and still be confident you are meeting the essential aims of the syllabus. We have reduced the number of words as much as possible to ensure everything you read has a clear meaning, is clearly related to the IB TOK Guide and will help you in your TOK assessments and beyond.

Format and approach

The content of the book is organized according to the stimulus questions for the WOKs and knowledge framework for the AOKs in the IB TOK Guide. Each section is looked at separately so that you can study each one without having read or understood previous sections. This allows you to use the book as a first text, or a review guide, or as a way to help you understand material you have been given from other sources.

Sub-headings

The pages are organized using logical sub-headings to help you understand the most important points of the IB TOK Guide.

Knowledge claims and knowledge questions

Knowledge claim: **Animals are particularly useful in research because researchers do not have the same level of moral obligation towards them as they do towards humans.**

Knowledge question: **To what extent is controversy a useful part of the academic process?**

Both knowledge claims and knowledge questions are clearly formatted to help you understand how they can be stated and addressed. Some knowledge questions are left unanswered – they serve as prompts to stimulate your thinking and can be used in essays and presentations.

Articulation sentences

Articulation sentence:
Language can affect how people experience the world and how they understand these experiences.

Articulation sentences are designed to summarize the main point within a piece of text to help you with understanding. They can be used in essays and presentations to show you understand the key points being discussed.

Vocabulary and synonym boxes

Useful words and phrases are colour coded in the text and given matching colour-coded explanations in the margins. There are three different sets: vocabulary related to the topic under discussion, **synonyms**, and **general vocabulary**.

These are included to help identify and support your understanding of academic and difficult words. In order to make the text more accessible to students whose first language is not English, we have avoided using a highly academic tone. However, at the same time we have ensured that the complexity of the content is at the level required by successful IB Diploma students.

Essay and presentation sections

These chapters are intended to help you design, write, present, and independently mark your own work. They are organized around the key phrases and expectations of the IB markschemes to help you see what is required to achieve the top marks.

eBook and audio

In the accompanying eBook you will find a complete digital version of the book. There are also links to spoken audio files of the vocabulary terms and definitions to help with comprehension and pronunciation. In addition, all the vocabulary lists are located together as downloadable files.

Above all, we hope this book helps you to understand and consolidate your TOK course more easily, helping you to achieve the highest possible results in your essays and presentations.

Christian Bryan and **Geoffrey Thomas**
September 2015, Budapest

How to use your enhanced eBook

Jump to any page

Switch from single- to double-page view

Highlight parts of the text

Search the whole book

Create notes

Zoom

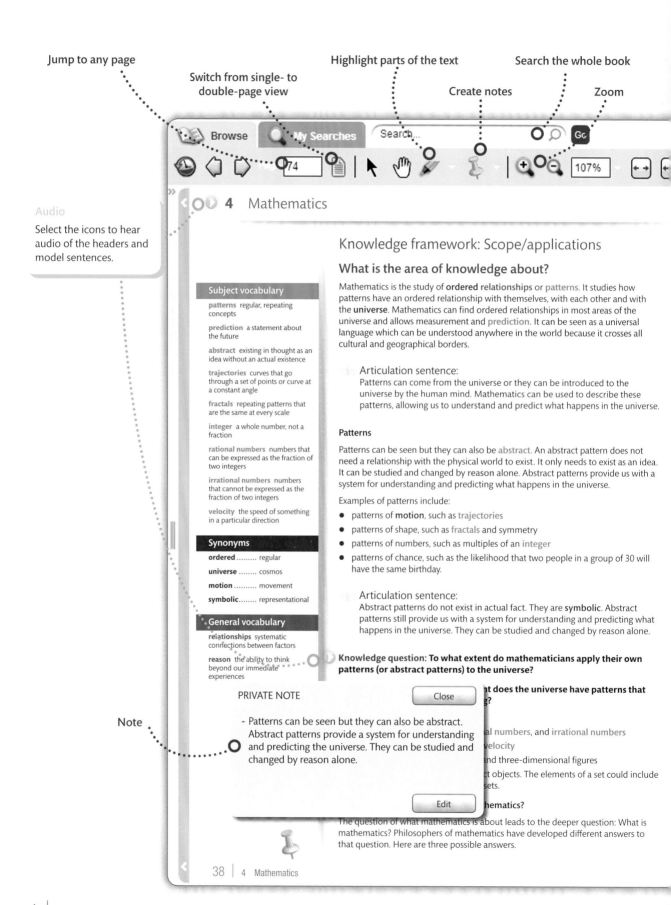

Audio

Select the icons to hear audio of the headers and model sentences.

4 Mathematics

Knowledge framework: Scope/applications

What is the area of knowledge about?

Mathematics is the study of **ordered** relationships or patterns. It studies how patterns have an ordered relationship with themselves, with each other and with the **universe**. Mathematics can find ordered relationships in most areas of the universe and allows measurement and prediction. It can be seen as a universal language which can be understood anywhere in the world because it crosses all cultural and geographical borders.

> Articulation sentence:
> Patterns can come from the universe or they can be introduced to the universe by the human mind. Mathematics can be used to describe these patterns, allowing us to understand and predict what happens in the universe.

Patterns

Patterns can be seen but they can also be abstract. An abstract pattern does not need a relationship with the physical world to exist. It only needs to exist as an idea. It can be studied and changed by **reason** alone. Abstract patterns provide us with a system for understanding and predicting what happens in the universe.

Examples of patterns include:

- patterns of **motion**, such as trajectories
- patterns of shape, such as fractals and symmetry
- patterns of numbers, such as multiples of an integer
- patterns of chance, such as the likelihood that two people in a group of 30 will have the same birthday.

> Articulation sentence:
> Abstract patterns do not exist in actual fact. They are **symbolic**. Abstract patterns still provide us with a system for understanding and predicting what happens in the universe. They can be studied and changed by reason alone.

Knowledge question: To what extent do mathematicians apply their own patterns (or abstract patterns) to the universe?

Subject vocabulary

patterns regular, repeating concepts

prediction a statement about the future

abstract existing in thought as an idea without an actual existence

trajectories curves that go through a set of points or curve at a constant angle

fractals repeating patterns that are the same at every scale

integer a whole number, not a fraction

rational numbers numbers that can be expressed as the fraction of two integers

irrational numbers numbers that cannot be expressed as the fraction of two integers

velocity the speed of something in a particular direction

Synonyms

ordered .... regular

universe .... cosmos

motion .... movement

symbolic........ representational

General vocabulary

relationships systematic connections between factors

reason the ability to think beyond our immediate experiences

Note

PRIVATE NOTE   [Close]

- Patterns can be seen but they can also be abstract. Abstract patterns provide a system for understanding and predicting the universe. They can be studied and changed by reason alone.

[Edit]

...t does the universe have patterns that ...g?

...al numbers, and irrational numbers
...velocity
...nd three-dimensional figures
...ct objects. The elements of a set could include ...sets.

...hematics?

The question of what mathematics is about leads to the deeper question: What is mathematics? Philosophers of mathematics have developed different answers to that question. Here are three possible answers.

See the definitions of key terms in the glossary

Create a bookmark

Switch to whiteboard view

Formalism

Formalism is the idea that mathematics is a game with rules that humans invented. If maths is like a game, then it must have rules. Formalism says that all axioms are true because of convention and that all mathematics is a kind of game. Formalism suggests that mathematicians introduce their ideas to the universe.

Formalism fits well with how modern mathematicians work. They invent formal systems and explore them. They do not worry about practical consequences. But applied mathematicians often find a practical use for these formal games. However, formalism has two problems. Why does mathematics apply in the real world? What are mathematical things like numbers and geometric objects?

Platonism

The Greek philosopher Plato said that mathematical statements describe an eternal world of abstract objects. Platonism says that the mind has mathematical intuition that enables it to see the truth of things like lines and points. Platonism suggests the universe has patterns that are independent of human thinking.

Logicism

Logicism states that mathematical proof uses reason and logic, which are used in many other areas of knowledge. Logicism states that mathematical proof is just a form of logical proof.

The mathematician Gottlob Frege argued that all mathematics could be deduced from logic. He was a strong supporter of logicism. The mathematician and philosopher Bertrand Russell noticed a problem with Frege's argument that causes problems for the idea of logicism. Russell imagined a believable situation that is logically impossible. He sent Frege a problem, now known as 'Russell's paradox'. Russell's paradox can be illustrated by the 'barber paradox'. This problem shows how logic and reason have limitations.

The barber paradox

There is a town with just one barber. The barber is male. In this town, every man keeps himself clean-shaven. Each man can either shave himself or go to the barber. All men who do not shave themselves go to the barber. The barber only shaves men who do not shave themselves.

But this creates a paradox. Who shaves the barber? The barber cannot shave himself because he only shaves men who do not shave themselves.

In 1931, the mathematician Kurt Gödel proved that there are mathematical statements that are neither provable nor disprovable. The barber's paradox is an example of this. Gödel's work created a crisis in the world of mathematics and damaged the case for logicism.

What practical problems can be solved through applying this knowledge?

Mathematics can be divided into two broad areas: pure and applied.

- Pure mathematics deals with abstract patterns. Mathematicians working in this area are less focused on solving practical problems.
- Applied mathematics deals with developing tools to be applied to other areas of knowledge, for example, computer programming, population predictions. Mathematicians working in this area are more focused on solving practical problems.

Definitions with audio

Click on highlighted terms to see the definition and hear the audio.

Vocabulary lists

Select the icons at the back of the book to see complete vocabulary lists.

Shared and personal knowledge

In many languages, the verb 'to know' has two first-person forms: 'I know' and 'we know'. 'I know' refers to the possession of knowledge by an individual – personal knowledge. 'We know' refers to knowledge that belongs to a group – shared knowledge. It can be useful in TOK to **draw a distinction** between these two forms of knowledge. The relationship can be shown in Figure 1.1.

Personal knowledge
'I know because ...'

Shared knowledge
'We know because ...'

Figure 1.1 *Shared and personal knowledge.*

Shared knowledge and personal knowledge interact. For example, **academics** use their personal experiences in their work when they develop theories and write about their subjects in a shared knowledge system. People who study those academic subjects in a shared knowledge system will have their personal knowledge influenced.

A useful **metaphor** for examining knowledge in TOK is a map. A map is a representation of a particular aspect of the world. It is a **tool** that serves a particular purpose. A map that illustrates one aspect of a city (e.g. an underground/metro map) may look very different from a map that illustrates a different aspect of the same city (e.g. a street map). The same can be said for knowledge.

Shared knowledge

Shared knowledge is highly structured, is systematic in its nature and the product of more than one individual. Shared knowledge is **dynamic**. It changes and evolves over time. Shared knowledge changes in response to the contributions of individuals over time. Shared knowledge is a collection of small pieces of individual knowledge that have been put together to form one coherent whole that users can interact with. The coherent wholes are distinct areas of knowledge.

Shared knowledge is malleable. It changes over time as different individuals share different knowledge and change the shape of the coherent whole. The changes can be **dramatic** and sudden, or they can evolve more slowly. When dramatic changes happen it is often known as a paradigm shift.

Academic areas of knowledge

Academic disciplines are very specific areas of knowledge. For example, those studied in the IB Diploma Programme. Academic knowledge creation does not depend only on the contributions of particular individuals. The process of knowledge creation in this area means many individuals can add to the shared knowledge system as well as edit and remove contributions made by others.

Knowledge communities

People are also members of **ethnic** groups, national groups, age groups, **gender** groups, religious groups, **interest groups**, class groups, political groups, and so on. There might be areas of knowledge that we share as members of these groups which are not available to those outside, such as knowledge that is **anchored** in a particular culture or in a particular religious tradition.

Subject vocabulary

coherent whole a single entity that has a clear label and identity

malleable changeable and open to influence

paradigm a model or example that shows how something works, or is produced

Synonyms

dynamic .... active, changing

dramatic .... sudden, striking

anchored .... fixed firmly

General vocabulary

draw a distinction to make different and clear from other categories

academics individuals who work with ideas and theory in academia

metaphor a way of describing something by referring to it as something different and suggesting that it has similar qualities to that thing

tool a useful piece of equipment, method, or skill

ethnic relating to a particular race, nation, or tribe and their customs and traditions

gender being male or female

interest groups groups of people who join together to try to influence the government in order to protect their own particular rights, advantages, etc.

This might raise questions regarding the possibility of knowledge transgressing the boundaries of the group.

Here are some examples of knowledge questions.

Knowledge question: Is it really possible to have knowledge of a culture in which we have not been raised?

Knowledge question: Are those outside a particular religious tradition really capable of understanding its key ideas?

Knowledge question: Does there exist a neutral position from which to make judgements about competing claims from different groups with different traditions and different interests?

Knowledge question: To what extent are our familiar areas of knowledge embedded in a particular tradition? To what extent might they be bound to a particular culture?

> Articulation sentence:
> Shared knowledge is highly structured, is systematic in its nature and the product of more than one individual. Shared knowledge is dynamic. It changes and evolves over time. Shared knowledge changes in response to the contributions of individuals over time.

Personal knowledge

Personal knowledge depends on the experiences of a particular individual. Like shared knowledge, personal knowledge is not static, but changes and evolves over time. Personal knowledge changes in response to experience.

Personal knowledge is gained through experience, practice and personal involvement and is intimately bound up with the particular local circumstances of the individual such as biography, interests, values, and so on. We can see shared knowledge as a coherent whole, and personal knowledge as one tiny piece of that whole.

Personal knowledge is made up of:

- skills and procedural knowledge that an individual has acquired through practice
- what an individual has learned through experience in their life beyond academia
- what an individual has learned through their formal education.

Personal knowledge therefore includes what might be described as skills, practical abilities and individual talents. This type of knowledge is sometimes called procedural knowledge, and refers to knowledge of how to do something, for example, how to play the piano, how to cook a soufflé, how to ride a bicycle, how to paint a portrait, how to windsurf, how to play volleyball and so on.

> Articulation sentence:
> Personal knowledge depends on the experiences of a particular individual. Personal knowledge is dynamic. It changes and evolves over time. Personal knowledge changes in response to experience. Personal knowledge includes what might be described as procedural knowledge.

Subject vocabulary

acquired to have taken possession or ownership of

Synonyms

bound .... tied

General vocabulary

transgressing moving over

raised looked after as children and helped to grow and understand cultural values

neutral position an objective stance

embedded believed very strongly

values ideas about what is right and wrong, or what is important in life

academia the activities and work done at universities and colleges, or the teachers and students involved in it

The eight ways of knowing

The ways of knowing assume knowledge is dynamic and is influenced by:

- how knowledge is received
- how knowledge is mentally **processed**
- how knowledge is emotionally processed
- how knowledge is **constructed**
- how knowledge is communicated
- how knowledge is shared
- how knowledge is **retained**, Figure 2.1.

Synonyms

processed ...... dealt with

constructed .... built

retained .... kept

General vocabulary

balanced giving equal attention to all sides or opinions

tools useful pieces of equipment, methods or skills

complex consisting of many different parts and often difficult to understand

gestures movements of a body part (especially hands or head) to show meaning or feeling

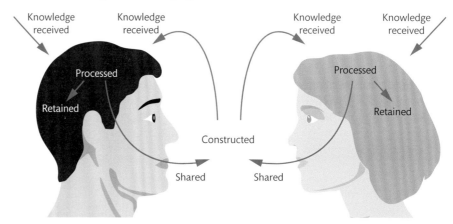

Figure 2.1 *Knowledge is received, processed, constructed, communicated, shared and retained.*

The ways of knowing also assume the *way* an individual or group of individuals knows is as important as *what* they know.

Students must explore a range of ways of knowing. The IB has identified eight ways of knowing. It is suggested that studying **four** of these eight in depth would be appropriate. The ways of knowing selected for detailed study should be carefully selected to ensure a coherent and **balanced** approach.

There are two central purposes to the ways of knowing in TOK. On the one hand they are the **tools** that answer the question 'how do we know?' and on the other hand they help us answer the question 'how do I know?', Figure 2.2.

Figure 2.2 *Eight ways of knowing.*

Language

Language can refer to the mental faculty which allows people to learn and use **complex** communication systems, or it can refer to those systems themselves. The systems are based on agreed rules and signs such as letters, symbols, sounds, **gestures**, images, and so on.

Sense perception

Sense perception is the process by which we can gain knowledge about the outside world. Traditionally, there were believed to be five senses: sight, touch, smell, taste and hearing. However, many now argue that there are others such as a sense of heat, sense of pain, sense of movement, sense of balance and the senses of hunger and thirst, or a sense of where our body parts are.

Emotion

Emotions are strong feelings humans experience. They are the products of natural processes and have a physiological element, a cognitive element, and a behavioural element. The IB seems to regard *feelings*, *moods*, *emotions*, and *emotion* as the same. The plural and the singular are used interchangeably.

Reason

Humans do not form judgements based solely on facts. We 'go beyond' the facts to form our judgements. This is because we have the *ability* to think beyond our immediate experiences. Judgements are formed through thinking or arguing in a logical manner. We reason in many ways: using comparison, rational thinking, deductive and inductive reasoning. When we reason, we seek causes, explanations and justifications.

Imagination

Imagination is the ability to create mental ideas without the input of sense perception. Imagination is connected with images, both real and imaginative. It is about imagining things that do not exist or that we have not seen.

Faith

The term 'faith' is most frequently used to refer specifically to religious faith, but can also be used in a secular sense as a synonym for trust. Although most associated with belief in a God or gods, faith can be religious without being theistic. Alternatively, it can be seen as a commitment to a particular interpretation of experience and reality.

Intuition

Intuition is knowing something without knowing why. Intuition just happens and does not require evidence or justification. Intuition includes beliefs that have no apparent source. It is associated with instinct and innate knowledge.

Memory

Memory is the processing, storage, and retrieval of information. Some people (e.g. Christopher Hitchens) have suggested a further function of memory is to *forget*. If we could not forget, we would be overburdened with events and unable to function.

> Articulation sentence:
> The ways of knowing assume knowledge is dynamic and active. Knowledge can be seen as malleable and relative. Ways of knowing are the tools we can use to answer the question 'How do we know?' and they can also help us answer the question 'How do I know?'

Language

Language can refer to the mental faculty which allows people to learn and use complex communication systems. Language is also about that system itself. Language is **made up of** a system of signs with agreed or conventional meanings combined according to a set of rules for the purposes of communication, formulation of ideas, storage of knowledge or as a medium of thought. There are many different kinds of sign used in a language. The term 'signs' can be interpreted very broadly to include letters, symbols, sounds, gestures, images and even objects. Language is a **crucial** part of our daily lives, but is also filled with potential problem areas, for example, ambiguity, sarcasm, irony and translation issues.

> Articulation sentence:
> Language can affect how people experience the world and how they understand these experiences.

Communicating knowledge is one of language's main jobs. But language may have an even more important job in shaping knowledge and human thinking. Language may affect how people experience the world and how they understand these experiences. Language may be a part of knowledge itself. Some kinds of knowledge may be made up of language. Certain kinds of knowledge may not exist without language. One theory says that facts about the world are made by language. This theory is called linguistic determinism.

Knowledge question: In what ways can language affect knowledge?

Knowledge claim 1: Language creates categories.

Language helps to create categories in the world. Categories help people understand the world. For example, English speakers have a variety of **expectations** when they hear the word *cat*, Figure 2.3. This word is a symbol that **stands for** a certain kind of animal. But the relationship between the sound of the word *cat* and the meaning of the word *cat* is arbitrary. There is nothing in the sound of the word that would tell a non-English speaker what the word means. There is nothing catlike about the word *cat*.

Figure 2.3 *A cat.*

The word *cat* divides the world into cats and non-cats. When people hear the word *cat*, they make certain mental **associations**; they have expectations about what a cat will or will not do. They may or may not know that **lions** and **tigers** are related to cats. When people see a photograph of a cat, they often point and say, 'Oh, that is a cat.' Of course, the photograph is not a cat. It is a photograph. So people have a range of ideas that they associate with the word *cat*. Typically, people who own a pet cat will think first of their cat. So, a word as simple as *cat* conveys a great deal of knowledge. Much of this knowledge is implicit. The knowledge only becomes explicit when a person is asked a series of questions.

Knowledge claim 2: Language conveys thoughts and communicates information.

Language communicates information. For example, 'The test will be on Wednesday.' With language, this information is quite easy to communicate. Without language, this would be much more difficult. People would have to rely on pictures or **pantomime**.

Communication always involves at least two people. It also involves **intention**. Speakers have a message they wish to convey. They must also believe that the listener has the ability to understand the message.

Knowledge claim 3: Language creates abstractions.

Language names, and perhaps creates, abstractions. The world contains children running, water flowing, and nuts falling – all of which we can see. But it is not possible to observe physical examples of truth, justice, and beauty. Truth, justice, and beauty are abstract ideas. Abstractions are a key aspect of **higher-order thinking**. Abstractions play a key role in the sciences. Language plays a key role in both naming and communicating such abstractions.

> Articulation sentence:
> Language names, expresses, communicates and perhaps even creates abstractions.

Knowledge claim 4: Language changes conditions and states.

Language can be performative. This means that just saying some words can be enough to change it to something important. For example:

- 'I now declare you man and wife.'
- 'You are under arrest!'
- 'You agree to pay back $10 000 with **interest** during the next five years.'

All three of these statements have changed a person's **state**. A person who has got married has new legal obligations and may be viewed differently by society. A person who is arrested may lose his or her freedom. A person who takes out a loan has new financial obligations. In all three examples, language itself creates new knowledge.

Knowledge question: Does a particular language cause people to think in a particular way?

This question seems to be asking if linguistic determinism is correct. In other words, does the language a person speaks affect that person's thinking? Many people who are multilingual may feel that they change according to the language they speak. So, they may have a feeling that different languages affect thinking in different ways.

Knowledge claim 1: Language gender can affect how speakers view objects.

Some languages contain gender. Latvian and Urdu have masculine and feminine. Romanian and German contain masculine, feminine and neuter. Zande, a Bantu language from Africa, contains masculine, feminine, **animate**, and **inanimate**. There is some evidence that people who speak languages with gender think of objects differently. For example, the gender for *death* in German is masculine but the gender for *death* in French is feminine. German artists tend to paint death as a man and French artists tend to paint death as a woman. In Portuguese, when a man says *thanks* he says, *obrigado* – a masculine form. When a woman says *thanks* she says, *obrigada* – a feminine form.

Subject vocabulary

abstractions things reduced to their most basic characteristics

obligations duties, responsibilities

gender being male or female

Synonyms

animate......... living

inanimate ...... not living

General vocabulary

pantomime communicating actions, emotions, or ideas without speech

intention a plan or desire to do something

higher-order thinking knowing and processing the facts (e.g. analysing, interpreting, manipulating, categorizing)

interest the extra money that must be paid back above the original sum borrowed

state the physical or mental condition that someone or something is in

Subject vocabulary

Aboriginal people the people who have been in a region since ancient times

linguists people who study language

connotations meanings or feelings that are not in the main or literal meaning of a word

Synonyms

speck.............. small piece

crack the code understand the code

low-down...... dishonest, unkind

General vocabulary

intercepting listening to

radio transmissions voices and other information sent by radio waves

code a system of words, letters, or symbols used instead of ordinary writing, so that the information can be understood only by someone who knows the system

extensive covering a wide area or range

spirits overall mood, feelings or attitude

depression a feeling of great sadness and unhappiness

high-minded having very high moral standards or principles

stoop to to do something bad or morally wrong (which the person would not normally do)

Knowledge claim 2: Language can affect how speakers perceive direction.

The Kuuk Thaayorre, an Aboriginal people from Australia, do not speak about left and right. Instead they describe direction using compass points, such as north, northwest, or southeast. For example, 'You have a **speck** of food on the southwest corner of your mouth.' The Kuuk Thaayorre do not learn to dance using left and right, or forwards and backwards. Instead, they learn to dance with north, south, northwest, southeast.

 Articulation sentence:
The Kuuk Thaayorre learn to dance using north, south, northwest, southeast.

Although these examples are interesting, linguists like John McWhorter and Steven Pinker believe the differences are small. One example supports this idea.

Knowledge claim 3: Very different languages can communicate the same information.

In the Second World War, Japanese radio operators became very good at intercepting and understanding US radio transmissions. This meant the Japanese military rapidly learned about US operations and could quickly react. To solve this problem, the US military began using Navajos, a Native American people. These men became soldiers in the US army and were called the Navajo code talkers. They created a special code using the Navajo language. The Navajo soldiers could speak English to their officers and could send military information (which had originally been in English) to other Navajo speakers in Navajo. They could freely communicate military information over the radio because the Japanese had no knowledge of the Navajo language. The Japanese were never able to **crack the code** of the Navajo code talkers, which was a great help to the US military.

The two very different languages had the same the content – but the Japanese could not understand Navajo. This example demonstrates that the same information can be communicated in very different languages. The content does not depend on a particular language. Understanding the content depends on understanding the language.

 Articulation sentence:
Very different languages can communicate the same ideas and information.

Knowledge question: How are metaphors used in the construction of knowledge?

A metaphor is a word or phrase that is applied to an action or an object. A metaphor describes something by referring to it as something different and suggesting that it has similar qualities to that thing. George Lakoff and Mark Johnson have done extensive work on metaphors. One of their ideas is that metaphors help to connect abstract ideas to the physical world. Metaphors also connect familiar concepts to less familiar concepts.

Knowledge claim 1: 'Up' and 'down' have positive and negative connotations.

- I'm feeling up. That raised my **spirits**.
- I was feeling down. I fell into **depression**.
- The number of people listening to Kanye West is up this year. Madonna's income is down since last year.
- He is **high-minded**. She has high standards.
- That was a low trick. I wouldn't **stoop to** that. That was a **low-down** thing to do.

Knowledge claim 2: 'In front' and 'behind' can refer to time.

- The future lies ahead.
- Let's put that behind us.

Knowledge claim 3: War and argument are linked by metaphors.

- Your claim is a bombshell.
- He attacked every weak point in my argument.
- His criticisms were right on target.
- If you use that strategy, he'll wipe you out.

Knowledge claim 4: Science uses metaphors to explain concepts.

- The atom is a small solar system.
- Biologists speak of the genetic code.
- Some environmentalists describe Earth as a living organism. This is the Gaia hypothesis.

In the end it is difficult to say how important metaphors are. But it is clear that people think in metaphors because metaphors connect the known to the unknown. Metaphors are the bridges that connect new to old, known to unknown.

> Articulation sentence:
> A metaphor is a word or phrase that is applied to an action or an object. A metaphor describes something by referring to it as something different and suggesting that it has similar qualities to that thing. The metaphor uses this word or phrase in a different way to create a new meaning.

Sense perception

Sense perception is the process by which we can gain knowledge about the outside world. Traditionally, there were believed to be five senses: sight, touch, smell, taste, and hearing. However, many now argue that there are other senses such as a sense of heat, sense of pain, sense of movement, sense of balance, the senses of hunger and thirst, and a sense of where our body parts are.

Knowledge question: To what extent is sense perception a passive or dynamic process?

There is debate over whether we *directly* perceive the world as it is, or whether we supply much of the content of our experiences ourselves and perceive the world *indirectly*, because we have constructed our understanding of it. Therefore, the process of sense perception can be seen as either a passive process, or a dynamic process.

Direct perception

Knowledge claim: **Direct perception assumes a passive approach to knowledge creation. It assumes perception is not itself a source of knowledge. It assumes the process of sense perception does not change information that passes through it. It is also known as top-down perception.**

How does this view influence knowledge creation?

Subject vocabulary

passive process without active involvement whereby the process is not changed as a result

dynamic process with active involvement whereby the process is changed as a result

Synonyms

perceive......... understand, interpret

It places an **emphasis** on useful knowledge. It places an emphasis on the individual **detecting** enough useful knowledge (ecological knowledge) to behave meaningfully in his or her environment (Shaw, Turvey and Mace, 1982). Thus, knowledge becomes a **pragmatic** entity leading to useful action. This view assumes an animal is not trying to perceive all the information in its environment. It is acquiring enough information to do something appropriate and effective.

Articulation sentence:
Direct perception assumes the process of sense perception does not change information that passes through it. Indirect perception assumes the process of sense perception adds and removes information as it passes through it.

Indirect perception

Knowledge claim: **Indirect perception assumes a dynamic approach to knowledge creation. It assumes sense perception actually helps construct knowledge. It assumes sense perception adds and removes information as it passes through the sense perception system. It does this based on prior expectations, schemas, and theories about the world. It is also known as indirect perception, constructivism, or bottom-up perception.**

How does this view influence knowledge creation?

It places an emphasis on the individual creation of knowledge. It places an emphasis on humans creating knowledge which will influence how they think, feel, and behave. This has implications for empiricism. Empiricism is a philosophy that places the emphasis on evidence to build theory. Evidence is usually collected by carrying out experiments and making observations. It is a key part of the scientific method that all hypotheses and theories must be tested under scientific conditions rather than using reasoning, revelation, or imagination. Therefore, indirect perception causes scientists to ask the knowledge question below.

Knowledge question: **To what extent is the world the way humans perceive it?**

For the Swiss psychiatrist Carl Jung (1875–1961), the place humans occupied in the world was a central question. He argued that humans give meaning to the world and without humans, the world would still exist as a physical entity but in the 'profoundest night of non-being'. For Jung, the meaning humans brought to the world added to the world.

Knowledge question: **What is the role of expectation in sense perception?**

Expectations are an anticipation of what is about to happen next. They can be guided by schemas. Schemas are an example of indirect/constructivist perception. Schemas are mental plans for action and **frameworks for thinking**. They serve as frameworks through which we can perceive the world. Schemas allow humans to navigate a complex world through pre-existing guides for action and thought.

Example 1: Schemas for the appearance of a 'brat' will influence how people attribute blame

Dion (1972) asked female **participants** to read reports about **severe** classroom **disruptions** by elementary schoolchildren. In some cases, the report was accompanied by a photograph of an '**attractive**' child. In other cases, the report was accompanied by a photo of an 'unattractive' child. The participants tended to blame the disruptive behaviour on the less 'attractive' children, saying that it was easy to see that they were 'brats.' Alternatively, when the photo was of an 'attractive' child, the women were more likely to **excuse** him or her. This study suggests the perception of physical attractiveness influences perception of **guilt**.

Example 2: Schemas for what is considered a 'criminal' appearance will influence eyewitness **testimony** (EWT)

Parker and Carranza (1989) tested the difference between children and older people's ability to recognize a criminal. Equal numbers (48) of elementary school children and college students viewed a slide sequence of a **mock** crime. This was followed by photo identification of the 'criminal'. The results showed child witnesses had a higher success rate of choosing the correct criminals than the adult witnesses. When photos were shown that did not show the criminal, children were more likely to say they could not identify the criminal. Adults were more likely to identify the wrong person. This suggests children do not have a fixed schema of what a typical 'criminal' looks like. The adults have more fixed expectations of what a criminal should look like, and so were more likely to blame an innocent person if the person 'looked like' a criminal.

> Articulation sentence:
> Schemas support an indirect/constructivist approach to perception and show how expectations can influence perception.

Knowledge question: How does language influence sense perception?

Language uses words to communicate meaning. Words can influence what people perceive and remember.

Example 3: Effect of the emotional intensity of verbs on speed perception

Loftus and Palmer (1974) aimed to investigate the effect of the **emotional intensity** of verbs on speed perception and the consequences of a car crash. Films of traffic accidents were presented and played in a **random** order to each group of participants.

The participants were asked 'About how fast were the cars going when they hit each other?' This critical question, acted as the independent variable. It was manipulated in five ways by changing the emotional intensity of the verb 'hit'. Some participants heard the sentence with the verb 'hit' in it. Other participants heard the sentence with the verb 'smashed', 'collided', 'bumped', or 'contacted' instead of 'hit'. The estimated speed was the dependent variable.

Results: *Speed estimates in miles per hour (mph)*

Verb	Mean speed estimate
smashed	40.8
collided	39.3
bumped	38.1
hit	34.0
contacted	31.8

The results show sense perception can be influenced by the wording of a question. The study has **implications** for the legal **profession** and has influenced how police officers and lawyers are allowed to ask questions when dealing with witnesses and **defendants**.

> Articulation sentence:
> Language influences sense perception because different words have different emotional intensities.

Subject vocabulary

independent variable (IV) the variable a researcher manipulates

dependent variable (DV) the variable a researcher measures

Synonyms

excuse .... forgive

mock .... fake

General vocabulary

guilt responsibility or blame for something bad that has happened

eyewitness someone who has seen a crime

emotional intensity how emotional something is

random without any definite pattern

implications the indirect results of an action or thought

profession job

defendants people who are accused of a crime

Knowledge question: How do emotions influence sense perception?

Knowledge question: How does sense perception influence emotions?

Subject vocabulary

psychological mental, emotional

empirically placing emphasis on evidence (usually collected by carrying out experiments and making observations)

appraisal the act of assessing or considering something in detail

significant important*

Synonyms

accelerated .... speeded up

signals .... indicators

General vocabulary

wielding holding in a threatening manner

alley a narrow street between or behind buildings, not usually used by cars

stooge a person with a supporting role in the experiment

arousal heightened sense of awareness

Emotions are biological *and* psychological events. For example, one part of the experience of emotions is the process of *interpreting* biological messages from the body.

Example 4: Comparing the perception of reaction of the body to different stimuli

The reaction of the body on a roller-coaster and the reaction of the body when being confronted by a knife-wielding stranger in a dark alley is the same (adrenaline release) but the *perception* of the events is different.

The roller-coaster rider interprets the bodily reaction as 'being excited' and perceives the experience as 'fun'. The person in the dark alley interprets the bodily reaction as 'being scared' and perceives the experience as 'dangerous'.

Knowledge question: To what extent can emotional influence on sense perception be tested empirically?

Key study: The adrenaline and the stooge experiment (Schachter and Singer, 1962)

The aim of the study was to investigate if the appraisal of a situation could influence emotion.

Schachter and Singer injected participants with either a placebo substance or adrenaline. The adrenaline group were either told it was adrenaline (informed) or were not told what it was (ignorant). They were then put in a room with either a happy or an angry stooge. They were then asked if they felt happy or angry.

Results

● Adrenaline-informed group – participants who were told of the real side-effects of adrenaline (general arousal of the sympathetic nervous system causing accelerated heartbeat, breathing, etc.) reported no significant* increase in happiness or anger.

Why did this happen?
The participants had an explanation for their physiological arousal and did not need to justify (give meaning to) their new-found physiological state.

The participants processed the stimuli as: *My body is reacting and I have been given a substance to make me feel a certain way. The reason why I am feeling this way is because of the substance.*

● Adrenaline-ignorant group – participants who were told of no side-effects reported being either happier (if they were in the room with a happy stooge) or angrier (if they were in the room with an angry stooge).

Why did this happen?
The participants needed an external explanation for their new-found aroused state. They now needed to justify the situation when they found their bodies reacting (accelerated heartbeat, etc.). They could not 'blame' the substance they had been injected with as they had been told it would not give them side-effects. They found the 'cause' of their new-found aroused state in the form of the angry or happy stooge. And then they labelled the emotion being felt as either happiness or anger, depending on which stooge they were placed with.

The participants processed the stimuli as: *My body is reacting and I am in a room with an angry person. So I should perceive these biological signals as anger.*
Or
My body is reacting and I am in room with a happy person. So I should perceive these biological signals as happiness.

* extent to which a researcher has confidence the IV caused the DV (confidence is measured using statistical processes; if a result is 'significant', then a researcher is confident the IV caused the DV and the hypothesis can be supported)

Articulation sentence:
The participants' perception of their situation had led them to feeling nothing, happier, or angrier. The appraisal or perception of the situation had influenced their emotions.

Emotion

What are emotions? / What is emotion?

Literature can often lack a clear definition of feelings and emotions, and this causes problems for analysis.

The IB appears to regard *feelings*, *moods*, *emotions*, and *emotion* as the same. The plural and the singular forms of these words are used interchangeably. In the light of this, this book uses the words *emotion* and *emotions* to cover all aspects of this area.

The following are some perspectives worth considering.

- Emotions can be seen from a purely biological perspective. They are a series of neural impulses sent from the brain.
- Emotions can be viewed as the interpretation of a change in bodily arousal (e.g. Mandler, 1975).
- Emotions can be viewed as being incomplete. They can be seen as **vague** and unformed (e.g. Oatley and Jenkins, 2003).
- Feelings can be viewed as what we experience, while emotions are the behavioural expression of those feelings (e.g. Forgas, 1992).
- Emotions can be viewed as 'noise' or **interference** in the cognitive system (e.g. Forgas, 1992).
- Feelings and emotions can be viewed as dynamic. They can **enhance** cognition by working with it to make things clearer to the individual. For example, Kagan (2007) outlines how humans can attach emotions to imagined events and creatures that do not exist (such as a dragons). Another example is attitudes: few consider attitudes without a cognitive and emotional component. An individual feels an attitude as well as thinks it. Cognition and emotion are now seen as important in influencing behaviour (e.g. Millar and Tesser, 1992).
- Emotions can be viewed as **primarily** private (e.g. Harding and Pribram, 2004).
- Emotions can be seen as primarily social (e.g. Bartky, 1990).
- Emotions can be seen as central to **artistic expression**. Emotions are needed for the creation of art and an emotional experience is needed to experience art (Fellous, 2006).

Are emotions biologically based?

Knowledge question: To what extent can emotions be considered universal?

Another way of asking this question is:

Knowledge question: To what extent are emotions biologically determined?

Knowledge claim: The naturalistic view of emotions is that they are the products of natural processes, with physiological causes and effects. For example, one supporter of this view was Darwin, who believed that emotions are purely physiological and therefore universal and experienced in all cultures.

Charles Darwin (1809–1882) was an English geologist and naturalist famous for his theory that species change over time by the process of natural selection. Darwin also researched the behavioural expression of emotions. He argued emotions had **evolved** over time. Darwin studied facial expressions in animals and humans, and noted **similarities** between them.

Darwin observed how the body and facial expressions of individuals who had been born **blind**, were similar to those of anyone else, even though the blind person could never have seen these expressions.

An example which supports Darwin's position comes from Ekman and Friesen (1971). They told people in a non-Western culture a story involving certain emotions. They also showed them photographs of Western people showing specific facial expressions. When asked to choose the emotion they thought was being expressed in the story, the choices made by non-Western participants matched those of the Western participants most of the time. These results suggest certain expressions are universally associated with particular emotions.

> Articulation sentence:
> Emotions are a vital part of the human communication system. They are **rooted in** evolutionary processes and they are partly shared with similar species.

Are emotions social constructs?

Knowledge question: To what extent can emotions be considered culturally specific?

Another way of asking this question is:

Knowledge question: To what extent are emotions socially constructed**?**

Knowledge claim: Social constructionists assume emotions have no, or very little natural basis. They state that emotions are socially constructed. For example, emotions such as **shame** seem to **presuppose** a **notion** of right and wrong. Notions of right and wrong are culturally specific as one culture may not look at things the same way as another.

The following is an example of culturally specific emotions.

Example 1: A Japanese culture-specific syndrome

Taijin kyofusho symptoms (TKS) is a Japanese culture-specific syndrome. The term taijin kyofusho translates as the disorder (sho) of fear (kyofu) of **interpersonal relations** (taijin). It is concerned with social anxiety. Those who experience TKS are likely to be extremely embarrassed about their bodily functions or their appearance. These bodily functions and appearances include their faces, **odour**, actions, or physical looks. They do not want to embarrass other people with their presence. There are further sub-divisions of TKS: for example, sekimen-kyofu, which is the phobia of **blushing** (Slayor A., 2012).

Is there a conflict between reason and emotion?

Knowledge question: To what extent are humans conflicted between reason and emotion?

The question presents human nature as conflicted between emotions and emotion-free reasoning. This view has been articulated in various ways throughout history.

Example 1: Erasmus's view

Desiderius Erasmus Roterodamus (1466–1536), known as Erasmus of Rotterdam, or simply Erasmus, was a Dutch scholar. He saw the quiet voice of 'reason' being bullied by two raging tyrants – anger and lust. Anger and lust are 'noisy and offensive' – reason is presented as a victim, a female, and ultimately likely to surrender.

Example 2: Freud's view

Sigmund Freud (1856–1939) was an Austrian neurologist who theorized about the unconscious. His basic assumptions were:

- the unconscious is a major contributor to behaviour
- the unconscious is in constant conflict
- thoughts, feelings, and behaviours are influenced by forgotten events which have been repressed.

He argued the unconscious contained the *id*, the *superego*, and the *ego*. The *id* is seen as the impulsive part of the unconscious personality structure. It is the source of a human's basic instinctual desires and impulses. In particular, the *id* is the source of the sexual and aggressive drives. The *id* is controlled by the *superego* and the *ego*. The *superego* works in direct contradiction to the *id*. The *superego* tries to act in a socially appropriate way, whereas the *id* simply wants self-gratification. The *ego* has to find a moderate path between the two. Its task is to find a balance between the primitive drives of the *id* and the high moralizing of the *superego*. Therefore, we can say that the *id* represents animalistic emotion and the *superego* represents extreme reason.

Knowledge question: To what extent does emotion help thinking processes?

An alternative view to seeing emotions and reason in conflict with one another is seeing emotions as *contributing* to cognition. In this view, emotions help rather than hinder perception. They can indicate what is worth attending to more and what is worth attending to less. Therefore, they can be viewed as having an *informational* role that helps us understand the world. Emotions can be viewed as helping people make sense of social and cultural experiences and behaviours. They can be viewed as a source of social, ethical, and political knowledge because they help us form an understanding of the world around us.

> Articulation sentence:
> Emotions can be viewed as helping people make sense of social and cultural experiences and behaviours.

Example 3: Damasio's view

The neurologist Damasio, presented the somatic marker hypothesis (SMH) in his book *Descartes' Error: Emotion, Reason, and the Human Brain* (1994). The hypothesis states: *Emotional processes guide reasoning.* The central piece of evidence Damasio presents is people who have damage to the frontal lobes of the brain.

Frontal lobe damage can lead to:

- reduced ability to organize and plan behaviour properly
- socially inappropriate behaviour
- inappropriate personal and social decision-making (e.g. people with frontal lobe damage can choose unsuitable friends and partners, and engage in activities that are harmful)
- an apparent lack of concern for other individuals
- difficulty in expressing and experiencing appropriate emotions.

However, people with frontal lobe damage appear to have normal intellect in other areas such as memory, attention, and language.

Damasio hypothesized that people who have suffered frontal lobe damage are unable to use past experiences to guide future behaviour. Their decision-making ability is hindered by their inability to use emotions.

In sum: The damage prevents emotional signals that help guide behaviors. Reasoning is guided by emotions and when emotions are removed, reasoning becomes impaired.

Reason

Reason allows individuals to go beyond the immediate experience of their senses. Reason is closely linked to logic in that it involves deducing **valid** conclusions from **given** starting points and using specific rules.

What is the difference between reason and logic?

Humans do not form judgements based solely on facts. They go beyond the facts to form their judgements.

Reason is the **ability** to think beyond our **immediate** experiences

Logic is reasoning based on **strict** rules or principles.

Reason and logic are closely linked. Here is a simplified list of their differences.

- Reason focuses on human action – an ability to think in a certain way and go beyond strict rules.
  Logic focuses on sets of rules which may not include human action.
- Reason is closely linked to human thought processes.
  Logic is closely linked to rules.
- Reason goes beyond the rules and may include more human elements in the calculations.
  Logic sticks very closely to the rules and all conclusions can be **traced** back to them.
- Reason focuses on the 'what' of an argument; the specific content that has been presented as being relevant.
  Logic focuses on the 'form and structure' of an argument; how an answer was created, and the premises that led to the answer.

Example 1: Analysing a football match

An approach using *logic* to analyse a football match would focus on the strict rules of football. It would analyse the proper structure of where everyone should be on the pitch at any given time according to the rules; and how the players *should* react to whatever else happens on the pitch according to the rules. The players would either react correctly or incorrectly in the eyes of the logician.

An approach using *reason* to analyse a football match would focus on the human element of football. It would go beyond merely looking at the rules. It would analyse player **interactions**, **motivations**, off-pitch relationships, relationships with supporters, previous successes and failures, as well as the rules of the game and decisions of the **referee** as the match progressed, and how these influenced the actions of the players.

> Articulation sentence:
> Reason is closely linked to logic in that it involves deducing valid conclusions from given starting points and using specific rules. However, reason goes beyond the rules and may include more human elements in the calculations.

Reasoning can be divided into two parts: inductive reasoning and deductive reasoning.

Inductive reasoning

Inductive reasoning starts at the **particular** and moves to the **general**, Figure 2.4.

Inductive reasoning uses a premise to draw broader conclusions. The conclusions go beyond the basic premise but they can be traced back to the premise. They are considered more or less probable. They are not considered either true or false.

Figure 2.4 *Reasoning from the particular to the general.*

Example 1: Correct inductive argument

Premise: 90% of humans are right-handed.
Premise: Charlie and Fyodor are human.
Probable conclusion: Therefore, the probability that Charlie and Fyodor are right-handed is 90%.

The particular **characteristic** of *humans being right-handed* is applied to the general group of humans which Charlie and Fyodor belong to.

Example 2: Correct inductive argument

Premise: 100% of life forms that we know of depend on liquid water to exist.
Probable conclusion: Therefore, if we discover a new life form, it will probably depend on liquid water to exist.

> Articulation sentence:
> Inductive reasoning suggests truth but it does not **guarantee** it. The truth of a conclusion is probable based on the evidence, but not certain. Inductive reasoning allows for the possibility that a conclusion is false.

Knowledge question: What are the implications for language use?

In the English language, there are certain responsibilities on the part of the writer when showing inductive reasoning. Definitive language has to be avoided and notions of uncertainty have to be respected.

Example 3: Incorrect inductive argument

An incorrect inductive argument was presented by John Vickers.
Premise: All of the **swans** we have seen are white.
False conclusion: Therefore, all swans are white.

This is known as a fallacy.

The conclusion is false because it is **expressed** as a 'truth ' in a definitive way. The example can be improved.

Premise: All of the swans I have seen so far are white.
Probable conclusion: Therefore, it is probable the next swan I see will be white.

Example 4: Incorrect inductive argument
Premise: The Sun has risen every day for the last thousand years.
False conclusion: Therefore, the Sun will rise tomorrow.

This is probably true, but it is not necessarily true. The conclusion is false because it is expressed as a 'truth' in a definitive way. The example can be improved:
Premise: The Sun has risen every day for the last thousand years.
Probable conclusion: Therefore, the Sun will *probably* rise tomorrow.

 Articulation sentence:
Language showing inductive reasoning should avoid being definitive. Notions of uncertainty have to be respected.

Deductive reasoning

Deductive reasoning starts at the general and moves to the particular, Figure 2.5.

Deductive reasoning uses a general premise to draw specific conclusions. The conclusions do not go beyond the basic premise. They are not considered strong or weak – they are either true or false. And it is assumed they are true.

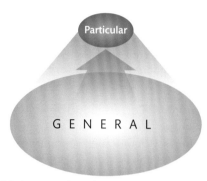

Figure 2.5 *Reasoning from the general to the particular.*

Example 1: Correct deductive argument
Premise: All men are **mortal**.
Premise: Aristotle is a man.
Conclusion: Therefore, Aristotle is mortal.

The first premise states all 'men' have the characteristic 'mortal'. The second premise states 'Aristotle' is a 'man' – a member of a set known as 'men'. The conclusion then states that 'Aristotle' must be 'mortal' because he inherits this characteristic from his classification as a 'man'. The general characteristic of *men being mortal* is applied to a particular man, Aristotle.

Example 2: Correct deductive argument
Premise: All apples are fruit.
Premise: A granny smith is an apple.
Conclusion: Therefore, a granny smith is a fruit.

Deductive reasoning guarantees truthful conclusions if the premises are true. The truth of a conclusion is certain because each step on the chain of reasoning is based entirely on the previous step. Therefore, deductive reasoning from true premises does not allow for the possibility that a conclusion is false.

Deductive reasoning is as reliable as the premises. If the premises are true, then the conclusion is *guaranteed* to be true. But if one or more of the premises are false, the conclusions will not be *necessarily* true – although they may still be true **accidentally**.

Example 3: Erroneous deductive argument
Premise: If the Moon is made of blue cheese, it is delicious.
Premise: The Moon is made of blue cheese.
Conclusion: Therefore the Moon is delicious.

Logic focuses on structure. The structure of the above is valid, but the second premise is false. Therefore, the Moon cannot be guaranteed to be delicious. It may *accidentally* be true (the Moon may indeed taste delicious), but the logic behind the argument would still not be valid as the Moon is not made of blue cheese.

> **Articulation sentence:**
> Deductive reasoning uses a premise to draw specific conclusions. The conclusions do not go beyond the basic premise. They are not considered strong or weak; they are either true or false. And it is assumed they are true.

Are we predictably irrational?

Knowledge question: How does reason influence our rationality?

Rationalism uses reason as a source of knowledge or justification. According to rationalism, reason can be used to reach 'truth' without the need for empirical evidence. Irrationality is an action or opinion based on an inadequate use of reason. Humans often behave in ways that are not based on predictable reasoning.

Example 1: The fallacy of supply and demand

Supply and demand is the notion that the price of a product depends on the demand there is to buy it.

According to Braeutigam (2010) the basic laws of supply and demand are as follows.

1 If demand for a product increases and supply remains unchanged, a **shortage** of the product occurs. This leads to a higher price.

2 If demand for a product decreases and supply remains unchanged, a **surplus** of the product occurs. This leads to a lower price.

3 If demand for a product remains unchanged and supply increases, a surplus of the product occurs. This leads to a lower price.

4 If demand for a product remains unchanged and supply decreases, a shortage of the product occurs. This leads to a higher price.

According to these rules, prices (and human behaviour) can be predicted. These rules are based on the rationale that the demand for a product will affect its supply and then price. However, in terms of the products we buy, humans do not always follow rational rules. The value of a product is not always determined by supply and demand. It can be influenced by:

- anchor prices
- the Veblen effect
- the zeitgeist.

Influence 1: Anchor prices (Ariely, 2008).

When consumers buy a product at a certain price, they become 'anchored' to that price. Over time, they still associate the initial price with the same product. An anchor price of a certain product will influence the way consumers perceive the value of future variations of the product. Anchor prices establish a form of rationale for future purchases. Future purchases become coherent after an initial anchor price has been established in the consumer's mind. However, anchor prices are difficult to predict – there are plenty of examples of products that did not become successful because the initial price was too high (an anchor price was not achieved). Fixing an anchor price to influence future buying perceptions is difficult to achieve.

Subject vocabulary

irrational unconnected to reason

empirical evidence evidence collected by carrying out experiments and observation

Synonyms

anchored .... fixed firmly

coherent .... logical, consistent

General vocabulary

supply and demand a way of determining price in a market

shortage lack, not enough of something

surplus an excess amount of something

consumers the people who buy products

Influence 2: The Veblen effect

The Veblen effect is named after the economist Thorstein Veblen (1857–1929), who first identified the concepts of **conspicuous consumption** and **status-seeking** in 1899.

The effect is as follows. For some goods, decreasing their price decreases people's desire to buy them – the less expensive they become, the less they sell.

This effect appears to contradict basic predictions about human buying patterns. However, it can be explained by the fact that the goods are no longer perceived as **exclusive** or high-status products (Wood, 1993). Similarly, a price increase may increase the perception of high status and **exclusivity**. This will make the product more desirable. Typical Veblen goods are: wines, handbags, luxury cars, jewellery, and shoes.

It is difficult for manufacturers to predict which goods will become Veblen goods. Pricing items too highly usually turns consumers away.

Influence 3: The zeitgeist

Anchor prices and Veblen goods are probably linked to the *zeitgeist*. The *zeitgeist*, or the spirit of the age, refers to **dominant** fashions or *ways of thinking* that influence the culture of a particular time. It is difficult to predict what products or ways of thinking will capture the *zeitgeist*.

An example of a zeitgeist trend is the popularity of diesel cars in Europe. It became a commonly held belief that *diesel cars were more friendly to the environment* because they use less fuel. Therefore, large numbers of people began to buy **diesel** cars. However, diesel cars produce far more harmful gasses and other pollutants that damage the environment, and are poisonous to humans than petrol cars. While diesel cars still remain popular, it can be predicted the *zeitgeist* will become more negative towards them. Car manufacturers have to try to predict these trends. Despite the popularity of diesel, many manufacturers are now concentrating on producing more economical petrol engines to compete with diesel engines.

> Articulation sentence:
> Humans can be irrational. Irrationality can be observed in their buying behaviour. Reasoning is used to dictate the laws of supply and demand. However, humans are influenced by other factors: anchor prices, the Veblen effect, the zeitgeist. These other influences make the buying behaviour of humans difficult to predict.

Imagination

There are many ways to understand imagination. Imagination is the ability to create mental ideas and images without the **input** of sense perception. Imagination is about things that do not exist. Imagination can be **influenced by** medical conditions. For example, severe **autism** can limit imagination and **schizophrenia** can cause illusions.

A wider definition of imagination includes solving problems, or being original and creative. Imagination can involve connecting ideas from very different areas. Imagination is critical for creating scientific theories and solving artistic problems. Sometimes imagination is **unreliable**. Imagination comes from the mind alone and can therefore be **subjective**. It is easy to imagine things that are not true. Imagination can entirely ignore facts. Imagination opens the door to possibilities such as, 'What if ...' or 'Imagine what would happen if ...'. Imagination can be used to discover what is and what is not possible. Imagination plays an important role in films, television programmes, and entertainment. Imagination also plays a role in ethics. It is possible to understand the lives and situations of other people through imagination. Imagination can lead to greater understanding of the human condition.

> Articulation sentence:
> Imagination is critical for creating scientific theories and solving artistic problems.

Knowledge question: What is the role of imagination in producing knowledge about the real world?

According to Albert Einstein, imagination is even more important than knowledge. He said that knowledge has limits but imagination can **take in** the entire world. Einstein imagined flying on a **beam** of light to help him understand the relationship between space and time.

Imagination can also be the ability to invent new ideas. Imagination is strongly connected to creativity, **innovation**, entrepreneurship, invention, discovery, and vision. Columbus imagined a western route to India. He was wrong about India, but made Europe aware of the existence of the Americas. Imagination can be the creative starting point, the **spark** that starts the fire, or the idea that allows ships to **set sail**. Imagination also includes things that are not true.

Imagination and sense perception

Knowledge often begins with input from sense perception. But sense perception can have gaps and the brain must fill in these gaps with imagination. The focus of the human eye is actually quite narrow. What we see to the side of us is largely constructed by the mind. In addition, there is a 'blind spot' in each eye created by the optic disc. For each eye, the brain fills in the missing information using information from the other eye, so we have no sensation of the blind spot. The visual field contains no holes, despite the blind spots. Sense perception is a mixture of information from the outside world and the brain's imaginative reconstruction of the world.

Optical illusions

The rational brain and the imaginative, perceiving brain are at war when viewing Photo 2.1. It is clear to the rational brain that it is nothing more than black lines. However, the imaginative, perceiving brain sees a three-dimensional figure that seems to move and shimmer. This creates an interesting and confusing problem for the viewer: Which part of the brain is telling the 'truth'?

Source: 123RF.com

Photo 2.1 *An optical illusion.*

Subject vocabulary

human condition the positive and negative aspects of being a person, such as birth and death

entrepreneurship the process of developing a business from the very beginning

vision thinking about and planning for the future with intelligence and imagination

optic disc the raised point on the retina where the optical nerves enter; there are no visual receptors at the optic disc

imaginative reconstruction idea or image in which the mind fills in missing parts and creates a sense of completeness

Synonyms

take in .... include

General vocabulary

beam a line of light or energy

innovation the process of creating new and useful products, processes, or ideas

spark very small piece of burning material produced by a fire, or by hitting or rubbing two hard objects together

set sail begin a journey

Imagination and creativity

Imagination is a **crucial** part of childhood. Children imagine that their dolls and soft toys are real people. They imagine that their toy cars and **trucks** and houses are real. To some extent, they understand the distinction between their fantasy world and the real world. Nonetheless, they can become completely **absorbed** in their imaginative world. Listening to stories may be another way children develop imagination.

Imagination can be creative in combining ideas in new and unexpected ways. Imagination can create sense perception without sense input. Imagination opens up new and different perspectives. It is possible to take the perspective of a person living in a different part of the world or even the perspective of an animal. It is possible to imagine better and worse future worlds.

> Articulation sentence:
> Imagination can be part of a creative process, combining ideas in new and unexpected ways.

Imagination and science

Scientific theories begin as imaginative constructions. The German chemist, August Kekulé (1829–1896), imagined the shape of the benzene ring in a daydream. He imagined a snake biting its tail. This was a significant **breakthrough** because understanding the structure of **molecules** is critical in chemistry. Progress in science often comes from explanations that are not finished. These explanations, hypotheses, and theories are developed in the imagination. The imagination helps scientists go from the known to the unknown.

Imagination and mathematics

Mathematics seems to be the area of knowledge that is the most connected to reason and logic, and the least connected to imagination. But much of mathematics is about things we never experience such as infinity. Mathematicians **set up** axioms that are sometimes like the rules of a game. They then imagine what would happen if they use these axioms. Solving difficult mathematical problems often involves great imagination.

Imagination and innovation

Imagination and vision can inspire the creation of new knowledge. In the 1960s, the US **set out** to put a man on the Moon. When President Kennedy spoke about this goal, the US did not know how to send a man to the Moon. Groups of engineers, scientists and politicians worked together to realize this imaginative vision. A huge range of technical and scientific problems had to be solved in order to put a man on the Moon. America's goal began in the imagination and then became a reality. Thus, imagination produced an enormous amount of knowledge.

> Articulation sentence:
> Imagination and vision can inspire the creation of new knowledge leading to important discoveries and scientific breakthroughs.

Imagination and reality

In many cases, facts are missing and imagination is required to fill in the gaps and **connect the dots**. Sherlock Holmes is famous for making **imaginative leaps** from limited knowledge. In one case, he deduced that a dog in a **barn** knew the man who stole the horse. Holmes knew this because the dog did not **bark** the night the horse was stolen. This showed that it was not a stranger who stole the horse. Imagination goes beyond the **available** facts. Imagination can jump across time and space.

Imagination and history

In history, there are gaps between what is known and what is not known. Imagination can help fill in the gaps. In ancient history, knowledge is often **scarce**. Historians must often connect limited documents, myths, and legends to archaeological findings. For centuries, scholars thought that the city of Troy was a legend. Troy is the scene of a war in Homer's epic poem the *Iliad*, which was written about 750 BCE, about a war between the Greeks and the Trojans. But in the 19th century, the site of Troy was discovered in Turkey. Thus a city went from reality to imagination and back again to reality.

Historians sometimes explore new ideas by imagining something that did not happen. What if Hitler had not become the leader of Germany? What if Hitler had not decided to invade the Soviet Union? Imagining such possibilities can lead historians to new **insights**. In history, it is easy to believe that what happened had to happen. This is known as **hindsight** bias. In some cases, small changes would have led to very different outcomes.

Knowledge question: To what extent is imagination reliable?

Imagination's strengths are also its weaknesses. Imagination is able to create things in the mind that do not exist. Imagination has no limits. It does not have to be controlled or limited by reality. It can be **delusional** and lead to conspiracy theories. Popular conspiracy theories include the claim that the 1969 landing on the Moon was staged and that the 9/11 attacks on the World Trade Center in New York City involved members of the US government. Imagination can **blur** the line between fact and fiction. Because imagination is free from limitations, it can be a source of real pleasure, but also of unnecessary suffering. It is possible to imagine wonderful possibilities. It is also possible to imagine terrible or horrifying events such as the death of loved-ones, or **nuclear holocaust**. This can cause fear and even mental illness. Thus, imagination can produce many different results.

Imagination and storytelling

Imagination includes the making of creation myths. These stories tell how the world began. They often start from a state of **nothingness**. The idea of nothingness is very hard to imagine. Hence the jump from nothingness to our world is a great mystery. Throughout history, people have tried to imagine this great jump. Religions speak of things that cannot be seen or experienced. **Faith** often requires imagination. Faith involves accepting unseen concepts such as **hell**, God, angels, **devils**, and spirits without empirical evidence.

Imagination and empathy

Psychologists and philosophers talk about a 'theory of the mind'. This means that a person has the ability to imagine what other people think, feel, and believe on the basis of what they say and do. There is much evidence that most people have similar thoughts, feelings, and beliefs. Psychologists now believe that some people with autism **lack** this ability and are not able to understand, or imagine what other people think, feel, and believe.

Subject vocabulary

deduced inferred or worked out

archaeological findings physical evidence dug up from ancient sites (e.g. pots, tools, building materials)

psychologists people who study emotion, intelligence, cognition, and human development

Synonyms

barn............... farm building

available........ easily found

scarce............ limited

lack............... do not have

General vocabulary

bark short, loud sound made by a dog

legends old, well-known stories, often about brave people, adventures, or magical events

insights clear understandings

hindsight the understanding of a situation after it has happened

delusional likely to have illusions, misbeliefs

blur to make the difference between two ideas, subjects, etc. less clear

nuclear holocaust the idea of very many people dying by nuclear weapons

nothingness complete absence of everything

faith belief and trust (usually in a god)

hell the place where the souls of bad people are punished after death

devils powerful evil spirits in some religions

Imagination and ethics

The ability to imagine another person's situation or problems is critical to developing ethical understanding. An ethical person understands that another human being has similar needs and desires. Immanuel Kant (1724–1804), a central figure in modern philosophy, said that a person has a duty to treat other people as individuals. Other people should not be treated simply as ways to gain what we want and fulfil our desires. Psychopaths and sociopaths lack this imaginative empathy. They see people only as a way to fulfil their wishes and desires. In war situations, people imagine the enemy as a beast, a rat, or an insect. This negative use of imagination allows people to kill, torture, and rape.

> Articulation sentence:
> The ability to imagine another person's situation or problems is critical to developing ethical understanding.

Imagination and the arts

Art is the greatest realm of imagination. For example, literature allows people to imaginatively identify with others. It allows them to go beyond the people that they know. The English poet, Samuel Taylor Coleridge talked about the 'willing suspension of disbelief.' This means that a person reading a book, watching a film, or sitting in the theatre forgets that the action is not actually true. It is possible to fully enter into a story with imagination. It is possible to even lose the sense of self. As people watch a play by Shakespeare, they can imagine what the characters on stage are imagining. At the end of *Romeo and Juliet*, Romeo believes that Juliet is dead. The audience knows that Juliet is not dead, but it can imagine how Romeo feels. In the play *Othello*, Iago misleads Othello. Othello believes that his wife Desdemona is having an affair. This false imagination leads him to kill her in a fit of jealous rage. The audience watches in horror as Othello and Desdemona are destroyed by false imagination.

> Articulation sentence:
> Imagination helps people understand the lives and situations of other people. Imagination can lead to a greater understanding of the human condition.

Faith

Religion is the most common link to faith. This kind of faith is normally linked to belief in a god or gods. However, Buddhism is a religion without belief in a god or gods. Faith can also include non-religious interpretations of the world, such as humanism. Some philosophers do not accept faith as a valid way of knowing. But for many religious believers, faith is the most important way of knowing. Faith is how they understand and explain the world. For this reason alone, it is important to carefully consider faith as a way of knowing.

Types of faith

A common definition of faith is complete trust in yourself, or someone, or something else. It may not be based on the same kind of evidence required in science.

Religious faith may reject the need for justification. It can be based on tradition, experience, sacred texts, and authority.

Students may have faith that they will pass the next test. They may rely on past experience. Therefore, their faith that they will pass the test is based on some reasons. They may have good reasons to believe that they will pass the test, but they will not know for sure until they receive their grades.

People might also have faith in their parents and teachers. Parents and teachers are not perfect, but over time they may have shown that they are reliable.

Faith is important because it can lead to action. This action might be as simple as attending a religious service or continuing with a difficult challenge. However, it might also lead to war and the destruction of other peoples.

Faith and religion

Many religions claim evidence for their beliefs. This is where the **controversies** often begin. Many religions see their sacred texts as infallible and use these texts to support their faiths. People outside a religion are unlikely to view these texts as infallible.

Christianity and Islam are the two most dominant and widely practised religions in the world. Faith plays a strong role in both religions. Is the emphasis on faith the reason why these two religions have such large numbers of followers? It is difficult to answer that question, but it would be hard to deny that faith is a central part of Christianity and Islam. Some of history's great **conflicts** – such as the Thirty Years' War in Europe in the 17th century, or the present conflicts in the Near East – involve conflicting religions.

Religions typically contain ethical systems. The faithful are instructed to follow these ethical systems. Followers of Judaism, Christianity and Islam are told to follow the Ten Commandments. Buddhism has the five precepts or virtues. People often demonstrate their religious faith by following the practices of their religion.

What role does faith play in humanism or atheism?

As is often the case in TOK, the answer depends on the definitions of key terms in the knowledge question. The word 'faith' is sometimes used as a synonym for religion. For example, people speak of the Christian faith. However, not all definitions of faith have a religious aspect. Humanism and atheism are both broad categories and come in many forms. On the simplest level, an atheist is a person who does not believe in a god or gods. Atheists are also people who have no religious beliefs or practices in their lives. They may not actively reject religious ideas; religious beliefs simply play no part in their lives. Humanism is somewhat harder to define. Humanists usually place emphasis on rational thinking and focus on human beings; not on gods, or **supernatural** powers.

If faith is defined as strong belief in the doctrines of a religion, then it is difficult to argue that atheism or humanism is a faith. It is not logical to say that a lack of belief in the doctrines of a religion is a religion. Therefore, humanists and atheists do not appear to have religious faith. But if faith is defined as complete trust and confidence in someone or something then the answer is different. Many humanists and atheists have this kind of faith in reason and science. They might have faith in the goodness of humanity, or in technology, and progress. Therefore, this second kind of faith does play a role in humanism and atheism.

Faith and reason

Some argue that faith is neither rational nor logical; others argue that faith goes beyond mere reason. Some argue that faith and reason are opposites; others argue that faith and reason work together.

Subject vocabulary

infallible without mistake or flaw

five precepts basic guidelines that Buddhists follow

practices application of beliefs and ideas such as (in the case of religion) prayer, meditation, attending religious services)

Synonyms

conflicts......... wars

General vocabulary

controversies serious arguments about something important (may involve many people)

supernatural not explained by natural causes, and therefore seeming to involve the powers of gods or magic

Faith and belief

Some traditions see belief that is not based on evidence as superior to belief that is based on evidence. They see the demand for evidence as showing a lack of faith.

Relatively little knowledge comes from direct experience. Almost no one alive today has seen Stalin. Very few people have been to the Moon. Most people do not know how to measure the speed of light. Nonetheless, we can reasonably accept many claims about Stalin, or the Moon, or light. This is because we have faith in the reliability of the sources and the methods used to find this knowledge.

Plato's definition of knowledge is that knowledge is justified, true *belief*. This suggests that faith is necessary and it is not possible to be completely certain. Perhaps most knowledge claims rely on beliefs accepted by faith. In standard epistemology, the quality of reasons converts true beliefs into knowledge.

Faith and assumption

Many assumptions are based on faith. It is rational to assume that there is a real world and that life is not merely a dream. Scientists assume the universe has laws that can be discovered. They also assume that that their results in specific cases may apply broadly to all similar cases. Mathematicians assume that logic will provide correct answers. The United Nations assumes that there are **fundamental** human rights. All of these involve faith.

Faith and science

The scientific revolution, the Enlightenment, and evolutionary theory have challenged faith-based knowledge. Many see science and faith as opposites. Modern science does not allow the use of the supernatural in its explanations or justifications. It does not use explanations based on faith. However, science is based on the belief that the universe has laws that can be discovered. Science is also based on the belief that it is possible to make generalizations based on limited evidence. One example is the **pressure–volume law of gases**. If universal, this law should apply in all cases. Experiments and theories support the pressure–volume law of gases. But it is not possible to test all gases, and so some degree of faith is required to claim that this is a universal law.

Knowledge question: Can theistic beliefs be considered knowledge because they are produced by a special cognitive faculty or 'divine sense'?

Some religious thinkers, such as the theologian John Calvin, argue that it is possible to sense **the divine**. Calvin argues that God gives people a sense of the divine from birth. He states that this sense is 'engraven' on the human heart.

Some developmental scientists believe that children are born with the tendency to look for causes. Research shows that children believe events must have causes. Therefore, children might be more likely to accept that God or some other supernatural source causes things to happen. It might be natural for children to look for religious explanations of the world. This suggests that there might be some psychological basis for theistic beliefs.

Faith and emotion

Faith has an emotional **aspect**. Many believers feel a strong emotional connection to their religious beliefs. This emotion may be the strongest basis for their beliefs. Conversion experiences are sometimes powerfully emotional. Faith is often connected to hope, such as the hope for life after death. A life with hope feels very different to a life without hope. Faith can be an attitude and can form the basis

Subject vocabulary

epistemology theory of knowledge

United Nations an international organization to promote peace and cooperation among countries

the Enlightenment a philosophical and intellectual movement that began in the 18th century and emphasizes the power of reason

evolutionary theory a scientific theory concerned with the origins of life on Earth, and its change and development over time

cognitive faculty thought concerned with memory, perception, and attention

theologian a person who studies God and religious ideas

conversion experiences experiences of changing religions

Synonyms

the divine ...... God

aspect .... part

General vocabulary

fundamental forming a base or core

pressure–volume law of gases this law describes the relationship between pressure, volume and temperature for a gas

engraven etched, marked into

for doing well in life. Losing faith is emotionally damaging for some. Fear may accompany faith. Some beliefs are very hard to support with logic or reason, but we hold onto them, explaining them through emotions or **gut feelings**.

Faith as personal or shared knowledge

Believers often see faith as something intensely personal. Yet religious belief is often practised in a community of faith. Groups with shared beliefs can often act in powerful ways. Communities of faith can unite through clothing, language, food, and **customs**. But these unifying features also separate them from other groups. Believers typically practise the religion of their parents and their community.

Faith and intuition

One study showed that people who rely on their intuition are more likely to believe in God. Encouraging people to think **intuitively** increases their belief in God. But encouraging people to think **analytically** reduces their tendency to believe in God. Therefore, intuition may increase faith and reason may reduce faith.

Intuition

What is intuition?

Intuition can be seen as:

- a gut feeling or sixth sense
- knowing something without knowing why
- being immediate and not requiring evidence or justification
- the opposite of reason, because intuition is quick, whereas reason is slow and methodical
- a form of perception, which comes from the unconscious
- beliefs, feelings, and actions that have no obvious source although they may be based on extensive experience.

Intuition is also associated with instinct and innate knowledge. Innate knowledge is knowledge that a child is born with. Most current research assumes children have an innate ability to learn language. This is not an ability to learn one particular language; it is the ability to learn *any* language. Many people also believe that children are born with some kind of moral intuition. This moral intuition is an inborn sense of what is right and wrong. People who acquire expertise in a field of knowledge may develop an intuitive feeling for their area.

Intuitive knowledge seems to pop into **awareness** without preparation. It does not seem to require justification. Some people seem to be more intuitive than others. They seem to be able to make quick decisions without a clear reason for those decisions. Some people deny that intuition is a separate way of knowing. They see intuition as a combination of previous experience, imagination, and sharp sense perception.

> Articulation sentence:
> Intuition comes immediately and does not require evidence or justification.

Subject vocabulary

community of faith a group of people that share the same religious beliefs

expertise high-level skill or knowledge in a field

Synonyms

intuitively ...... instinctively

analytically .... rationally

awareness ...... consciousness, wakefulness

General vocabulary

gut feelings reactions or feelings that you are sure are right, although you cannot give a reason for them

customs things done by people in a particular society because they are traditional

intuition the ability to understand or know something because of a feeling rather than by considering the facts

Is intuition expertise?

Knowledge question: To what extent is intuition a form of expertise?

Expertise is a high-level of skill or knowledge in a particular field. Experts go about their work with **apparent** intuitive ease. For example, expert football players, surgeons, or jazz pianists do not have to stop and think carefully about each step. They make decisions with great rapidity. Therefore, experts seem to be more intuitive in their field.

However, experts are not born with expertise. The expertise is acquired over time. The psychologist Dr Anders Ericsson estimates that it takes 10 000 hours of practice to achieve expertise in a field. For example, a beginner chess player starts with very little knowledge, or ability, and gradually improves to a level of expertise. A high-level chess player is able to recognize more patterns. High-level chess players are able to do this because they have memorized hundreds of games. Their intuition has a rich store of examples to draw on. Therefore, expert intuition is based on experience and practice. The extensive practice makes the process nearly automatic. As a result, this quick, automatic ability feels intuitive and not linked to conscious thought but it is actually based on practice and experience.

> Articulation sentence:
> Expert intuition is based on experience and practice. The extensive practice makes the process nearly automatic and therefore intuitive.

Is intuition innate knowledge?

Knowledge question: To what extent is intuition a form of innate knowledge?

The English philosopher, John Locke, speaks of the tabula rasa or the blank slate. This means that humans are born without built-in or instinctual knowledge. Therefore, all knowledge is gained through experience and sense perception. Locke's idea suggests that the environment forms the child. The environment includes the family, the culture, the language, and the natural world. The role of intuition in this conceptual framework is not clear.

However, there is important evidence against the idea of the blank slate.

Example 1:

Studies with twins and adopted children show that important characteristics can be inherited. Abilities, or qualities such as IQ, the tendency towards alcoholism, and gender identity have a genetic basis.

Example 2:

Developmental psychologists, like Andrew Meltzoff and Alison Gopnik, have shown that babies have an innate sense of physics. They will look at something longer when it is unexpected because it goes against normal physics or statistics. This demonstrates that babies have some innate or intuitive understanding of how the world works.

> Articulation sentence:
> Inherited characteristics provide a starting point for intuition because humans are born with certain knowledge.

Intuition and learning

Although babies have an innate ability to learn language and some sense of physics, it is clear that they must also learn. A child must have exposure to a language. Deaf children need to be exposed to fluent signers. The sign language of the deaf is a **fully fledged** language. Deaf children in an isolated **rural** community may never come into contact with a fluent signer. If so, they will never learn to sign properly or have real language abilities. In the same way, a child must **interact** with the physical world to develop their innate sense of physics or logic. The key point here is that a child must practise to take an innate ability to a fluent, intuitive level. In their native tongue, people instantly recognize grammatical mistakes. This is not an analytical process; it seems to come automatically or intuitively. However, this fluent, intuitive ability comes after hundreds or even thousands of hours of exposure to a language. Therefore, intuition and learning are deeply connected.

Is intuition useful?

Knowledge question: To what extent is intuition useful?

Knowledge claim: **Intuition is useful because it allows quick decisions to be made that may aid survival.**

Example 1: Facial recognition

Recognizing faces quickly would have aided survival for early humans. It appears to be an intuitive rather than learned skill. For example, newborn babies find faces interesting even though their actual vision is still quite weak. Babies quickly learn to recognize faces because facial recognition is so important to their survival. However, there are some conditions which cause difficulties in recognizing faces (e.g. autism). People with autism may find recognizing emotions in other people's faces difficult. People with a condition called prosopagnosia cannot recognize faces.

Therefore, facial recognition skills are not intuitive for everyone, and are probably under genetic influence.

Example 2: Confirmation bias

Confirmation bias is the tendency to:

- look for evidence that supports beliefs and habits
- ignore evidence that goes against beliefs and habits.

According to the argumentative theory (Mercier and Sperber, 2011) people are largely unable to overcome confirmation bias. People are motivated to find support for their own view of the world because they want to maintain their self-esteem. Maintaining self-esteem is a major force in people's lives. People can also be seen as 'cognitive misers'. This means they do not wish to spend more cognitive effort than necessary, so they take short cuts to reach quick conclusions. In sum: humans tend to simplify information.

> Articulation sentence:
> Intuition is useful because it allows quick decisions to be made about important information (e.g. face recognition); this provides a boost to self-esteem and saves cognitive energy.

Subject vocabulary

fluent signers people who can use sign language with the speed and expertise of normal spoken language

self-esteem ability to think of oneself in a positive light

cognitive concerning mental processes such as memory, perception and attention

Synonyms

fully fledged... complete

rural.............. countryside

General vocabulary

interact have a relationship

Intuition and cognitive energy

Knowledge claim: Intuition saves cognitive energy.

The psychologist Daniel Kahneman argues the brain is divided into two systems: System 1 and System 2.

- System 1 is fast, intuitive and easy to use.
- System 2 is slow, more difficult and uses reason, problem solving, and concentration.

According to Kahneman, people prefer to use System 1 because it is easy and intuitive. System 2 is harder to use and it is much less intuitive.

According to the assumptions of evolutionary theory, System 1 must be fairly useful. If System 1 were not accurate most of the time, early humans would have stood less chance of surviving. However, the kinds of intuitions that served early humans well may no longer serve modern humans so well. The research of Kahneman and others shows that System 1 makes many errors.

Memory

Memory is the processing, storage, and retrieval of information. Some (e.g. Christopher Hitchens) have suggested a further function of memory is to *forget*; otherwise we would be overburdened with events and unable to function.

Memory can be broadly divided into three categories, Figure 2.6.

- ***Attention***
  Attention is a **filtering** system. It is the ability to decide which information is important and how it will be dealt with. It is possible that attention is mostly sub-conscious. This means why and how we deal with some information is not immediately obvious to conscious thought.

- ***Retention***
  Retention is a storage system. Items have to be coded and then put aside for later use.

- ***Recall***
  Recall is a retrieval system. It is the ability to withdraw information. Memory researchers are interested in how, and in what way we recall information. Items have to be recalled so we can 'remember' them and use the information.

Subject vocabulary

coded have labels or markers attached

Synonyms

filtering .... sorting

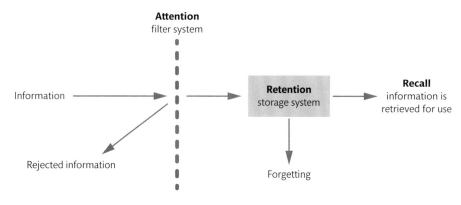

Figure 2.6 *A model of a memory system.*

Articulation sentence:
The function of memory is the processing, storage, retrieval, and possibly the forgetting of information.

Memory and recall

The only way researchers can research what information is retained in storage is to ask research participants to *recall* information. However, as soon as they ask participants to recall information, they are researching *recall* and not just *retention*. Researchers have to assume that what is recalled is similar to what is retained.

Knowledge question: How does memory influence knowledge?

Many discussions of knowledge tend to focus on how knowledge is formed rather than on how it is remembered by individuals. However, most of the knowledge that individuals have is in the form of memory. Therefore, the way they retain and recall information is an important aspect of how knowledge is formed.

Memory refers to things which are not currently happening. Memory can be contrasted with:

- perception – deals with information after it has been passed through the attention filter
- imagination – deals with information that has not happened in 'reality' but has been constructed by the individual.

> Articulation sentence:
> Memory is important to knowing because most of the knowledge that individuals have is in the form of memory.

Memory and experience

Memory should be distinguished from *experience*. Experience is the ongoing interpretation of an event as it unfolds. Memory is the edited version. When we see a movie, we have a continuous experience. When we remember a movie, we do not remember the entire film. Our memory of the film is not 2 hours long. We remember edited highlights of the event as well as how the movie made us feel. Different people will remember the movie differently. How and why memories are recalled differently by different people is a key area for memory researchers.

> Articulation sentence:
> Memory should also be distinguished from experience. Experience is the ongoing interpretation of an event as it unfolds. Memory is the edited version.

Memory: Passive or dynamic?

The process of memory can be seen as a passive process or a dynamic process.

- A passive approach assumes memory is not itself a source of knowledge. It assumes memory does not change information that is stored within it and then recalled.
- A dynamic approach assumes memory actually helps construct knowledge. It assumes memory changes information that is stored within it and then recalled.

TOK takes a dynamic approach to memory.

Memory and models

A model is a simplified representation of a process. There are two main models for memory.

Subject vocabulary

model a simple representation of a complex process

General vocabulary

distinguished made or seen as different from

Example 1: The multi-store model by Atkinson and Shiffrin (1968)

These researchers introduced the notion of memory being divided into two main stores: a short-term store (STS) and a long-term store (LTS), Figure 2.7. Information flows through the system, and is processed and stored, or processed and deliberately forgotten. The model does not explain *why* or *how* some events are remembered or lost.

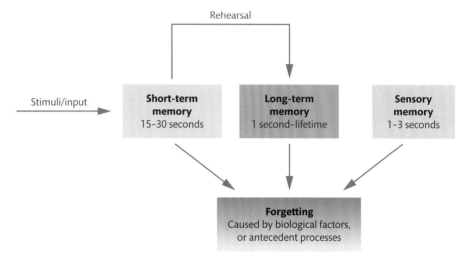

Figure 2.7 *Multi-store model of memory.*

Example 2: The levels of processing approach (LOP) by Craik and Lockhart (1972)

According to memory researchers Craik and Lockhart, memory is a **by-product** of perception. Memory is a direct consequence of the way information is perceived or encoded. Therefore, if information is processed at a deep level, the memory it creates will be longer lasting.

> Articulation sentence:
> According to Craik and Lockhart (1972), **shallow** processing leads to a **fragile** memory **trace**. Deeper processing leads to a strong memory trace.

Memory and emotion

Knowledge question: How do emotions shape memories?

Knowledge claim: Emotions influence depth of processing.

The levels of processing approach assumes memory is caused by the depth of processing. The assumption is: if an event is particularly emotional, it will be processed more deeply and the individual will be more likely to remember it. The relationship between emotions and memory can be further illustrated by the idea of **flashbulb** memories (FBM) by Brown and Kulik (1977). Flashbulb theory supports the basic assumptions of levels of processing by Craik and Lockhart (1972): emotional events are more likely to be processed deeply and therefore remembered.

Flashbulb memories usually:

- form in situations where we **encounter** surprising and highly emotional information
- are maintained in memory by means of **overt** rehearsal (for example, talking about it with others) and **covert** rehearsal (for example, daydreaming)
- differ from other memories in that they are more vivid, last longer, and are more **consistent** and accurate.

Flashbulb memories have six characteristic features:

- place (where the event happened)
- **ongoing** activity (what I was doing)
- **informant** (who broke the news)
- own emotion (how I felt)
- other emotion (how other people felt)
- **aftermath** (what I did next; what happened in the long run).

> Articulation sentence:
> Flashbulb memories are highly detailed, exceptionally clear 'snapshots' of a moment (Brown and Kulik, 1977).

Knowledge claim: There is empirical evidence for the existence of flashbulb memories (FBM).

Brown and Kulik (1977) asked 80 American participants (40 white and 40 black) to answer questions about ten events. Nine of the events were mostly **assassinations** or attempted assassinations of well-known American personalities (e.g. JF Kennedy, Martin Luther King). The tenth was a self-selected event of personal relevance and involving unexpected shock. Examples included the death of a friend or relative, or a serious accident. Participants were asked to recall the circumstances they found themselves in when they first heard the news about the ten events.

Results

- 90% of the participants recalled the assassination of JF Kennedy in 1963 and where they were in vivid detail.
- African Americans reported more flashbulb memories for leaders of civil rights movements (e.g. the assassination of Martin Luther King) than white Americans.
- Most participants recalled a personal flashbulb memory which tended to be related to learning about the death of a parent.

Conclusion

Surprising information is likely to be remembered. Events which have high personal and emotional relevance/**resonance** are likely to be remembered. This is shown by the African Americans having flashbulb memories for the assassinations of civil rights leaders.

Knowledge claim: Emotions cause memories to be structured as stories.

Neisser (1982) suggests memories are so clear because the event itself is **rehearsed** and *reconsidered* after the event. What is actually being remembered is not a memory of an event but a memory of a *story* about an event. People remember their reconstruction rather than the actual event. For example, flashbulb memories usually appear in the form of stories with a storytelling structure, such as place (Where were we?), activity (What were we doing?), a character (Who told us?), and emotion (How did we feel about it?).

Knowledge claim: Emotions cause memories to be altered.

- The use of stories/narratives ('I was sitting on the floor when I heard …') helps people deal with the emotional situation they found themselves in. It does not help them remember the actual information accurately.
- Emotions cause people to have more confidence in a memory.
- Flashbulb memories usually produce a great deal of confidence from the individual that their memories are accurate. However, the levels of inaccuracy are so high it is possible to argue that flashbulb memories could not actually be considered as 'memory.'

Synonyms

ongoing .... continuing

rehearsed ...... practised

altered .... changed

General vocabulary

informant an individual who secretly passes on information

aftermath consequence

snapshots pieces of information that quickly give an idea of what the situation is like at a particular time

assassinations murders of well-known people

resonance the special meaning or importance that something has because it relates to experience

Memory and language

Knowledge question: How does language shape memory?

Language carries meaning. When we process language through memory we are also processing meaning. An example that shows this is Bartlett (1932) who asked English participants to read *The War of the Ghosts*. This is a Native American folk **tale** containing details about hunting **seals** in **canoes**. The participants' memory of this story was tested by asking them to repeat the details **over time**. Over time, the story became increasingly shorter and changed to **suit** the English language. (*Remember*: English was the cultural background of the participants.) For example, 'hunting seals' became 'fishing' and 'canoes' became 'boats'. What started as a strange story with strange words to the participants became a traditional English story with more familiar words.

Synonyms

tale .... story

over time .... gradually

General vocabulary

seals large sea animals that eat fish and live around coasts

canoes long, light boats that are pointed at both ends and are moved with a paddle

suit be acceptable to

3 What is the knowledge framework?

The knowledge framework provides a systematic way to compare and contrast areas of knowledge. TOK seeks to understand the unique character of each area of knowledge. The course also seeks to understand what the areas of knowledge have in common. TOK looks at how knowledge is created and how reliable that knowledge is.

This book uses the knowledge framework to explore and investigate the different areas of knowledge. The knowledge framework includes a series of questions that are used for every area of knowledge. In some cases, a question from the knowledge framework does not fit a particular area of knowledge. Therefore, that question is not included in a particular section. But in all cases, the book uses each of the five parts of the knowledge framework, as illustrated in Figure 3.1

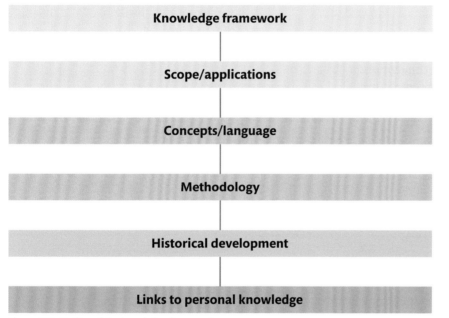

Figure 3.1 *Outline of the knowledge framework.*

Subject vocabulary

framework a structure that supports thought and different ideas and investigations

examines looks at or investigates closely

organisms living things, life forms

cloning creating a genetically identical life form

General vocabulary

systematic organized carefully and done thoroughly

unique specific

fit be suitable for

fields subjects that people study or areas of work

ethical about moral principles and practices

Knowledge framework: Scope/applications

The scope and applications part of the knowledge framework examines an area of knowledge as shown in the table below.

The scope and applications part of the knowledge framework ...	Example
Defines the area of knowledge.	Biology is the study of living organisms and how they function.
Looks at the problems the area of knowledge solves.	Biology looks at how living organisms reproduce and develop.
Looks at how the area of knowledge is used.	Biology is used in many fields including medicine.
Includes important questions about the area of knowledge.	How did life on Earth first develop?
Examines ethical problems in the area of knowledge.	What are the ethical questions linked to cloning?

Knowledge framework: Historical development

Areas of knowledge change and develop over the course of time. Every area of knowledge has changed from what it was in the past. Some areas of knowledge have changed **radically**. It is important to understand that knowledge is not static. Knowledge is dynamic; it changes, develops, and **evolves**.

For example:

- the theory of evolution completely changed the life sciences
- the English naturalist and geologist Charles Darwin's theory was a challenge to religious explanations of life on Earth
- the Czech scientist ('the father of genetics') Gregor Mendel's work on **inheritance** gave a biological mechanism as an explanation for evolution
- chemistry and physics have come to play an increasingly important role in understanding evolution
- genetic modification and artificial intelligence raise new ethical issues.

Knowledge framework: Links to personal knowledge

Areas of knowledge are examples of shared knowledge. Shared and personal knowledge are often connected. Shared knowledge is often built by the personal knowledge **contributions** of individuals. These contributions must be examined and tested by the group to become shared knowledge.

Shared knowledge is very important to the knowledge of each person. Shared knowledge helps people to make sense out of the world. For each person, there is a **give and take** between shared and personal knowledge. People want to know what shared knowledge is important. How does shared knowledge affect individual human lives? How does shared knowledge change or alter perspectives?

For example:

- listening to music can give us new **insights** about the world
- music can have an emotional effect on listeners who understand the musical style or the musical convention
- musicians play music written by great **composers**
- musicians play music that comes from **folk** or other cultural traditions
- musicians create their own music
- musicians participate in various musical traditions
- some music is created by individuals working and **improvising** together
- music can create common **bonds** between people
- music can be a deeply personal experience that is also shared with other people.

Knowledge framework: Scope/applications

What is the area of knowledge about?

Mathematics is the study of **ordered** relationships or patterns. It studies how patterns have an ordered relationship with themselves, with each other and with the **universe**. Mathematics can find ordered relationships in most areas of the universe and allows measurement and prediction. It can be seen as a universal language which can be understood anywhere in the world because it crosses all cultural and geographical borders.

Articulation sentence:
Patterns can come from the universe or they can be introduced to the universe by the human mind. Mathematics can be used to describe these patterns, allowing us to understand and predict what happens in the universe.

Patterns

Patterns can be seen but they can also be abstract. An abstract pattern does not need a relationship with the physical world to exist. It only needs to exist as an idea. It can be studied and changed by **reason** alone. Abstract patterns provide us with a system for understanding and predicting what happens in the universe.

Examples of patterns include:

- patterns of **motion**, such as trajectories
- patterns of shape, such as fractals and symmetry
- patterns of numbers, such as multiples of an integer
- patterns of chance, such as the likelihood that two people in a group of 30 will have the same birthday.

Articulation sentence:
Abstract patterns do not exist in actual fact. They are **symbolic**. Abstract patterns still provide us with a system for understanding and predicting what happens in the universe. They can be studied and changed by reason alone.

Knowledge question: To what extent do mathematicians apply their own patterns (or abstract patterns) to the universe?

Knowledge question: To what extent does the universe have patterns that are independent of human thinking?

Mathematics examines things such as:

- numbers, including integers, rational numbers, and irrational numbers
- quantity such as height, mass, and velocity
- space, including two-dimensional and three-dimensional figures
- sets, which are collections of distinct objects. The elements of a set could include plants, numbers, letters, and other sets.

Explaining mathematics: What is mathematics?

The question of what mathematics is about leads to the deeper question: What is mathematics? Philosophers of mathematics have developed different answers to that question. Here are three possible answers.

Subject vocabulary

patterns regular, repeating concepts

prediction a statement about the future

abstract existing in thought as an idea without an actual existence

trajectories curves that go through a set of points or curve at a constant angle

fractals repeating patterns that are the same at every scale

integer a whole number, not a fraction

rational numbers numbers that can be expressed as the fraction of two integers

irrational numbers numbers that cannot be expressed as the fraction of two integers

velocity the speed of something in a particular direction

Synonyms

ordered .... regular

universe .... cosmos

motion .... movement

symbolic........ representational

General vocabulary

relationships systematic connections between factors

reason the ability to think beyond our immediate experiences

Formalism

Formalism is the idea that mathematics is a game with rules that humans invented. If maths is like a game, then it must have rules. Formalism says that all axioms are true because of convention and that all mathematics is a kind of game. Formalism suggests that mathematicians introduce their ideas to the universe.

Formalism fits well with how modern mathematicians work. They invent formal systems and explore them. They do not worry about practical consequences. But applied mathematicians often find a practical use for these formal games. However, formalism has two problems. Why does mathematics apply in the real world? What are mathematical things like numbers and geometric objects?

Platonism

The Greek philosopher Plato said that mathematical statements describe an eternal world of abstract objects. Platonism says that the mind has mathematical intuition that enables it to see the truth of things like lines and points. Platonism suggests the universe has patterns that are independent of human thinking.

Logicism

Logicism states that mathematical proof uses reason and logic, which are used in many other areas of knowledge. Logicism states that mathematical proof is just a form of logical proof.

The mathematician Gottlob Frege argued that all mathematics could be deduced from logic. He was a strong supporter of logicism. The mathematician and philosopher Bertrand Russell noticed a problem with Frege's argument that causes problems for the idea of logicism. Russell imagined a believable situation that is logically impossible. He sent Frege a problem, now known as 'Russell's paradox'. Russell's paradox can be illustrated by the 'barber paradox'. This problem shows how logic and reason have limitations.

> ### The barber paradox
>
> There is a town with just one barber. The barber is male. In this town, every man keeps himself clean-shaven. Each man can either shave himself or go to the barber. All men who do not shave themselves go to the barber. The barber only shaves men who do not shave themselves.
>
> But this creates a paradox. Who shaves the barber? The barber cannot shave himself because he only shaves men who do not shave themselves.

In 1931, the mathematician Kurt Gödel proved that there are mathematical statements that are neither provable nor disprovable. The barber's paradox is an example of this. Gödel's work created a crisis in the world of mathematics and damaged the case for logicism.

What practical problems can be solved through applying this knowledge?

Mathematics can be divided into two broad areas: pure and applied.

- Pure mathematics deals with abstract patterns. Mathematicians working in this area are less focused on solving practical problems.
- Applied mathematics deals with developing tools to be applied to other areas of knowledge, for example, computer programming, population predictions. Mathematicians working in this area are more focused on solving practical problems.

Here is an example of a pure mathematics problem.

Example 1: Twin primes

A twin prime is a pair of prime numbers that are separated by only two numbers. For example, 41 and 43. One area of pure mathematics is number theory, which looks at the properties and relationships of numbers. An open question in number theory is this: Are there an infinite number of prime pairs? Many number theorists suspect that there may be an infinite number of twin primes. However, no mathematician has been able to prove or disprove this conjecture.

Here is an example of a practical problem that applied mathematics addresses: making estimates to understand social problems.

Example 2: Indian gendercide

It is thought that in the past three decades up to 12 million unborn girls have been deliberately aborted in India. This is known as *gendercide*: a specific gender (usually female) is **discriminated against**. This is done because it is a cultural **norm** to have a male **heir**.

In a 2011 Indian census it was revealed that in the under-7 age group:

● there are 7.1 million fewer girls than boys
● the sex ratio is 915 girls to 1000 boys
● in families where the first child was a girl, the gender ratio for second births fell from 906 girls per 1000 boys in 1990 to 836 in 2005.

Mathematicians are able to **generate** and present these numbers. Researchers in the human sciences then draw conclusions from the data. For example, one conclusion is that parents welcome a first daughter but take measures to ensure that their second child is a son.

This conclusion raises difficult questions for the government: should medical technology (such as **abortion**) be given to families in India if the data shows female unborn babies are discriminated against?

Example 3: Exponential growth of human populations

The **population** of the world **doubled** between 1804 and 1922. It doubled again between 1922 and 1959. And it doubled again between 1959 and 1974. Such rapid growth is known as **exponential growth**, Figure 4.1. Exponential growth in a population means more people have to be clothed, fed, housed, and cared for.

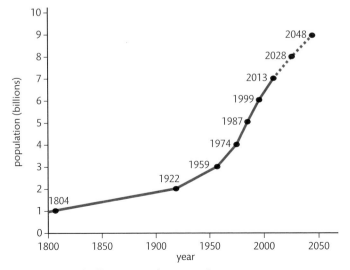

Figure 4.1 *Graph of human population growth.*

Applying mathematics to this problem allows **policy makers** to:

- predict how many people will be alive in certain areas of the world
- predict what their needs will be.

For example, in economically developed countries people are living longer (**life expectancy** is longer) but they are having fewer children (birth rate is low). This means the population contains more elderly people, who need to be cared for. However, there are fewer working people in the population, whose taxes will pay for the care of the elderly (tax income is lower).

> Articulation sentence:
> Mathematicians are able to help predict trends in human populations. Policy makers are able to change policies based on these predictions.

What makes this area of knowledge important?

Example 1: Soil loss

Soil loss can be predicted using the following equation:

A = R × K × L × S × C × P

In this equation:

    A = predicted soil loss

    R = the rainfall erosivity index (rainfall totals)

    K = soil erodibility (how much the soil is likely to **erode**)

    L = slope length (how long the slope is)

    S = slope gradient (how steep the slope is)

    C = cover and management (how covered the slope is)

    P = erosion control practice (practices such as **contour ploughing** to reduce erosion).

Mathematics is important because it is the basis for understanding and predicting a range of human interactions. For example:

- computer programming
- economic understanding (personal, national and international)
- economic security
- engineering – including transport (cars, railways, etc.), bridges, buildings
- modelling the spread of **epidemics**
- business predictions
- population predictions.

Example 2: Crude birth rate (CBR)

CBR is the number of live births per thousand people in a population.

The equation is:

$$CBR = \frac{\text{total number of births}}{\text{total population}} \times 1000$$

In the USA in 2005, there were 4 138 349 births from a population of 295 895 897. The CBR is 13.98 per thousand.

In Mauritius in 2001, there were 19 600 births from a population of 1 189 000. The CBR is 16.5 per thousand.

General vocabulary

policy makers people who recommend what action government should take

life expectancy how long people are expected to live

soil earth, mud

erode graduallly be destroyed or removed by the weather

contour ploughing ploughing is turning over the soil before planting; contour ploughing is ploughing around a hill rather than up and down the slope of a hill

epidemics widespread occurrences of disease

> Articulation sentence:
> Mathematics is important because it allows measurements and predictions to be made about the universe, and about human interactions.

As before, mathematicians are able to generate and present these numbers. Researchers in the human sciences then draw conclusions from the data. For example, an obvious conclusion is parents in poorer countries have more children.

Reasons for this include:

- parents in poorer countries want more children to take care of them in old age
- women in poorer countries have fewer rights and have less control over their own bodies
- poorer countries have placed more importance on **superstition** and religion, and so **contraception** is less available.

What are the current open questions in this area?

In the natural sciences, new evidence is researched and then presented. Theories change or are replaced. Asking questions is a normal part of the research process. Mathematics is slightly different from the natural sciences because it is **cumulative**. Mathematics from the past is still **valid** and is still used today. There are open questions within mathematics waiting to be answered. They are usually in the form of complex problems. Here are two open, unanswered questions in mathematics.

Open question 1: To what extent can beauty be reduced to a mathematical equation?

Example 1: Beauty and the golden ratio

The golden ratio refers to **proportions** that conform to the mathematical equation:

$$\frac{a+b}{a} = \frac{a}{b} \overset{\text{def}}{=} \varphi,$$

Where the Greek letter phi (φ) represents the golden ratio. Its value is:

$$\varphi = \frac{1 + \sqrt{5}}{2} = 1.6180339887 \ldots$$

The golden ratio is thought to play a role in human **perception** of beauty. It can be applied to *facial* **symmetry** using a 'mask' developed recently, Photo 4.1. Perfect facial symmetry is rare in humans and requires 'good' **genes**. Therefore, facial symmetry is a sign of genetic health. However, it should be noted perceptions of beauty are complex, personal, and open to influence. Reducing such a complex process to a mathematical equation has significant flaws.

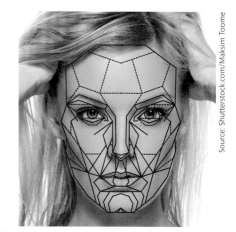

Source: Shutterstock.com/Maksim Toome

Photo 4.1 *The 'beauty mask' overlaid on the face of a model.*

> Articulation sentence:
> The golden ratio is a mathematical equation that can measure 'beauty'. It has been applied to facial symmetry.

Open question 2: Can a mathematic equation predict how human factors influence behaviour? Examples of human factors are: natural ability, practice, injury and psychology.

Example 2: Stephen Hawking's formulae for predicting England's World Cup chances

Hawking took factors such as weather, shirt colour, time of day, temperature, and nationality of the **referee**, and calculated England's best chances of success. It should be treated as a hypothetical exercise rather than a serious attempt to predict football matches.

For example:

- England are twice as likely to be successful when playing below 500 m above sea level
- a 4-3-3 team shape has a success rate of 58%, compared to 48% when playing 4-4-2
- professional footballers should be able to score from the **penalty** spot more than they do; the reason why they do not is because different people react differently under pressure.

Knowledge framework: Concepts/language

What role does language play in the accumulation of knowledge in this area?

Numbers are the basic building block of mathematical language. They are **represented** by numerals and symbols.

Numerals

Example 1: The tally system

Used for thousands of years, the tally system helped **traders** count effectively. It is very simple and only useful for small amounts:

////= 4   ǂǁǁǁ = 5.

Example 2: Roman numerals

These form a more advanced tallying system:

I = 1   II = 2   III = 3   IV = 4   V = 5.

Example 3: Hindu–Arabic numerals

These are the most **common** representation of numbers. They are the ten digits:

0   1   2   3   4   5   6   7   8   9

They were probably adopted by the Muslim–Persian and Arabic mathematicians in India and then passed on to Arabs further west. There is some evidence the numerals developed from Arabic letters.

Symbols are a more complex system to represent numbers

Example 1: Fractions

$$\frac{1}{3} \quad \frac{2}{6} \quad \frac{3}{9}$$

These fractions all represent the same number.

Subject vocabulary

numbers objects used to count, label, and measure

numerals parts of a writing system that represents numbers

tally to mark

Synonyms

represented … symbolized

common …….. usual

General vocabulary

injury a wound or damage to part of your body caused by an accident, or attack

referee someone who makes sure the rules of a game are followed

penalty a chance to kick the ball or hit the puck into the goal in a game of football, rugby, or ice hockey; given because the other team has broken a rule

traders people who buy and sell goods

Example 2: Decimals

0.9999 ...

The three dots mean 9 is repeated indefinitely. Therefore, this is a complex representation of the number 1.

Knowledge question: To what extent does the representation of numbers influence how we think about them?

Knowledge question: Do Roman numerals force us to think differently?

 Articulation sentence:
A number is an object used to count, label, and measure. A numeral is a writing system that represents numbers.

What are the roles of the key concepts and key terms that provide the building blocks for knowledge in this area?

The key concepts and terms in mathematics are:

- axioms
- conjecture
- theorems.

Key concept 1: Axiom

An axiom is a starting point of reasoning. A mathematical axiom is a statement which is a starting point for the development of further mathematical statements. Axioms do not have to represent 'truth' outside of the statement they represent. They are simply formal logical expressions which build mathematical theory.

Different mathematical branches have different axioms. For example, algebra has five basic axioms:

- reflexive axiom
- symmetric axiom
- transitive axiom
- additive axiom
- multiplicative axiom.

An example of a reflexive axiom is: a number can be equal to itself (e.g. $a = a$). This is known as the first axiom of equality.

An example of a symmetric axiom is: if $a = b$ then $b = a$.

An example of a transitive axiom is: if $a = b$ and $b = c$, then $a = c$.

An example of an additive axiom is: if $a = b$ and $c = d$, then $a + c = b + d$.

An example of a multiplicative axiom is: if $a = b$ and $c = d$ then $ac = bd$.

 Articulation sentence:
Axioms provide a building block because they are the starting point for the development of further mathematical statements.

Key concept 2: Conjecture

Conjecture is a statement that appears correct but has not been proven (or disproven).

Conjectures are supported by cases that appear to make the conjecture correct. It does not matter how many cases support the conjecture: it does not become truth. A single **counter-example** can disprove the conjecture. Conjectures disproven through counter-examples are called false conjectures.

Example: The next number in the pattern 2, 6, 11, 17 will be 24 because it will have increased by 7.

The terms increase by 4, then 5, and then 6.

> Articulation sentence:
> Conjectures provide a building block because they enable mathematicians to make guesses about patterns based on experience and knowledge. This allows mathematicians to test their ideas.

Key concept 3: Theorem

A theorem is a major mathematical result that has been proved to be true. It has been proved to be true on the basis of previously accepted theorems and generally accepted axioms. A theorem is the **product** of other theorems and axioms.

Example: Pythagoras's Theorem proved that for a right-angled triangle, $a^2 + b^2 = c^2$, Figure 4.2.

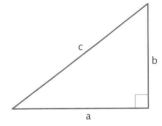

Figure 4.2 *A right-angled triangle.*

> Articulation sentence:
> Theorems provide a building block because theorems have to be proved true by the use of a logical argument. They provide examples of pure logic and proof.

What metaphors are appropriate to this area of knowledge?

Example metaphor 1: 'Fact families' (Benjamin, 2013)

A fact family is a collection of number sentences about addition, subtraction, multiplication, or division. Each number sentence has the same numbers:

$7 + 4 = 11$

$4 + 7 = 11$

$11 - 4 = 7$

$11 - 7 = 4$

The metaphor here is the notion of a 'family'. The metaphor of family helps us understand meaning because it shows how members of a family 'go together'.

Example metaphor 2: Equations as 'sentences' (Benjamin, 2013)

Viewing equations as 'sentences' shows they have two sides. Applying the notion of a 'sentence' to describe an equation makes the equation appear 'complete'.

Consider this equation: $x + 15 = 25$

The two sides are: '$x + 15$' and '$= 25$'.

The answer is: $x = 10$

General vocabulary

pursuit the act of trying to get, achieve, or find something in a determined way

standard accepted as normal or usual

geometric having or using shapes and lines such as circles or squares, especially when these are arranged in regular patterns

dictates controls or influences something

What is the role of convention in this area?

A convention in mathematics is a fact, a name, or usage which is generally agreed on by other mathematicians. It is a **standard** way of doing things. Mathematicians follow conventions to allow other mathematicians to understand what they write.

Example of a convention 1: The labelling of geometric figures

Convention **dictates** points are usually labelled with capital Latin letters such as A, B, and C. Convention dictates straight lines are usually labelled with lower-case Latin letters, such as a, b, and c. For example, see Figure 4.3.

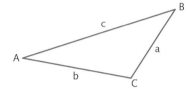

Figure 4.3 *Triangle with conventional labelling of points and sides.*

Example of a convention 2: Congruent angles (angles having the same measure or angle size) and arcs

Convention dictates that congruent angles are indicated with arcs, as in Figure 4.4.

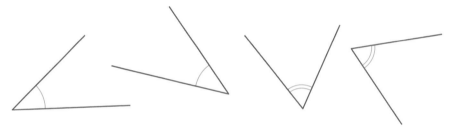

Figure 4.4 *Congruent angles are indicated with arcs.*

Example of a convention 3: Congruent segments and ticks

Convention dictates congruent segments (sides having the same length) are indicated by tick marks. Convention also dictates if there is more than one pair of congruent segments, then additional tick marks are used, Figure 4.5.

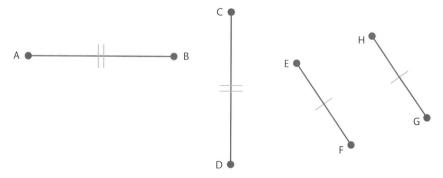

Figure 4.5 *Congruent segments are indicated with tick marks: line AB is congruent to line CD. Line EF is congruent to line HG.*

Knowledge question: **Are mathematical conventions useful or do they hinder new knowledge production?**

Knowledge framework: Methodology

What are the methods or procedures used in this area and what is it about these methods that generates knowledge?

Mathematics uses a special methodology to produce knowledge. It is designed to **guarantee** correctness.

In mathematics, the starting points are axioms and the conclusions are called theorems, lemmas, or propositions. A theorem is a big result. Less important results are called lemmas or propositions.

Axioms are statements that cannot be proved. The axiom is the starting point of mathematical reasoning. Different axioms produce different kinds of mathematics.

Proof

Proof is at the centre of mathematics. Mathematical statements must be **justified** with proof. Proof is a formal method that makes mathematical statements true. Proof is the logical sequence of steps that makes it possible to deduce one thing from another thing. Each step can be checked. A mathematical **argument** is either right or wrong, **sound** or **unsound**. The truth of each **premise** contributes to the truth of the conclusion. Logical arguments in mathematics guarantee truth. This arguably makes mathematics different from other areas of knowledge. Science and philosophy also use logical deduction but mathematics uses proof with symbols in ways that are more strict and **systematic**. This gives it a claim to specialized knowledge.

> Articulation sentence:
> Proof is at the centre of mathematics. Mathematical statements must be justified with proof. Proof is a formal method that makes mathematical statements true.

Example: Finding proof using English words

This word example shows that it is possible to construct a proof without numbers. Mathematicians use a range of symbols including letters. The procedure used to find the proof is not dependent on the symbols used.

The proof begins with the word SHIP. This is the premise of the proof. Each step must use a four-letter English word. Each word **differs** from the one above it by changing only one letter. These are the rules or axioms of the proof. The aim is to arrive at the word DOCK. This is the conclusion of the proof. Here are two possible solutions.

SHIP	SHIP
SHOP	SLIP
SHOT	SLAP
SOOT	SOAP
LOOT	SOAK
LOOK	SOCK
LOCK	DOCK
DOCK	

Each step must be correct. There are no unexplained jumps. The logic flows from the beginning to the end.

> Articulation sentence:
> A premise is a previous statement on which another statement can be built.

After solving this problem, it is possible make a conjecture. A conjecture is a mathematical statement that has not yet been proven. The conjecture might be that to solve this problem, we must use a word with two vowels in the middle. (In this proof it is assumed that the vowels are *a*, *e*, *i*, *o* and *u*.) To solve this problem, a vowel must move from position three to position two. The problem only permits a change of one letter in each step. There is an axiom in English spelling: every word must contain at least one vowel; there are no words with no vowels. Therefore, any solution to this problem must contain a word with two vowels. The word with two vowels in the middle allows the problem to be solved. This proves the conjecture and thus creates a theorem.

> Articulation sentence:
> A conjecture is a mathematical statement that has not yet been proven.

What are the assumptions underlying these methods?

Below are five assumptions or knowledge claims that could be made about mathematics.

Knowledge claim 1: **Mathematics is a universal language.**

Knowledge claim 2: **Mathematics is a self-contained logical system that is true.**

Knowledge claim 3: **Mathematics is independent of the real world.**

Knowledge claim 4: **People can make sense of the world with logic.**

Knowledge claim 5: **A collection of statements can only be true if it is internally consistent.**

Examination of knowledge claim 1: Mathematics is a universal language.

This assumption or knowledge claim raises many questions. What is meant by universal? Does this mean that mathematics is the same throughout the universe? Mathematics seems to describe the universe and is central to physics. It can also make predictions that later prove to be true. For example, mathematics predicted the existence of the planet Neptune and the Higgs boson. Some cosmologists even believe that the underlying reality of the universe is mathematical.

'Mathematics is a universal language' could have another meaning. It could mean that all human beings have mathematics. Is this true? School systems throughout the world teach mathematics. Numeracy, the ability to understand and use numbers, is a basic part of education. But the fact that numeracy must be taught suggests that it is not universal. Numeracy is also different from literacy. Children start primary school fluent in one or more languages but they must be taught literacy, which is the ability to read and write. But most children must be taught almost all aspects of mathematics.

Some languages also suggest that mathematics is not universal. There are languages with very few numbers. For example, the Pirahã language of Brazil has words for one and two: hói and hoí. Hói and hoí can also mean 'small quantity' and 'larger quantity'.

Counting is not limited to human beings. Animals that **count** include:

- chimpanzees
- black bears
- desert ants
- crows.

The claim that mathematics is a universal language raises another question: Is mathematics a language? The answer is dependent on the definition of 'language'. If the definition of 'language' is based on a detailed definition of spoken human language, then the answer is 'no.' Mathematics does not contain phonemes, morphology, phonology, and lexicons. People do not speak 'mathematics' to one another to communicate states of emotion. However, it is common to hear people speak of the language of maths or the language of music. Defining words is not a strict science. So a word like language has a range of meanings.

> Articulation sentence:
> The claim that mathematics is a universal language depends on how language and universal are defined.

What counts as a fact in this area of knowledge?

When children learn mathematics, they learn facts such as addition and multiplication tables. However, professional mathematicians prefer not to speak of facts. So, the idea of facts in mathematics is a problem

Mathematical empiricism does say that mathematical facts are discovered by empirical research. Science uses empirical methods to gather data. However, there is a problem with the idea of mathematical empiricism. It means that it is necessary to go out into the world to discover mathematical facts. But, that's not how most mathematicians think or work. It is not even clear that mathematical facts can be found.

Knowledge question: If mathematics is discoverable, where can it be found?

Does mathematics even have facts?

- Yes: there are an infinite number of facts: 1 + 1 = 2, 1 + 2 = 3, etc.
- No: mathematical ideas are abstractions.

Mathematicians create axioms and then work with them. The axioms do not have to relate to the world. Mathematicians have invented mathematical systems that seem to have no relation to the real world. But scientists and mathematicians may find uses for these mathematical systems later. Number theory once seemed very abstract but it is now essential for **cryptography**.

Scientists rely heavily on mathematics and they regard the measurements, graphs, equations, and formulae as logical support for their work.

What role do models play in this area of knowledge?

Models can help us understand complex, real-world problems. A mathematical model is a mathematical representation of a complex real-life problem in simpler form. The idea is to **translate** a practical problem into a mathematical one and then solve the mathematical problem. That solution can then form the solution to the original physical problem.

Subject vocabulary

phonemes fundamental speech sounds, such as p, b, and t

morphology the structure of words

phonology the sounds of words

lexicons dictionaries

empirical based on evidence (usually quantitative) collected from experiments and observation

General vocabulary

count to say numbers in order, one by one or in groups

chimpanzees intelligent African apes

crows large black birds with a loud call

cryptography the study of secret writing and codes

translate express the same idea, or concept in another system, or language

Articulation sentence:
A mathematical model is a mathematical representation of a complex real-life problem in simpler form.

Look at Figure 4.6. The yellow parts are bridges and the blue parts are a river running through a city. Is it possible to walk around the city and cross each bridge only once? Try to trace a path so that you cross each bridge only once. You must complete the route with one continuous pencil stroke.

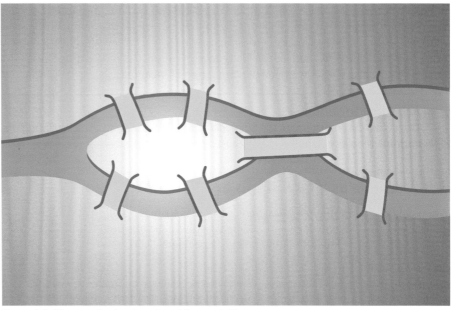

Figure 4.6 *Diagram of a river in a city, with seven bridges.*

To solve this problem, people use **graph** theory. Graph theory is the study of points and lines. It studies how sets of points, called vertices, can be connected by lines or **arcs**, called edges.

The mathematician Leonhard Euler realized that problems like this could be solved with a model. In the model in Figure 4.7, land is represented with red points and the bridges are represented by black arcs. The points are called vertices.

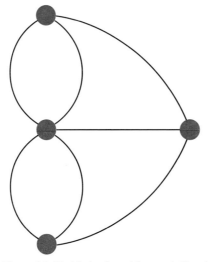

Figure 4.7 *Model of a river with seven bridges in a city.*

Each red vertex connects to an odd number of arcs. You are not allowed to use an arc more than once. Therefore, unless the vertex is your final stop, you need an even number of arcs at each vertex. You need one arc for each arrival and one arc for each departure. In this model, every vertex has an odd number of arcs. Therefore, there is no solution to this problem. This is an example of proof by contradiction. In mathematics and science it is useful both to prove and disprove. Proof by contradiction relates to falsification in science.

How models generate knowledge in mathematics

This model generates knowledge because people can use it to **construct** a generalization. Models enable people to connect and solve problems that seem different on the surface. Models remove details and show basic structures. Mathematical models are powerful tools for analysis and people can use them for real-world problems. The seven bridges model is useful for transportation, planning, scheduling, and understanding the internet.

Knowledge question: How do mathematical models relate to the real world?

What are the roles of imagination in mathematics?

Mathematicians use imagination to find solutions to real-world problems and to clarify complex ideas.

Role 1: Solving real-world problems

- The ancient Egyptians used calculations to position the pyramids in line with the stars.
- The ancient Chinese created advanced computation formulae for volume, area, and proportion to build the Great Wall.
- Chess is a highly mathematical game. It is interesting to compare how computers play chess and how humans play chess. Humans use intuition and mental images. A computer uses pure logic. It **rapidly** runs through a long list of possible moves.

Role 2: Showing complex ideas in a simpler manner

Mathematicians use imagination in finding ways to show proof. The mathematician Georg Cantor proved that there were different types of infinity. A set is countably infinite if its elements can be put in one-to-one correspondence with the set of natural numbers, Figure 4.8.

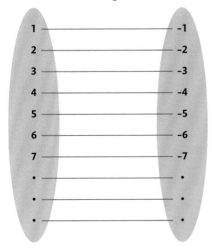

Figure 4.8 *Model of countable infinity.*

However, the set of real numbers cannot be counted. Real numbers include whole numbers (like 0, 1, 2, 3, 4), rational numbers (like $\frac{3}{4}$, 0.125, 0.333 ..., 1.1), and irrational numbers (like π, √3). Infinity is very useful to mathematicians, but it is difficult to imagine. Cantor found that the number of points on a line between two numbers is uncountably infinite. The points between two lines include numbers that cannot be counted: irrational numbers.

Knowledge framework: Historical development

What is the significance of the key points in the historical development of this area of knowledge?

Key point 1: The development of writing and mathematical notation

People have a fundamental need to count and to measure distance. They also need to understand basic geometry. The historical evidence of mathematics begins with writing. Writing is a form of communication that uses signs and symbols to communicate meaning. As human societies developed there was a need to exchange more complex information such as land ownership, financial accounts, and contracts.

Key point 2: The development of numbers and their representation

Numbers are the basic building blocks of mathematical language. They are represented by numerals and symbols (see page 43).

How has the history of this area led to its current form?

- The Mayans, the Chinese, the ancient Indians, the Egyptians, and the Babylonians all developed mathematical knowledge. This knowledge goes back at least 4000 years. There is a strong link between the development of government and mathematics.

- The early mathematicians looked at practical problems. They discovered important areas of maths, but they did not have the idea of proof. Their mathematics was more like a cookbook with specific examples.

- The Greeks were the first to develop the idea of proof. This was an enormous advance in mathematics. Euclid's proofs are still valid today, more than 2000 years later.

- Algebra is the one of the most important contributions of the Muslim Golden Age. It was developed in the period 800–850 in Persia (now Iran).

- By the 1600s, Europe had become the centre of mathematical history.

- René Descartes developed analytic geometry.

- Isaac Newton and Gottfried Wilhelm Leibniz simultaneously invented calculus.

- Algebra, geometry, and calculus played key roles in the development of physics, chemistry, and medicine.

- In the 19th century, Lobachevsky and Bolyai discovered non-Euclidean geometry. This type of geometry uses spheres and other shapes that are not flat. The results are very different from traditional Euclidean geometry.

The history of mathematics is quite international. It is also cumulative, meaning that it builds up over time. New mathematical knowledge seldom replaces old knowledge, as often happens in the sciences. Instead, new mathematical knowledge is added to the larger store of mathematical knowledge.

fundamental forming a base or core

algebra the part of mathematics that uses letters and other general symbols to represent numbers, and quantities in formulae and equations

analytic geometry the branch of algebra that models geometric objects such as points, lines, and circles

calculus the study of how things change, it provides a way to model systems in which there is change

General vocabulary

geometry the study in mathematics of the angles and shapes formed by the relationships of lines, surfaces, and solid objects in space

building blocks the pieces which together make it possible for something bigger to exist

Muslim Golden Age the period from the 7th century to the 17th century

Knowledge framework: Links to personal knowledge

Why is this area of knowledge significant to the individual?

- Mathematics plays a key role in many professions including science, economics, finance, and **engineering**. Many important concepts in physics are explained through mathematical formulae. Statistics plays a central role in some of the human sciences. Engineers rely heavily on mathematics to solve practical problems. In all of these fields, mathematical expertise is critical. People who plan to go into these fields must have strong mathematical skills. Thus, mathematics has an important practical purpose for many people.

- Some people find the world of mathematics itself attractive. They love the **order** and coherence of mathematics. Problems in other areas of knowledge often seem messy and lack clear solutions. But mathematical problems have definite solutions. More complex problems may have more than one solution.

- Mathematics looks at patterns and some of these patterns are **symmetrical** and pleasing. Mathematics expresses proportions and relationships. Mathematical symmetry can be found in architecture, music, painting, and in nature.

What is the nature of the contribution of individuals to this area?

People with special talents can contribute greatly to the production of shared knowledge. This seems to be particularly true in mathematics. There are many individuals who have made great **contributions** to mathematics including Pythagoras, Archimedes, Euclid, Galileo, Newton, Leibniz, Euler, Gauss, Riemann, Laplace, Lagrange, Hilbert, Neumann, Wiles, and Perelman.

Key individual 1: Pythagoras

Pythagoras is often called the first 'true' mathematician. He is a **controversial** figure. He did not write down his theories himself. Most of what people know about Pythagoras's thoughts and ideas comes to us from his followers. It is not clear if any of the theorems were solved by Pythagoras personally or by his followers. 'Pythagoras's Theorem' is very famous. It proved that for a **right-angled** triangle:

$$a^2 + b^2 = c^2$$

Key individual 2: Euclid

Euclid was a Greek mathematician. He is referred to as the 'Father of Geometry'. Geometry is an area of mathematics concerned with questions of size, shape, the relative position of figures, and the properties of space. He lived during the reign of Ptolemy I (367–283 BCE) and wrote *Elements*, his most famous work. It was the main textbook for teaching, especially geometry.

What are the implications of this area of knowledge for one's own individual perspective?

To some extent mathematics is not only an area of knowledge, it is also a way of knowing. Mathematics involves perceiving the world as a series of patterns and abstract relationships.

General vocabulary

engineering profession in which people are trained to design, or build roads, bridges, machines, etc.

order organization and correct arrangement

symmetrical balanced or exactly the same in some way

contributions input, involvements, addition of something

controversial produces different opinions that cause arguments

right-angled with an angle of 90°, like the angles at the corners of a square

Here are some examples of looking at the world from a mathematical perspective:

- estimating percentages
- noting fractions
- estimating rates of change
- using statistics
- noticing geometric shapes
- making time estimates.

If a person consistently asks for proof, this may also be a mathematical perspective. Perhaps the search for order and structure is a way of seeing the world from a mathematical perspective.

5 Natural sciences

Knowledge framework: Scope/applications

What is the area of knowledge about?

The natural sciences look for laws of nature. The term 'laws of nature' refers to observable laws relating to natural phenomena. These laws are generalized statements about how the natural world works. They are usually based on systematic observation and are constructed using reason and imagination.

The list of natural sciences includes, but is not limited to:

- physics – the study of matter and energy
- chemistry – the study of the composition, structure, and properties of chemical elements and how they interact with each other
- biology – the study of living organisms, including their structure, growth, and interactions with each other
- oceanography – the study of the ocean
- climatology – the study of climates.

> Articulation sentence:
> The natural sciences seek to find laws of nature that connect different aspects of the natural world.

To understand the natural world, natural scientists do the following.

- Use measurement and other quantitative techniques. For example, they measure things like mass, size, softness or hardness, and thickness or thinness. Quantitative techniques give mathematical results. Science organizes this quantitative data into charts and graphs. This is one reason why mathematics plays a very important role in the natural sciences.
- Use evidence to support any knowledge claim. This evidence is based on observation.
- Use experiments, which must be repeatable, to test data.
- Use peer review. This means that the opinions and research of other experts are used to analyse and criticize conclusions.
- Use standardized language which does not vary from country to country. For example, there is no difference between Chinese chemistry and Brazilian chemistry.

Science typically looks for cause and effect. If event A happens, then event B will happen. The end goal is to understand phenomena and then to establish underlying laws, mechanisms, and principles that cause the effect. If natural scientists discover laws and principles, then they can make predictions.

> Articulation sentence:
> The natural sciences seek to uncover, demonstrate, and explain mechanisms of causation in the natural world.

Subject vocabulary

laws a system of rules

generalized broadly understood from a small sample

reason the ability to think beyond our immediate experiences

imagination the ability to create events, scenarios, causations in one's head that do not exist in reality

properties characteristics

organisms living things, life forms

mass the number of atoms in an object; a measure of the amount of matter in an object

peer review the process whereby other experts evaluate a study and conclusions

mechanisms the means by which a cause produces an effect

Synonyms

interactions.... relationships

General vocabulary

phenomena (singular: phenomenon) facts or events that can be observed

systematic organized carefully and done thoroughly

causation the action of causing something to happen or exist

What practical problems can be solved through applying this knowledge?

Natural science has solved many problems.

Example 1: The development of antibiotics to address the problem of illness

Antibiotics are naturally occurring chemicals that kill bacteria. They naturally occur as moulds or **fungi**. There are many examples of different cultures at different times using moulds and fungi to treat infection. For example, the ancient Greeks and the people of ancient India used moulds and other plants to treat infection. However, they could not control how the moulds and fungi were produced. During the 18th and 19th centuries, interest in producing antibacterial substances grew. The methodology for isolating and controlling the growth of helpful moulds or fungi became more developed.

In 1928, Sir Alexander Fleming noticed how bacteria could not grow around a mould, which he assumed correctly was *Penicillium notatum*. Over the following years, other researchers were able to isolate penicillin and began to produce it. The antibiotic has been used to treat the growth of harmful bacteria inside the body. It is considered one of the most **influential** discoveries and has saved the lives of millions of people.

The key point about the discovery is that it was made using:

- standardized methods to **isolate** key **variables**
- the knowledge and expertise of researchers who had studied the same process.

What are the current open questions in this area?

The natural sciences are driven by curiosity. They want to understand the natural world. Here are some of the open questions that encourage experts in the natural sciences to continue their work.

Examples of open questions

- What is the universe made of?
- How did life begin?
- Is the Solar System dynamically stable?
- What are comets made of?
- Are there other universes?
- What makes us human?
- What is at the bottom of the ocean?
- How can major diseases such as HIV/AIDS be cured?
- How do viruses spread through a population?

Some of these questions belong largely to pure science. Pure science produces theories and predictions. Applied science seeks to solve practical issues. For example:

- how to deal with the world's increasing population
- how to meet the world's energy needs
- how to maintain or improve the quality of the environment.

Many of these problems require **input** from other areas of knowledge in addition to the natural sciences (for example, the human sciences: sociology, law, politics, psychology, economics, geography). This overlap raises both **theoretical** and practical issues.

> Articulation sentence:
> Science does not operate in isolation. Its findings usually cross boundaries into other disciplines such as sociology, philosophy, ethics, law, politics, education, and psychology.

What are the ethical considerations that limit the scope of inquiry?

Ethical thinking concerns what is allowed and what is not allowed. Ethics can therefore limit the kinds of question the natural sciences can study and the kinds of method the natural sciences can use.

Example 1: Appropriateness of topics

Knowledge claim: There are topics that are not suitable for scientific study.

James Watson (b. 1928) is an American molecular biologist, geneticist, and zoologist. Together with Francis Crick, he discovered the structure of DNA in 1953.

Recently, Watson has suggested:

- There is a link between skin colour and libido. He argues darker-skinned people have stronger libido due to the melanin present in darker skin (Watson cited in Abate, 2000).
- 'Stupidity' should be cured through genetic engineering (Watson cited in Bhattacharya, 2007).
- 'Beauty' should be genetically engineered (Watson cited in Bhattacharya, 2007).
- There is a link between race and intelligence (Watson cited in Milmo, 2013).

These topics may be **distasteful** for some people to consider. Problems arise in the natural sciences when scientists are discouraged from considering these questions due to cultural **sensitivities**. Cultural sensitivities could include religious sensitivities in religious societies, or questions of **political correctness** in **Western** countries. If theories cannot be tested, it means humans cannot further their understanding of the natural world. For example, it may offend people to consider a link between race and intelligence, but if the theory cannot be tested, then it will remain an unanswered question. The resulting ignorance may actually encourage **prejudice** through a lack of understanding.

Example 2: Animal testing

Knowledge claim: Animals are particularly useful in research because researchers do not have the same level of moral obligation towards them as they do towards humans.

Animals are used in the following ways.

- *To advance scientific understanding:* Adding to scientific knowledge through basic biological research creates knowledge about how living things work.
- *To test models of disease:* Humans and animals suffer from the same diseases. Therefore, animals can act as models for the study of human illness. For example, rabbits suffer from emphysema, which is a disease of the lungs; and dogs suffer from diabetes.
- *To develop and test potential forms of treatment:* Once treatments for illness have been developed, they need to be tested and their potential side-effects and benefits need to be assessed.

However, there are strict guidelines that must be followed for animal use in research. These guidelines may limit the **scope** of inquiry. The British Society of Animal Science wrote a set of **ethical guidelines** for the use of animals in research experimentation, which they refer to as the 3Rs.

- *Refinement:* Any animal science research undertaken should be as focused as possible. It should have realistic and achievable aims of increasing knowledge of the species in relation to our understanding of its functioning, performance, health, or welfare.

- *Replacement:* Researchers must consider all available options to replace animals with other techniques that will fulfil the research objectives. Researchers should always actively look for non-animal methods of investigation (e.g. **computer models**).

- *Reduction:* There is a scientific, **moral obligation** and legal requirement to expose as few animals to pain, suffering, and distress as possible.

> Articulation sentence:
> Animals are particularly useful in research. It is commonly agreed by most natural science researchers that they do not have the same level of moral obligation towards animals as they do towards humans.

Knowledge framework: Concepts/language

What role does language play in the accumulation of knowledge in this area?

Role 1: The use of mathematical language

- In physics, almost all the key concepts are linked by mathematical relationships.
- Geologists use mathematical models to describe geomagnetic fields.
- Biological reports almost always include mathematics such as graphs, charts, and tables.

Role 2: The use of standardized language

The sciences use **standardized** and **specific** vocabulary. For example, each science aims to give very specific names to objects and processes. Scientific language aims for **precision** and seeks to avoid **ambiguity**. Students of science must learn many new words in order to **master** their topic.

Examples of standardized and specific vocabulary in biology include:

- cytoplasm
- nucleolus
- nucleus
- organ
- tissue
- vacuole
- cell wall
- chlorophyll
- chloroplast
- chromosome.

> Articulation sentence:
> The sciences use standardized and specific vocabulary to be precise and avoid ambiguity.

Knowledge question: To what extent can language mislead us in the natural sciences?

Example 1: 'Survival of the fittest'

The phrase 'survival of the fittest' is a phrase often associated with the theory of natural selection. It was **coined** by Herbert Spencer (1820–1903), who was a 19th-century English philosopher. It can be misleading because the word 'fittest' has changed its meaning over time. In the 19th century it meant 'best-fitted'; the correct modern-day interpretation should be: *survival of the organism best suited to its environment.*

However, the word 'fittest' can now be associated with 'the strongest' or even 'the most attractive'. **Notions** of the 'strongest' or 'most beautiful' being most fit for survival have influenced movements such as the Social Darwinists and the Eugenics Movement.

> Articulation sentence:
> The language used to describe the theory of natural selection led (in part) to **deformed** theories of how society should be **ordered**.

Social Darwinism is a name given to various social theories that became popular in Europe in the late 19th and early 20th centuries. The theories claimed to be able to apply the theory of natural selection and the notion of 'survival of the fittest' to problems facing society.

For example, Social Darwinists generally argue:

- wealth and power should increase for the 'strong'
- wealth and power should decrease for the 'weak'
- 'strength' should be encouraged
- 'weakness' should be discouraged.

There is usually debate over which groups should be considered 'strong' and 'weak', but there is typically a racial component to the theory. The above aims are achieved by encouraging competition between individuals.

> Articulation sentence:
> Social Darwinism is a movement based in part on misinterpretations of the word 'fittest'. Social Darwinists wrongly believe strength increases an organism's chance of survival.

Social Darwinism led to the development of the Eugenics Movement. The Eugenics Movement aims to 'improve' the genetic quality of the human population by selective breeding. This is achieved by encouraging people with 'desirable' **traits** to reproduce and discouraging people with 'undesirable' traits from reproducing – usually by sterilization. Many countries took an interest in the theories of eugenics as a way to 'improve' the genetic stock of their people. It should also be noted, that in many countries in the past, the theories of eugenics and forced sterilization had public support.

Example 2: In Nazi Germany

Nazi Germany passed the Law for the Prevention of Hereditarily Diseased **Offspring** (Gesetz zur Verhütung erbkranken Nachwuchses) in July 1933. According to the law, doctors were required to report patients who were classified **intellectually** disabled, mentally ill (including **schizophrenia** and **manic depression**), epileptic, blind, deaf, or physically deformed. The laws also applied to **homosexuals** and people from mixed race relationships. As a result, patients were **forcibly** sterilized.

Subject vocabulary

compatible results data that fit a previous theory and data

Synonyms

targeted......... focused on

unfit.............. unsuitable

acknowledges accepts

General vocabulary

undesirables people who are not liked or that other people are suspicious of

promiscuous having many sexual partners

disproportionate higher (or lower) than would be expected

ethnic minorities groups of people of a different race from the main ethnic group in a country

biases opinions about whether a person, group, or idea is good or bad, which influence how that person, group or thing is dealt with

interact have a relationship

on the right track going in the right direction

Example 3: In the USA

The USA enacted sterilization laws for **undesirables** during the early to mid-20th century. The targets of the American programme were the 'intellectually disabled' and the mentally ill. However, many individual state laws **targeted** the deaf, the blind, people with epilepsy, and the physically 'deformed'. **Promiscuous** women (but not men) were also targeted as they were more likely to have children out of marriage. A **disproportionate** number of people affected were from **ethnic minorities** such as Native Americans and African Americans.

Articulation sentence:
The scientific language used to explain the theory of natural selection led to (in part) deformed theories of how society should be ordered. This led to forced sterilization programmes of people considered **unfit** for reproduction.

What are the roles of the key concepts and key terms that provide the building blocks for knowledge in this area?

Key concept 1: Objectivity

An approach where sources of influence, such as personal and emotional influences, towards a feature are minimized (McLeod, 2008). Objectivity can be contrasted with *subjectivity*, whereby a researcher **acknowledges** how their own personal **biases** influenced the research process towards the feature being studied.

Articulation sentence:
Scientific objectivity is the idea that claims, methods, and results in science should not be affected by individual perspectives such as values or bias. It is the basis for the authority of science in society.

Key concept 2: Theory

The natural sciences seek to demonstrate theory. A theory connects the results of many experiments and observations to provide a framework of explanation. Theories provide a framework for understanding and expressing knowledge. They allow new ideas to be developed that support the basic assumptions of the original theory.

Key concept 3: Replicability

Researchers re-test their results to discover if the results repeat themselves. Replicability is when a repeated study gives the same or compatible results over time.

Key concept 4: Validity

Researchers re-test their results to discover if the results are correct and to check the correct methods have been used. The review procedure is examined to make sure it is appropriate. In an experimental setting, validity refers to the level of confidence a researcher has that the independent variable (IV) caused the dependent variable (DV).

Replicability and validity **interact** and indicate if scientists are **on the right track** with their theories.

However, it should be noted:

- results can be replicable but not valid
- results can be valid but not replicable.

Hypothetical example

A chemist conducts an experiment with test tubes wherein she mixes chemical a with chemical b to make product c: a + b = c

She replicates the experiment and finds the same result: a + b = c

The results are replicable. She is certain the results are valid. However, another chemist performs the same experiment with different test tubes and does not find the same result.

The new lack of reliability causes the two chemists to question their methods. They recheck the **apparatus** and find an additional chemical (chemical f) was present in the original test tubes. Therefore, the original statement a + b = c is not valid even though the same results appeared to be replicated. After further testing they **assert**: a + b + f = c

What is the role of convention in this area?

Conventions in natural science are used to standardize methodology and **terminology** to allow communication and understanding to take place across **national boundaries**. Conventions are rules or guidelines that are used and recognized by many people.

Convention 1: The metric system

The metric system is an internationally recognized decimal system of measurement. It was originally developed during the French First Republic in 1799. It is officially referred to as the SI or 'International System of Units' and is used by almost every country. It consists of a basic set of units of measurement known as base units.

The SI base units are:

- metres for length
- kilograms for mass
- seconds for time
- ampères for electric current
- kelvin for temperature
- candelas for **luminous** intensity
- moles for the amount of substance.

> Articulation sentence:
> The metric system allows the natural world to be studied in a standardized way by different people in different cultures.

Convention 2: The use of Latin and Greek

Latin and Greek are traditionally used for officially naming concepts in natural science. For example, the official name for a domestic dog is *Canis lupus familiaris*.

The reasons for using Latin and Greek as the standard language of the natural sciences are these.

- Latin was the language of the Christian Church in Europe, where a significant amount of early work in the natural sciences was **conducted**. It had **prestige** as a **sophisticated** language.
- Latin and Greek were the languages of the scholars and educated people throughout Europe.
- Latin and Greek were already dead languages as science developed in the Middle Ages. They were not spoken by everyday people. Using Latin and Greek for science meant the system did not favour a particular culture or group of people.

> Articulation sentence:
> Conventions in natural science are used to standardize methodology and terminology to allow communication and understanding to take place across national boundaries.

Knowledge framework: Methodology

What are the methods or procedures used in this area and what is it about these methods that generates knowledge?

Method 1: The scientific method

The scientific method begins with a theory or hypothesis about how the world works. Then an experiment is devised to test it. The results of the experiment are analysed and conclusions drawn. The original theory can then be modified as necessary and the process repeated, Figure 5.1.

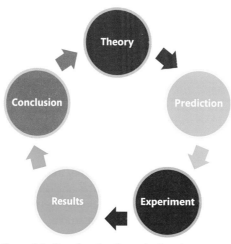

Figure 5.1 *How the scientific method works.*

Method 2: Peer review

The natural sciences are examples of shared knowledge. The results of scientific studies are published so that they are available for study by other researchers working in the same field. Peer review is the process whereby other experts in the knowledge community evaluate the study and its conclusions before it is accepted as shared knowledge.

How does it generate knowledge?

The results of scientific exploration are not final. Science is **provisional**. This means that it is always possible to improve or correct scientific ideas. Science should be self-correcting. The goal is to find a better theory, a better explanation, or a better understanding of cause and effect. This leads to the knowledge questions below.

Knowledge question: How can explanations be compared?

Knowledge question: If there are rival explanations, what are the criteria for judging which is better?

Peer review takes place at an official level in peer-reviewed journals. These are **periodically published** and read by experts in the field. They are very specific. For example, *The Journal of Neuroscience Methods* publishes papers that describe new methods specifically for neuroscience research conducted in invertebrates, vertebrates, or humans.

> Articulation sentence:
> Peer review is the process whereby other experts in the knowledge community evaluate research before it is accepted as shared knowledge.

Method 3: The use of scientific theory

A theory is an explanation of some aspect of the natural world that has been acquired through the scientific method (National Academy of Sciences, 1999). Therefore, it has been repeatedly tested and confirmed through observation and experimentation.

How does it generate knowledge?

Theories provide a framework for understanding and articulating knowledge. They allow new ideas to be developed that support the basic assumptions of the original theory over time.

The development over time of the Theory of Natural Selection

The following section demonstrates how theories change over time to take account of new findings and increase understanding of the natural world.

When Darwin presented his theory in the book *On the Origin of Species*, he was not aware of the biological processes through which traits are inherited. However, the theory provided a framework for understanding and articulating knowledge about the origins of life and how life forms change over time.

The key assumptions were:
- evolution is caused by natural selection
- evolution is caused by sexual selection.

The basic assumptions of natural selection are these.
- The resources needed for survival are limited.
- There is a struggle to survive in the environment.
- Environments present challenges to individuals and species.
- Individuals in the population have **variations** in their traits. These variations make the individual organism more or less suited to its environment.
- Individuals with better-adapted traits have a better chance of surviving and passing their better-adapted genes on to the next generation.
- Individuals with less well-adapted traits have a worse chance of surviving and passing their less well-adapted genes on to the next generation.

Sexual selection is a subset of natural selection because the sexual environment is part of the natural environment. The basic assumptions of sexual selection are these.
- There is a struggle to **breed** in the environment (Darwin referred to it as the 'sexual struggle').
- Sexual selection takes place between individuals of the same sex (generally the males) in order to **drive away** or kill their **rivals**, and to attract individuals of the opposite sex (generally the females) who then select the more **agreeable** partners.
- Better-adapted organisms have characteristics which make the individual more sexually attractive – and therefore more likely to **mate**.
- Individuals with better-adapted sexual traits have a better chance of breeding and passing their better-adapted genes on to the next generation.
- Individuals with less-well-adapted sexual traits have a worse chance of breeding and passing their less-well-adapted genes on to the next generation.

Subject vocabulary

assumptions unproven starting points, suppositions

species a class of individuals or organisms having some common characteristics and able to breed together

Synonyms

variations ...... differences

drive away ..... repel

rivals............. competitors

agreeable ...... appropriate

General vocabulary

subset a group of people or things that is part of a larger group of people or things

breed have sex to produce offspring

mate have sex to produce babies

How have new ideas been developed that support the basic assumptions of the original theory?

Darwin understood there was a biological mechanism that allowed traits to be **passed on** but appropriate methods had not been developed to enable him to fully investigate them. Others used his basic theory to uncover the mechanisms that allowed traits to be passed on. Figure 5.2 demonstrates how theories provide research focus to allow for the development of new additions to the original theory over time.

Subject vocabulary

classification putting organisms into groups or categories to enable study

prediction the act of making a statement about the future

General vocabulary

passed on given to offspring or children through genes

nuanced very slightly different

sound sensible and likely to produce the right results

Mendel (1822–1884) is seen as the founder of genetics. Mendel's pea plant experiments conducted between 1856 and 1863 established many of the rules of studying how traits are passed on. This led to a focus on how genes pass on biological instructions.

↓

Deoxyribonucleic acid (DNA) is a molecule that encodes genetic instructions. DNA was first identified and isolated by Friedrich Miescher in 1871.

↓

The structure of DNA was discovered by James Watson and Francis Crick in 1953. They based their work on the data collected by Rosalind Franklin and Maurice Wilkins.

↓

Epigenetics is the study of cellular and physiological trait variations that are not caused by changes in the DNA sequence. It developed in the early 21st century as new technology allowed closer inspection of the DNA molecule.

↓

Epigenetics focuses on how changes occur (on a genetic level) *over the lifetime of the individual* and the extent to which these changes are passed on to the next generation.

Figure 5.2 *How new ideas support the Theory of Natural Selection.*

In sum: Due to the development of the theory of natural selection using the principles of the scientific method, it is now believed the basic mechanisms of evolution are more **nuanced** than previously thought. Darwin himself stated he did not believe natural and sexual selection were the *sole* mechanisms for passing on characteristics from one generation to the next. The basic theory has stimulated new research over time by providing a **sound** basis for thought and articulation.

Articulation sentence:

Theories provide a framework for understanding and articulating knowledge. They allow new ideas to be developed over time that support the basic assumptions of the original theory.

Method 4: The use of classification

Science seeks to find patterns in the natural world. The knowledge has to be ordered to allow it to be studied.

How does it generate knowledge?

Classification helps explain relationships in the natural world and helps improve **prediction**, Figure 5.3, opposite.

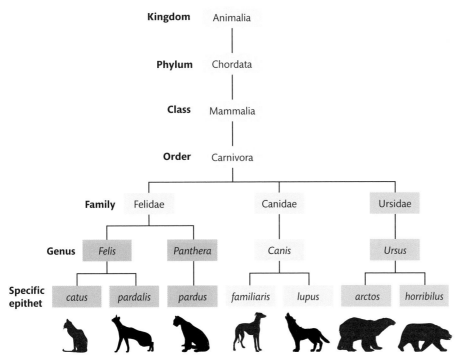

Figure 5.3 *Classification scheme showing the relationships between cats, dogs and bears.*

Method 5: The use of models

Models are representations of complex processes.

The characteristics of models are:

- a model is a simpler representation of an aspect or process in the world
- models **leave out** many aspects
- models can describe
- models can explain
- models are usually used to make predictions about the process they represent.

How does it generate knowledge?

Models are representations of complex processes. Models are useful because they simplify complex phenomena and make them easier to study.

Figure 5.4 is the Bohr model of the atom. It was developed by Niels Bohr in 1913. It shows the atom as a small, positively charged nucleus surrounded by electrons that travel in circular orbits around the nucleus. It is similar in structure to the Solar System. However, attraction is caused by electrostatic forces rather than gravity.

Subject vocabulary

atom the smallest component of an element or living thing

orbits circular paths around a central object

Solar System the name given to the Sun and all the planets and other bodies that revolve around it, including the Earth

Synonyms

leave out........ do not include, omit

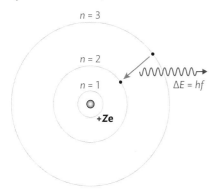

Figure 5.4 *The Bohr model of the atom.*

What are the assumptions underlying these methods?

Assumption 1: The world is rationally comprehensible

'Rationally comprehensible' means causes in the world can be uncovered and understood in terms of natural phenomena. Causes are demonstrated with scientific law.

Scientific law is a phenomenon that invariably occurs whenever certain conditions exist. The formal statement about such a phenomenon is called *natural law* – a generalized rule to explain a body of observations that show cause and effect.

For example, Newton's First Law states that an object will remain at rest or in uniform motion in a straight line unless acted on by an external force.

The subset of this assumption is: The world is a system of cause and effect.

Assumption 2: Empiricism

The emphasis placed on evidence (usually quantitative) to build theory. Evidence is usually collected by carrying out experiments and making observations. It is a key part of the scientific method that all hypotheses and theories must be tested under scientific conditions rather than using **revelation** or imagination.

Assumption 3: Induction

Science can never test all possible examples. For example, the natural sciences cannot study every polar bear to test if they are all white. So far, all polar bears seen have been white. However, it is not possible to say with absolute certainty that all polar bears are white. The natural sciences must *assume* that conclusions that apply to a few samples will apply to all examples. This is the process of induction. The natural sciences believe that nature has laws and principles which can be applied to individuals not included in the sample.

 Articulation sentence:
The process of induction is the assumption that conclusions that apply to a few samples will apply to all examples.

Assumption 4: Generalizability

The natural sciences seek to make valid generalizations. A valid generalization is a broad understanding based on a smaller sample that applies to a larger population. For example, scientists do not study all tree roots. They seek to discover things that are true for all tree roots by studying a small sample of tree roots. They seek to make generalizations that show the similarities and differences between different kinds of tree roots.

Articulation sentence:
Generalizations give us a broad understanding and link different areas.

Assumption 5: Positivism

Positivism emphasizes knowledge creation by the use of empirical evidence and scientific methods (Jakobsen, 2013).

Example: Falsifiability/disconfirmation

These ideas concern the *testing* of scientific ideas. The philosopher Karl Popper argues that scientific theories can be clearly separated from non-scientific theories through falsification: if a theory cannot be tested and thereby have the opportunity to be falsified by scientific means, then it is not scientific.

It should be noted:

- not all philosophers agree with Popper's assertion
- Popper also argued that unfalsifiable statements have a place in natural science because they allow creativity to influence the research process.

Falsification allows theories to progress and develop. Falsified theories are replaced by theories that can account for the phenomena that falsified the prior theory.

Assumption 6: Causation

This is the belief that one event leads to another and that events occur in predictable ways (Shepard and Greene, 2003).

Example: The peppered moth

The basic principles of natural selection are shown by the effect of pollution on the development of a darker-coloured peppered **moth** (Kettlewell and Ford, 1956). Moths in certain geographical areas evolved darker wings. It is assumed this was *caused* by pollution. Darker wings help the moths **blend in** better with the **bark** of the trees which are stained by pollution. Therefore, the following can be predicted.

- Moths with darker wings are less likely to be eaten than moths with lighter wings.
- Moths with lighter wings are more likely to be eaten than moths with darker wings.
- Lighter coloured moths will become less common.
- Darker coloured moths will become more common.

The principles of evolution dictate that environments present challenges to individuals and species. In this example, the environmental change from pollution presented challenges to the moths and *caused* a change. The prediction could then be made based on the principles of the theory: *Those who are better adapted through inherited characteristics stand more chance of surviving and passing their genes onto the next generation*. This prediction can be tested using observation over time and causation can be established.

Knowledge framework: Historical development

What is the significance of the key points in the historical development of this area of knowledge?

Key Point 1: The Age of Enlightenment and the scientific revolution

In Europe, Christianity offered a grand narrative to explain the world. This narrative could not be challenged. Christianity explained how the world came to **exist** and why. People who challenged this basic belief were dealt with **harshly** to discourage others from challenging Christianity.

The Age of Enlightenment, or the Age of Reason, is a label for a historical era from the 1650s to the 1780s. During this period, Christianity's grand narrative to explain the world was challenged. During the Enlightenment, cultural and intellectual figures (for example, John Locke, Isaac Newton) **promoted** reason, **analysis**, tolerance, science, **scepticism**, and **individualism** as the key building blocks of society.

Subject vocabulary

grand narrative large explanation that addresses many factors

Synonyms

blend in .... camouflaged

exist .... be present

harshly .... severely

promoted ...... encouraged

analysis .... detailed examination

scepticism ...... doubting, questioning

General vocabulary

moth an insect that flies mainly at night and is attracted to lights; related to the butterfly

bark the outer covering of a tree

individualism behaving as an individual

Synonyms

dominance..... superiority

General vocabulary

torture to deliberately hurt someone in order to force them to give you information, to punish them, or to be cruel

learned people people who have a lot of knowledge because they have read and studied a lot

This approach challenged the **dominance** of Christianity in explaining the natural world. Initially, **key thinkers** were at risk of **torture** and death. However, over time science became an accepted approach to explain the natural world.

The Age of Enlightenment was influenced by the period known as the Scientific Revolution. This was a period when developments in mathematics, physics, astronomy, biology, and chemistry began to explain the natural world using science as the main method.

Articulation sentence:
The Age of Enlightenment or the Age of Reason are labels for a historical era from the 1650s to the 1780s. During this era, it became possible to use reason, analysis, and science to explain the natural world.

Key point 2: Development of scientific academies

Scientific academies are societies of **learned people**. They promote science as an academic discipline. They use conferences, journals, sponsorship, academic training, and a sense of membership to ensure science remains scientific. Scientific academies play a key role in promoting scientific collaborations among nations to address common problems facing the natural world. Most countries have them as part of their cultural traditions.

Scientific academies act as:

● standard bearers – upholding standards, routines, and promoting the 'correct' way of doing things', while regulating how challenges can be best communicated and addressed

● communications hubs – like-minded individuals have a space to communicate, share knowledge, and develop ideas.

The Royal Society of London for Improving Natural Knowledge

This society acts as the UK's Academy of Sciences. It was founded in 1660 by King Charles II. It supports modern science by:

● funding research

● funding the careers of scientists

● promoting innovation

● awarding prizes for work.

Articulation sentence:
Scientific academies are societies of learned people. They promote science as an academic discipline. They are an example of a mechanism to share knowledge.

Knowledge framework: Links to personal knowledge

What is the nature of the contribution of individuals to this area?

Key individual 1: Nicolaus Copernicus

Nicolaus Copernicus (1473–1543) was a scholar who created a model of the universe that placed the Sun rather than the Earth at its centre. He spoke many languages but lived and died in an area known as Royal Prussia, which is now modern-day Poland. This period of history was dominated by religious thinking in Europe. Copernicus **proposed** that the Earth was not at the centre of the known universe – this challenged the notion that the Earth and humans were God's special creations. People who challenged this notion were tortured, imprisoned, and killed.

What is the nature of Copernicus's contribution?

The Copernican Revolution was a paradigm shift in how the natural world was viewed. He was one of many thinkers who gave scholars a theoretical framework for moving away from the notion that religious texts could fully explain the natural world and that God had placed humans at the centre of the universe. Therefore, Copernicus is seen as one of the 'fathers of the scientific revolution'.

His name is given to a principle to test for 'modern thought' known as the *Copernican principle*: 'It is evident that in the post-Copernican era of human history, no well-informed and rational person can imagine that Earth occupies a unique position in the universe' (Rowan–Robinson, 1996: 62–63).

> Articulation sentence:
> Copernicus proposed that the Earth was not at the centre of the known universe. This challenged the notion that the Earth and humans were God's special creations.

Key individual 2: Charles Darwin

Charles Darwin (1809–1882) was an English geologist and naturalist. Darwin was interested in religious thinking and his earlier work was an attempt to find evidence for divinity in nature. Darwin was also thinking and working at a time when competing theories of how species change over time were common. For example, Jean-Baptiste de Lamarck (1744–1829) was a French naturalist. His theory was a dominant explanation of evolution. He assumed:

- evolution happens according to a **predetermined** plan
- change is made by what the organisms *want* and/or *need*
- changes as a result of these wants and needs are then passed on to offspring.

An example of Lamarckian reasoning is: Giraffes used to have short necks. Over time, many generations reached up to trees and this gradually lengthened the neck of giraffes.

What is the nature of Darwin's contribution?

Darwin rejected the basic assumptions of Lamarckian reasoning.

He established:
- all species of life have **descended** over time from common **ancestors**
- species change over time by the process of natural selection
- species change over time by the process of sexual selection.

He was able to demonstrate his theory using fossils and studying animals in very specific ecosystems.

For example, Darwin studied **finches** which live on the Galápagos Islands, near Ecuador. The conditions on these islands represent an environmental challenge to finches because there is little food and the islands are all very different. Darwin noticed the beaks of the birds were adapted to their specific environmental niches, which contained very specific food sources, Figure 5.5, overleaf.

Subject vocabulary

paradigm shift a change in the way the world is seen

geologist an individual who studies the Earth and rocks

naturalist an individual who studies natural history and how life has changed over time

divinity God

fossils bones found in rock; bones that have turned into rock

environmental niches the specific living environments of organisms

Synonyms

ancestors .... forebears

General vocabulary

proposed suggested

predetermined decided or arranged before something happens, so that it does not happen by chance

descended to be related to a person or group who lived a long time ago

finches small birds with a short beak

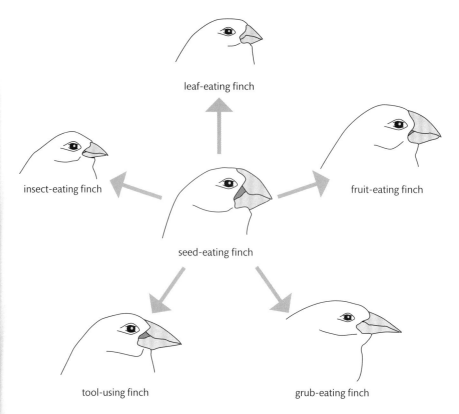

Figure 5.5 *Development of different beaks in Galápagos finches.*

> Articulation sentence:
> Charles Darwin articulated the theory of evolution, which shows how species change over time due to natural and sexual selection.

Due to recent advances in technology, some Lamarckian principles are being revisited. For example, epigenetics focuses on how changes occur (on a genetic level) *over the lifetime of the individual* and the extent to which these changes are passed on to the next generation.

> Articulation sentence:
> Darwin provided a sound theoretical framework to demonstrate how species change over time and adapt to environmental challenges. However, scientific theories have to adapt to new evidence. Epigenetics represents a new line of thinking for how species change over time without challenging the basic assumptions of Darwin's ideas.

Knowledge framework: Scope/applications

What is the area of knowledge about?

The following are examples of **academic disciplines** within the human sciences.

- Anthropology focuses on wider cultural and historical **influences** on **humankind**. It aims to answer the following questions:
  - *What is culture? How does culture influence human behaviour? How has culture changed over time? How and why are human cultures different from one another? How does the environment influence human development?*

- Economics focuses on **financial affairs**. It aims to answer the following questions:
  - *How is wealth produced? How is wealth used? How is wealth transferred?*

- Psychology focuses on the individual. It aims to answer the following questions:
  - *How do humans think, feel, and act in different environments? How do their thoughts, feelings, and behaviours influence themselves and others?*

- Sociology focuses on social and cultural influences on humankind. It aims to answer the following questions:
  - *How do the structures of society (e.g. government policies; laws; education) influence humankind? What are the social problems facing humankind and how can they be addressed? What groups are there in society and how do they form and change over time?*

The academic disciplines can usually be divided into *theoretical* and *applied* components (e.g. Applied Sociology).

- Theoretical human science: concerned with working with existing theories about human nature and creating new theories to explain and predict human behaviour.

- Applied human science: concerned with using theories to solve human problems in a practical way.

> Articulation sentence:
> The human sciences are about **investigating** and understanding human behaviour.

What practical problems can be solved through applying this knowledge?

Knowledge claim: Viewing humans through clearly defined perspectives can help our understanding of them.

Human science **theorists** and researchers consider humankind from different **perspectives** and take account of these different perspectives when writing and researching. They rarely consider humankind from the perspective of just one academic discipline. For example, it would be appropriate to look at crime in a residential area from anthropological, economic, psychological, and sociological perspectives.

Knowledge claim: Some practical problems can best be solved by addressing them within specific disciplines.

- Anthropological perspective: What are the cultural norms for drug use? What are the cultural norms for gun ownership? What are the cultural norms for contraception? What are the cultural norms for female employment? What are the cultural norms for male and female expectations?

- Economic perspective: What are the current levels of employment? What are the causes of unemployment? What is the average weekly family **budget**? How affordable is food and energy?

- Psychological perspective: What are the current levels of drug use? What are the current levels of single parent families? What are the causes of criminal behaviour?

- Sociological perspective: What are the current levels of literacy rates in schools? What are the current levels of government financial help? How accessible are government agencies (such as community centres and doctors)? What is the relationship between **residents** and the police?

The following examples are specific problems that might be addressed by the different disciplines.

Example 1: Anthropology

Practical problem: Organ donation *and use in the USA versus Japan (Lock, 2001).*

Anthropology focuses on cultural norms and how they influence human behaviour.

An anthropological study into organ donation and use has uncovered how Japan and the USA approach organ donation in different ways.

- In the USA, the human body is seen as separate to the mind and the person. It is viewed as a biological machine, whose worn out parts can be replaced. In Japan, there is no separation of body and person.

- In the USA, organs can be **harvested** and donated as **anonymous** gifts. In Japan, organs cannot be harvested as anonymous 'gifts' because any gift must be connected to the person doing the giving. Giving gifts in Japan has far greater social meaning.

> Articulation sentence:
> A different cultural norm in Japan has forced medical practitioners to re-think how they approach organ donation, as the American **model** is not appropriate for Japanese people.

Example 2: Economics

Practical problem: Identifying which areas a government should spend money on to improve the economy (for example, education spending).

A modern successful economy requires a well-educated and skilled workforce. Education is provided by the government and paid for through taxes. Without government intervention, not enough money would be spent on education and training. If education and training were in the private sector, it is likely there would be less education and training available. It is also likely that fewer people would take up education and training. Society would not enjoy all the benefits of a well-educated and well-trained population. The government might **intervene** to ensure that education is as comprehensive as possible. If workers have the skills industries need, unemployment will fall. If more companies have better access to trained people, the economy will improve. Governments can help improve the skills of the workforce by giving subsidies to firms to provide training, and by tailoring education to suit the needs of business.

Articulation sentence:
Economics can be used to identify the areas a government should spend money on to improve the economy. For example, education spending.

Example 3: Psychology

Practical problem: Identifying causes of (usually theories) and solutions to (usually practical therapies) individual problems by carrying out research studies. For example, using psychology to understand domestic violence.

Domestic violence is aggressive behaviour between people who are in a relationship, often married and usually living together. It can include violence between a man and woman, between a parent and child, and sometimes between children too.

- Causation: Social Learning Theory (SLT) can explain how we learn aggression from people around us. SLT assumes humans learn behaviour by observation: we watch others and imitate their behaviour. It has been shown that people are more likely to imitate **role models** of their own gender, role models who they identify the most with, and role models who are rewarded for their behaviour.

- Solution: The Broward County experiment in Florida aimed to test the **effectiveness** of 'group treatment' compared with 'no treatment' for men who had been convicted of domestic violence (Feder and Dugan, 2002). One group of men received 26 weeks of group treatment. A second group received no treatment. To judge the effectiveness of the programme, the researchers looked at police and **probation** records, and interviews with the men. They did this after 6 and 12 months. There was no significant difference between the two groups in terms of the amount of violence after treatment. The treatment could then be altered to take account of the results. The conclusion was that attention also needs to be paid to all the other factors that affect people's behaviour, such as whether they are employed or not.

Articulation sentence:
Psychology can be used to identify causes individuals experience in society and help formulate solutions. For example, domestic violence.

Example 4: Sociology

Practical problem: Making drug campaigns relevant for young people.

The UK Advisory Council on the Misuse of Drugs (1984) researched drug use among the target population of young people. It concluded that government **anti-drug campaigns** were not effective. The campaigns mainly used **scare tactics**. They aimed to shock young people about how dangerous drugs were.

Research was then **conducted** to find out the effects of government anti-drug campaigns. It found certain types of young people were more likely to try drugs because:

- governments specifically told them not to
- the scare campaigns made the drugs look **mysterious**
- the anti-drug campaigns made drug users look **rebellious**.

As a result, anti-drug campaigns became more subtle. Facts were presented coldly and maturely. Scary, dramatic tactics were **toned down**. Government symbols were removed (e.g. the label 'Department of Health' was removed from posters).

The sociological approach to drug research has shown government anti-drug use campaigns were in some cases actually *encouraging* young people to try drugs. Therefore, anti-drug campaigns became more factual, less official, and more subtle to make drugs appear less mysterious and rebellious.

> Articulation sentence:
> Sociology can be used to identify problems that certain groups experience in society and help formulate solutions. For example, young people who do not listen to anti-drug campaigns.

What are the current open questions in this area?

Open question 1: To what extent can human behaviour be investigated scientifically?

The scientific method aims to investigate phenomena through systematic observation, measurement, experiment, and through the formulation, testing, and **modification** of hypotheses. It is based on the notion of causation. The human *body* can be investigated with the scientific approach because we can use the principles of biology to do this.

However, investigating human feelings, thoughts, and behaviours **encompasses** many different **approaches**. This can cause problems for researchers for the following reasons.

- **Establishing** causation with human beings is difficult because there are so many different potential causes for human behaviour.
- Feelings are **transient**. They are **partly** based on biology and partly based in psychology.
- Human behaviour can be unpredictable. People do not behave consistently across space and time. Individual human beings can change their behaviour depending on their surroundings, their feelings, their diets, their sleep pattern, etc.

Open question 2: To what extent can human behaviour be predicted?

Some disciplines assume human behaviour is partly predictable. They aim to predict human behaviour (e.g. economics, psychology, sociology). Therefore, human science **inquirers** will often try and control the environment when they investigate human behaviour. They do this so they can find out how distinct variables influence human behaviour, and so they can have greater confidence in their predictions. However, controlling the environment (e.g. in a laboratory) means they are testing people in a strange environment and this in itself influences human behaviour as the setting is unrealistic. If this happens, the research method can be said to be lacking ecological validity.

Open question 3: To what extent are human behaviours the product of nature or nurture?

Biological determinism can be **contrasted with** environmental determinism – the notion that behaviour is influenced by the environment. This debate is known as the nature/**nurture** debate. Most human behaviours can be debated this way. For example, intelligence, sexuality, aggression, and criminality. It is usually accepted that both biological and environmental influences play a part in human behaviour but the question always remains: To what extent?

What are the ethical considerations that limit the scope of inquiry?

Ethical considerations refer to the correct rules when carrying out human science research. For example, human science researchers have a moral responsibility to protect research participants from emotional harm.

Key study: Milgram's *obedience* study (1963; 1974)

Aim
To investigate the role of authority figures in explaining behaviour.

Method
An authority figure stood next to the participant (the 'teacher') in one room at Yale University. In the next room was a 'learner'. The 'teacher' asked prepared questions. When the 'learner' made a mistake a (**fake**) electric shock was given. The 'teacher' assumed he/she was hurting the 'learner'. Every time a wrong answer was given, the **voltage** was increased. The 'learner' complained of a heart problem and banged on the wall. The participant (as the 'teacher') was encouraged to continue with these standardized instructions.

1   Please continue.

2   The experiment requires that you continue.

3   It is absolutely essential that you continue.

4   You have no other choice, you must go on.

5   Although the shocks may be painful, there is no **permanent tissue** damage, so please go on.

The dependent variable (DV) was the amount of obedience. It was measured according to the fake voltage level. The higher the voltage the participant 'teacher' was willing to use on the 'learner', the higher the level of obedience. The higher voltages up to 450 volts were labelled 'Danger: **Severe** shock' and 'XXX'. The participants thought they were hurting the 'learner'. When the screaming and banging stopped (at 300 volts), the participants had to conclude they had seriously hurt the 'learner'.

Results
No teacher stopped before 300 volts.

65% of all participants continued past 300 volts (when the screaming and banging stopped) to the maximum 450 volts.

The study was replicated with **variations**.

Variation 1: Yale University was replaced with less impressive offices: The obedience rate dropped to 47.5%.

Variation 2: Social support in the form of two more teachers (who were also confederates) who refused to obey: The obedience rate dropped dramatically to 10%.

Conclusion
The presence of an authority figure (in a **lab** coat) who issues instructions can lead to extreme obedience. **Prestigious** settings ('Yale University') lead to more obedience than more **modest** settings. The presence of social support in the form of people who are rebellious leads to less obedience.

inform........... tell

deception ...... lying

deceived........ lied to

findings .... results

**reflect
negatively**...... look bad

distress.......... emotional upset

guidelines rules or instructions about the best way to do something

test subjects people taking part in a study

protected kept from harm

fright a sudden feeling of fear

insightful perceptive, intelligent

identifiable features characteristics that allow an individual to be identified (for example, their name or what they look like)

Ethical consideration 1: The use of humans as test subjects

The British Psychological Society (2004) issued a set of **guidelines** for using humans as **test subjects**.

The have been summarized by McLeod (2007) as follows.

- **Informed consent**
  Researchers are usually expected to explain to the participants what the research is about, and then ask for their consent (i.e. permission) to take part.

  - How might this limit the *scope* of inquiry?
    If researchers reveal too much about the nature and purpose of the research, this will influence the results. It is not always possible or desirable to get informed consent from all participants. For example, if Milgram had informed his participants about the true nature of his research, he would have got lower levels of obedience. If researchers **inform** people they are being observed, this changes their behaviour (known as the *Hawthorne Effect*).

- **The use of deception**
  Researchers often choose to not fully inform participants about the nature of the research. This is to avoid participants trying to guess the nature of the study.

  - *How might this limit the scope of inquiry?*
    Deception can lead to distrust of psychological research. People know about human science research where deception has been used. Milgram is such a famous study that many people who have not studied human science subjects know about it. People who are asked to take part in research may assume they are being **deceived** and will try to guess the 'true' nature of any study they take part in. This will influence the results.

- **Explanation**
  Participants must be given a general idea of what the researcher is investigating and why. Their part in the research process should be explained. They must be told if they have been deceived and given reasons why. They must be given the opportunity to ask questions about the **findings** and publication.

  - *How might this limit the scope of inquiry?*
    Researchers may be reluctant to reveal the full extent of their inquiry because it may **reflect negatively** on the participants (e.g. research investigating prejudice). They may deliberately avoid certain types of topic that would cause **distress** to participants if the full extent of the research was revealed. Milgram chose to explain everything to his participants, which was wise as many of them thought they had actually hurt someone. He also learned that participants were 'pleased' to have taken part in the research because they learned something about themselves.

- **Protection of participants**
  Researchers must ensure participants will not be caused distress beyond what might be expected in ordinary life. Usually this means they will be **protected** from physical and mental harm in the form of embarrassment, **fright**, or personal offence.

  - *How might this limit the scope of inquiry?*
    Many interesting and **insightful** topics may be avoided if this is taken too literally. Milgram's research caused all three of these reactions and yet we learned a lot about the nature of human obedience. If Milgram was doing research today, he may not be allowed to conduct his research in the same way.

- **Confidentiality**
  Participants, and the data gained from them, must be kept anonymous unless they give their full consent. No names and **identifiable features** can be used in a research report.

- *How might this limit the scope of inquiry?*
  It is often difficult to keep the identity of participants truly anonymous in a small group of research participants. This is particularly true with research into small institutions (e.g. a school; a company; a hotel) whereby participant responses will be linked to their jobs. For example, a researcher might state: 'The head chef had serious reservations about how the food budget was spent by the senior managers.' In this situation, the head chef is clearly identifiable even though their name has not been revealed. The researcher may choose to re-label the person as 'a senior kitchen employee' but the head chef is still potentially identifiable. The researcher could avoid any identifiable characteristics and label the head chef as a 'hotel employee'. However, this makes what the researcher is saying less powerful because the staff member is no longer identified as a kitchen employee or as having anything to do with the food budget. In protecting the head chef's true identity, the research could lose some of its potential **impact**.

- **Right to withdraw**
  Participants must be aware of their right to stop participating in the study and may stop participating at any time.
  - *How might this limit the scope of inquiry?*
    It is in the interests of the researcher to keep as many participants as possible during the entire research process, as participants who stop will effect the results. Milgram deliberately **downplayed** the ability of the participants to stop, otherwise many of them would have done so.

  Articulation sentence:
  The British Psychological Society (2004) issued a set of guidelines for using humans as test subjects. They are:

  - informed consent – an explanation should be given where appropriate
  - the use of deception should be limited
  - participants should be protected from physical and mental harm
  - participants, and the data gained from them, must be kept anonymous unless they give their full consent
  - participants must be aware of their right to stop participating in the study.

Ethical consideration 2: The use of human personal material as research data

For example, research with genetics needs to have clear ethical guidelines for the following reasons.

- Research can reveal unexpected information that may harm research participants; for example, evidence of true **parentage**, secret **adoption**, or when a person discovers from the study that he or she carries the gene for a particular genetic **disorder**. Such information can cause undue stress to the participant.
- Research can often be **complex** and misunderstood. Careful consideration needs to be given to how participants and their families are kept informed about the nature of genetic research.

Here are some example guidelines that govern how genetic research is carried out.

- Participants should always know how their details will be protected, and what will happen to any genetic information obtained as part of the study.
- The aims and **procedure** of the study must be explained in plain language. Participants must sign an informed **consent** form to show they have a clear understanding of the study they are participating in, and the implications, including any potential harm.

Subject vocabulary

procedure the method used to gather data in a study

consent agreement to take part in a study

Synonyms

impact........... effect

General vocabulary

downplayed made to seem less important than something really is

parentage who the biological parents are

adoption parenting a child by non-biologically related adults

disorder a mental or physical illness which prevents part of your body from working properly

complex consisting of many different parts and often difficult to understand

coding placing markers on data (usually colours or numbers) so the source of the data cannot be identified

scientific value importance to scientists

rigorous tone reporting with an academic and scientific voice

variable a factor that plays some part in the research process or the phenomenon under investigation; a factor a researcher is controlling, manipulating, or measuring

neutral questions questions that are not biased

biases opinions about whether a person, group, or idea is good or bad, which influence how that person, group or thing is dealt with

Synonyms

determined.... caused

unwittingly .... unintentionally

implies .... suggests

positive connotations.. suggestions of goodness

negative connotations.. suggestions of badness

strive for........ aim for

General vocabulary

aboriginal people the native people or indigenous tribe of a country; the original or earliest known people of a country

follow-ups checks that earlier actions have been successful or effective

- Some groups, including **aboriginal people**, may have objections to genetic studies as a cultural principle. It is very important to consult with relevant community leaders and organizations, and explain research aims in language they understand. Consent is a community matter for many ethnic groups, not a matter for an individual.

- Privacy can be protected by coding information. Codes are assigned to the research material and only a small number of researchers have access to the codes. Researchers can make the sample fully anonymous so that they cannot link any information to particular people.

  - *How might this limit the scope of inquiry?*
    Coding can limit the scientific value of a study by preventing **follow-ups** and further investigation.

Knowledge framework: Concepts/language

What role does language play in the accumulation of knowledge in this area?

Human science researchers have to consider the impact of language in the following areas.

- Human science researchers often use scientific language to give their research a more rigorous tone. For example, words such as variable, control, causation, and **determined** are borrowed from the natural science discipline.

- Human science researchers need to know how to word questions, so that they can write questionnaires in a way that does not **unwittingly** influence the results.

Knowledge question: Is it possible to have neutral questions?

A question is considered to be a neutral question if it appears to have no biases. However, this is difficult to achieve. Suppose you have a questionnaire about gun control (this statement itself is non-neutral because it assumes guns should be 'controlled'). The question below might appear on such a questionnaire:

Many people have said that there is a need for stricter laws on dangerous weapons. Do you agree?

This is a non-neutral question because it contains the phrase 'many people'. This suggests that there is a common answer, and may influence the participant in his/her answer.

The question could be written:

Do you agree or disagree with this statement: There is a need for better gun regulation.

There is still a problem with neutrality because the word 'better' **implies** that current gun laws are not good enough.

A more neutral way might be to phrase it:

Do you agree or disagree with this statement: There is a need for stricter gun laws.

But there could still be a problem with the neutrality of this question because the word 'stricter' may have **positive connotations** for some people and **negative connotations** for others.

> Articulation sentence:
> The notion of neutrality might be seen as something to **strive for** rather than something that can be definitively achieved.

What are the roles of the key concepts and key terms that provide the building blocks for knowledge in this area?

Key term: Reliability

The term 'reliability' refers to *internal reliability* and *external reliability*. Internal reliability refers to results from research being consistent from different samples. External reliability refers to results from research being consistent from different researchers who have **replicated** the study and found the same results.

For example, consider a human science study that investigates the mental health of **prisoners**. Researcher A assumes the amount of time the prisoners spend in **cells** may be causing problems. The researcher issues questionnaires to prisoners about how long they spend in cells and their mental health. The results indicate 'being locked in cells causes mental health problems for prisoners'. Other researchers using the same questionnaire in other prisons find the same results. The conclusion might be to allow prisoners more time outside their cells.

Reliability gives us confidence that research methods used are a correct way to investigate a particular phenomenon. However, it does not mean that the results are valid.

Key term: Validity

The term 'validity' refers to the notion that a study has measured what it claims to measure. For example, a questionnaire is not necessarily an appropriate way to investigate such a personal matter as mental health. Researcher B decides to carry out an in-depth case study of one prison. She finds that 'being locked in cells' is not the cause of mental health problems. Rather, the cause is the availability of drugs, the **corruption** of **guards**, and the amount of violence. Therefore, the previous study which argued 'being locked in cells causes mental health problems for prisoners' could be considered to be lacking validity. Researcher B actually argues that if prisoners were given more time outside their cells, these problems would get worse. The prison management becomes alarmed and **commissions** other studies. However, other researchers are not able replicate Researcher B's findings. She makes the claim that although her research lacks reliability, it is still valid.

> **Articulation sentence:**
> The role validity plays is to act as a **check** for researchers (and their peer reviewers) to make sure the research shows what it claims to show.

> **Articulation sentence:**
> Human science research can have high levels of reliability and low levels of validity. It can also have high levels of validity and low levels of reliability.

Key term: Opportunity cost (economics)

The term 'opportunity cost' refers to the benefits a person would have received if they had not taken an alternative action. For example, an **investor** decides to invest in one company and receives a 2% **return on the investment**. However, in doing so, they gave up an opportunity to invest in another company that returned 6%. Therefore, the opportunity cost is 4%.

> **Articulation sentence:**
> The role opportunity cost plays in economics is to focus economists on consequences for business decisions.

Subject vocabulary

questionnaires copies of a formal list of questions, formulated by a researcher to be answered by participants

valid acceptable; in an experimental setting, the level of confidence a researcher has that the independent variable (IV) caused the dependent variable (DV)

peer reviewers other experts who evaluate the study and conclusions

Synonyms

replicated ...... repeated

check .... control

General vocabulary

prisoners people who are kept in a prison either as a legal punishment for a crime or while they are waiting for their trial

cells small rooms in a prison or police station where prisoners are kept

corruption dishonest, illegal, or immoral behaviour, especially from someone with power

guards people whose job is to protect a place or person

commissions formally asks someone to write an official report, produce a work of art, etc.

investor an individual who places money in a scheme or product

return on investment the profit made from an investment

Knowledge framework: Methodology

What are the methods or procedures used in this area and what is it about these methods that generates knowledge?

Method 1: Insider research

Insider research refers to the notion of the researcher studying the system in which they work. They acknowledge themselves as part of the system being studied.

Human scientists are concerned with the notion of *being human* and how humankind influences the environment. Therefore, because human science researchers are also human, the researcher has to consider how this influences the research process.

How does it generate knowledge?

This approach can be contrasted with a purely objective approach where the scientist rarely considers what impact they have on the environment and what impact the environment has on them. Insider research generates personal knowledge and insight from the researcher, who considers themself as part of the research process.

For example, an economist may conduct research in the company where he or she works. They would have to consider what impact they have in the environment they are studying and how their insider knowledge has influenced the research process.

What are the assumptions underlying this method?

The method assumes it is difficult for humans to separate themselves from the object of study. This can be contrasted with the way biologists can separate themselves from their objects of study (e.g. the process of photosynthesis in a plant). It assumes by acknowledging themselves as part of the research process, they will influence the research process.

> Articulation sentence:
> Insider research refers to the notion of the researcher studying the system in which they work. They acknowledge themselves as part of the system being studied.

Method 2: Qualitative data

Qualitative data is gathered through direct interaction with participants. For example, through one-to-one or group interviews, observation, diary entries. The data usually consists of text and is not usually numbered. It can be compared with quantitative data which is mathematical and usually numbered in some way.

How does it generate knowledge?

The aim of qualitative research is to describe and possibly *explain* events and *experiences*. It will rarely offer a **definitive**, **monolithic** conclusion. It is about **marshalling** *understandings* (note the plural) and generating insight.

What are the assumptions underlying this method?

Researchers using a qualitative approach usually assume there are many ways to interpret the data set. They assume decisions (e.g. choosing participants, deciding on questions, deciding on interview settings, choosing parts and not the entire interview, interpreting the responses) are subjective in nature and influence the research process. They acknowledge these subjective influences in a reflexive section of the final report.

Subject vocabulary

objective not influenced by personal feelings or opinions

insider knowledge knowledge gained from working within an organization

subjective influenced by personal feelings or opinions, which are thought to uncover greater understanding

reflexive acknowledging a researcher's own contribution to the construction of meaning in the research process; the researcher's own background and beliefs can influence the way the research is conducted

Synonyms

definitive .... correct, unchanging

monolithic ..... singular, dominating

marshalling .... organizing

General vocabulary

photosynthesis the production by a green plant of sugar that it uses as food; photosynthesis is caused by the action of sunlight on chlorophyll

Articulation sentence:
Qualitative data usually consists of text and is not usually numbered. It can be compared with quantitative data which is mathematical and usually numbered in some way.

Method 3: Experimental method

The experimental method involves manipulating an independent variable (IV) to measure the effect on a dependent variable (DV) (see page 75). At the same time, other variables are controlled as much as possible.

It is based on the notion of the scientific method. The term 'scientific method' refers to systematic observation, measurement, and experimentation; and the formulation, testing, and modification of hypotheses. It is based on the notion of causation – the idea that phenomena within the world have causes that can be uncovered and investigated.

The role the scientific method plays is to provide a consistent framework for study. Human phenomena can be investigated with an agreed set of rules and procedures that can be peer-reviewed by other social scientists.

Key study: An investigation into how oxytocin influences the perception of emotions (Guastella et al., 2009)

Aim
To test the effects of the hormone oxytocin on 'Reading the mind in the eyes' task.

Method
The IV was oxytocin. The DV was perception of emotions. Oxytocin or a placebo was given as a nasal spray to 16 males aged 12 to 19 who were diagnosed with autism or Asperger's disorder. Participants then completed the 'Reading the mind in the eyes' task, a widely used test of emotion recognition. Participants are shown a picture of a pair of eyes and asked to discern what emotion they are showing, Photo 6.1.

jealous   panicked

arrogant   hateful

Photo 6.1 *'Reading the mind in the eyes' task.*

Results
The participants who received oxytocin performed better in the task than those who were given the placebo.

Conclusions
Oxytocin improves the perception of emotions.

This study provides the first evidence that oxytocin nasal spray improves emotion recognition in young people diagnosed with autism spectrum disorders. Findings suggest that earlier intervention may be useful. They also highlight the potential of, and further evaluation of, oxytocin nasal spray as a treatment to improve social communication and interaction in young people with autism spectrum disorders.

Source: Shutterstock.com/ntstudio

How does it generate knowledge?

The experimental method allows variables to be identified and tested under controlled conditions to see if they have the impact the researcher assumes they do. Therefore, the researchers can be more confident the IV *caused* the DV. In the example above, it is oxytocin (IV) that has an effect on the emotional recognition (DV).

What are the assumptions underlying this method?

Variables should be controlled as much as possible to identify how they interact. The method also assumes that such controlled conditions do not affect human behaviour too much, and general conclusions can be drawn despite the unrealistic setting. For example, in the above study, all of the eyes shown were of white people. To what extent can we apply these findings generally to other cultures?

> Articulation sentence:
> The experimental method involves manipulating an independent variable (IV) to measure the effect on a dependent variable (DV). At the same time, other variables are controlled as much as possible.

What role do models play in this area of knowledge?

A model in human science is a deliberate simplification of the key elements of a real-world situation so it can be studied. All models have **inherent flaws** because they lose the detail of the process they are trying to represent.

Example: Psychology – multi-store model of memory

Cognitive researchers Atkinson and Shiffrin proposed the multi-store model of memory, which showed how information flowed through 'stores' of **sensory**, short-term and long-term memory (you can remind yourself of this by referring back to Figure 2.7, on page 32).

By simplifying the key elements, the **key processes** of memory can be shown, tested and revised. This allows psychologists to understand memory problems and treat those who have them.

Knowledge framework: Historical development

What is the significance of the key points in the historical development of this area of knowledge?
How has the history of this area led to its current form?

Example 1: Anthropology

Key point: A shift in focus from biology to culture to explain human differences

Franz Uri Boas (1858–1942) was a German–American **anthropologist** and has been called the 'father of American anthropology'. He **objected to** studying humankind through purely biological characteristics, which was fashionable in the late 19th and early 20th centuries. For example, it was considered scientific to **rank** humanity according to skull size and shape. Boas demonstrated how environmental factors such as health and nutrition can heavily influence skull size and shape. This view denied the claims made by racial anthropologists, who stated head shape was a **stable racial trait** and influenced intelligence. Boas also showed differences in

Subject vocabulary

cognitive referring to mental processes such as memory, perception, attention

anthropologist a person who studies the wider cultural and historical influences on humankind

Synonyms

key processes . important events

General vocabulary

inherent flaws mistakes or problems which cannot be removed

sensory relating to the traditional senses of sight, hearing, smell, taste, and touch

objected to felt, or announced opposition, or disapproval

rank place in order of importance

stable racial trait a trait or characteristic that is said to occur in the same way across members of the same race

human behaviour were not determined by **innate** biological factors, but could also be the result of cultural differences acquired through social learning. Therefore, Boas introduced culture as the primary notion for explaining behavioural differences between human groups. He also placed culture as the central focus of anthropology.

> Articulation sentence:
> Anthropology allowed a shift in focus from biology to culture to explain human differences.

Current form

Anthropology is now no longer concerned with innate racial or biological characteristics. It attempts to understand various cultures **on their own merits** rather than just comparing them to other cultures. It no longer presents cultures as part of a hierarchy, which had been the norm before Boas's influence. Boas also made popular the notion of living within the culture the anthropologist is studying (known as extended residence), learning the local language, and developing close relationships with the people to inform the research.

Example 2: Psychology

Key point: People have powerful urges *that need to be* repressed *for civilization to be maintained (Freud)*

Sigmund Freud (1856–1939) was an Austrian neurologist who developed the notion of the unconscious. He argued it played an active part in people's lives. The idea of the unconscious had been around since about 1700, but Freud showed how it could influence people's day-to-day lives. For example, he argued sex was a powerful **drive** that needed to be **restrained** otherwise it would cause problems. Society provides rituals (in thought and behaviour) as a defence against temptations presented by the sex drive. The rituals control instinctive forces. For example, religion was a key force in people's lives when Freud was writing. It promises an after-life in return for good thoughts and behaviour. A dead person will be rewarded with heavenly pleasures to **compensate** for the earthly pleasures he or she has had to **forgo** in the interests of civilization. Freud argued this repression of certain thoughts and drives leads to emotional problems in other areas of life.

Current form

Freudian theory is still very influential in many areas, such as approaches to therapy and advertising. Repressed thoughts and drives are still seen as a key influence on people's lives. Identifying them and talking about them (in the form of talking therapy) were key parts of the Freudian approach to psychology. However, there was also a negative reaction to the Freudian approach. Freud did not place much emphasis on empirical data to support his theories. There was a reaction to this, because psychologists wanted to build theories based on observable data (for example, the behaviourists) rather than on interpretation.

> Articulation sentence:
> Freud developed the notion of the 'unconscious'. He argued it played an active part in people's lives. For example, he argued sex was a powerful drive that needed to be restrained otherwise it would cause problems.

Example 3: Economics

Key point: When an individual pursues their self-interest*, they indirectly promote the good of society (Smith)*

Adam Smith (1723–1790) was a Scottish philosopher and is seen as the 'father of modern economics'. Smith is well known for two works: *The Theory of Moral Sentiments* (1759), and *An Inquiry into the Nature and Causes of the Wealth of Nations* (1776), usually shortened to *The Wealth of Nations*. He argued people who pursue self-interest in a market place tend to benefit society as a whole by keeping prices low. In basic terms, people want to dominate market places by selling the most products to make more money for themselves. If lots of people do this, the consumer benefits by having more choice at lower prices. However, he also warned against the reactions of businesses to unpredictable market places and falling prices. He argued businesses would form clubs (known as cabals or monopolies) to set prices. He warned against businesses trying to influence politics.

Current form

Smith's ideas have been very influential. Despite being written hundreds of years ago, the warnings about monopolies and attempts by the business community to influence politics are still very relevant. However, there have been two main reactions to Smith that have influenced modern economics.

- He was seen as over-emphasizing the price of 'goods' but not 'services', although this is forgivable as he was writing at a time before the service economy became so important.
- He placed emphasis on wealth creation and not on human welfare (believing wealth creation led to an increase in human welfare). Some modern economists try to place an emphasis on how wealth creation affects welfare.

Example 4: Sociology

Key point: Weak social systems result in deviant *behaviour*

David Émile Durkheim (1858–1917) was a French sociologist and is seen by some as the 'father of sociology'. His book *Le Suicide* (1897) was a unique book for the time. It was a case study of suicide and highlighted the link between social systems (notably religious factors such as Protestantism and Catholicism), and why people commit suicide.

Durkheim concluded suicide rates were higher for:
- men compared to women
- those who are single compared to those who are married
- people without children compared to people with children
- Protestants and Jews compared to Catholics
- soldiers compared to civilians
- people living in Scandinavian countries.

Current form

Durkheim's work influenced the formulation of control theory.

The assumptions are as follows.
- Deviant behaviour occurs when external controls on behaviour are weak.
- If people are given the chance to act in a deviant way, they will.
- Humans are selfish beings – they make decisions based on what will give them the greatest benefit. For example, having a job: most people do not want to have a job but they have a job to obtain the things they want.

- People who do not have a job will commit deviant acts in order to get what they want or need to survive.

> Articulation sentence:
> Durkheim (1858–1917) is seen by some as the 'father of sociology'. He highlighted the link between social systems (notably religious factors such as Protestantism and Catholicism), and why people commit suicide.

Links to personal knowledge

Why is this area significant to the individual?

Human sciences are significant to the individual because they suggest that the idea of the self is:

- a product of historical and cultural forces (anthropology)
- a product of individual consciousness (psychology)
- a product of economic forces (economics)
- a product of social forces (sociology).

What responsibilities rest upon the individual knower by virtue of his or her knowledge in this area?

Responsibility 1: In the human sciences, there is a responsibility on the researcher to reveal how their personal experiences influenced the research process.

Knowledge question: To what extent is it legitimate for an inquirer to draw on their personal experiences when approaching topics in human science?

Anti-positivism (also known as interpretivism) is the belief that social science should not be subjected to the same methods of investigation as the natural sciences. Inquirers must reject empiricism and embrace subjectivism.

Positivism assumes the human world can be investigated and discovered objectively.

Antipositivism assumes the human world cannot be 'discovered' as it 'is' but can only be experienced and interpreted. Therefore, the inquirer must acknowledge and discuss their biases, influences, motivations, personal histories, etc. and assess how these influenced the research process (especially data collection and interpretation).

Responsibility 2: In the human sciences, there is a responsibility on the researcher to achieve trustworthiness or credibility in their research.

There are two main ways to achieve trustworthiness or credibility in the human sciences: reflexivity and triangulation.

Reflexivity

Reflexivity is based on the assumption that it is important that the researcher is aware of his or her own contribution to the construction of meaning in the research process. Reflexivity is a process that occurs throughout the research. It allows the researcher to reflect on ways in which bias may occur, by acknowledging that his or her own background and beliefs could have influenced the way the research was conducted, Figure 6.1, overleaf.

Subject vocabulary

the idea of the self a person's beliefs about themself

empiricism placing emphasis on evidence (usually quantitative) when building a theory (evidence is usually collected by carrying out experiments and making observations); it is a key part of the scientific method that all hypotheses and theories must be tested under scientific conditions rather than by use of reasoning, revelation, or imagination

subjectivism the theory whereby judgements are encouraged when an attempt is made to be influenced by personal feelings or opinions, and to use them to uncover greater understanding

Synonyms

draw on .... use

embrace .... welcome

General vocabulary

legitimate ethically or legally fair

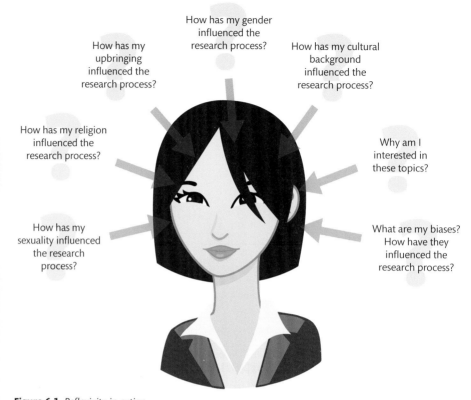

How has my gender influenced the research process?

How has my upbringing influenced the research process?

How has my cultural background influenced the research process?

How has my religion influenced the research process?

Why am I interested in these topics?

How has my sexuality influenced the research process?

What are my biases? How have they influenced the research process?

Figure 6.1 *Reflexivity in action.*

Researchers try to make their reflections and decisions in the research process as clear as possible. This is done so they can be analysed by other researchers. According to Sandelowski (1986), it means 'leaving a decision trail, so that the reader would be able to track and verify the research process '. There are no objective criteria for trustworthiness. However, a reflexive tone and sometimes an entire section is expected in human science reports.

This might include:

- lots of examples from the data, complete with explanations of how the data has been analysed
- an example of peer review to check the interpretations
- a decision trail explaining why decisions were made.

Triangulation

Triangulation supports the interpretation of the data. Triangulation involves the use of different perspectives, methods, and sources to check if the interpretation of data can be supported. There are different forms of triangulation, Figure 6.2, opposite.

Method triangulation involves comparing data created by using different methods. This could involve case studies, diary analysis, qualitative, and quantitative methods.

Data triangulation involves comparing data gathered from other participants or other sources.

Researcher triangulation involves the use of different researchers, who bring a different perspective.

Theory triangulation involves looking at the data using different theoretical perspectives.

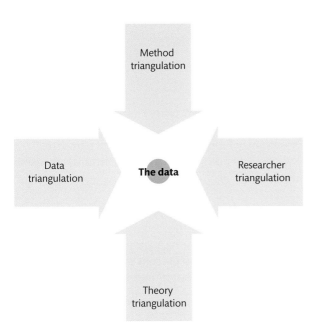

Figure 6.2 *Triangulation in action.*

Articulation sentence:
According to an anti-positivist position, the **notion** of validity in the human sciences should not be linked to 'truth' (e.g. Sandelowski, 1993). Validity should be linked to trustworthiness or credibility.

Articulation sentence:
Human science research strives for credibility and trustworthiness. This can be achieved by reflexivity and triangulation.

Synonyms

notion .... idea

Knowledge framework: Scope/applications

What is the area of knowledge about?

History is the systematic study of the past. The term 'history' usually refers to human history. It is about constructing explanations for events that happened using evidence from sources. These explanations are called historical narratives. Historical narratives are a method of telling history in story-based form, as opposed to merely listing chronological events.

What practical problems can be solved through applying this knowledge?

Practical problem: History helps us understand the present by outlining lessons from the past; for example, the development of Nazism **in Weimar Germany (1921–1945)**

Some of the most basic lessons from the development of Nazism are relevant today.

Lesson 1: Poverty can provide a catalyst *for extremist views*

The **extremism** of the Nazis appealed to people who had lost their **savings** and found themselves living in poverty **through no fault of their own**. The economic crisis of 1929 made the situation worse. People would not have supported the Nazis in such large numbers if there had not been an economic **collapse**.

Lesson 2: Extremist politicians are more likely to have an influence if they appeal to the middle class

In a democracy, the key to political success is usually to appeal to the centre ground – offering **moderate** policies that are usually supported by the middle class. The Nazis moderated some of their more extremist ideas to make sure they gained middle-class support. When Hitler became Chancellor in 1933, he initially softened his image and publicly criticized the more aggressive elements of the Nazi party.

Lesson 3: Democracy can be used to overthrow democracy

A significant number of Germans voted for Hitler, and so the Nazis joined the Weimar **parliament**. Although the Nazis never achieved an absolute majority, they were still the biggest party in 1933, with 43% of the vote. Once they had gained enough power, they made other political parties illegal and turned Germany into a one-party state.

Lesson 4: How the media is regulated is an essential issue for advanced societies

The Nazis understood they had to have influence in the German media. They made deals with media owners; they produced their own newspapers and attacked any news **outlet** which did not support them. Once they had gained enough support, they **outlawed** newspapers that did not **back** them.

Lesson 5: Educated and civilized societies can be willing to support extremist ideologies

Weimar Germany was seen as a modern and **civilized society**. The Weimar period had one of the highest levels of intellectual productivity in human history. Weimar culture was rich, with major advancements in science, technology, architecture, literature, philosophy, and art. Despite this, one of the most **destructive** ideologies in human history **flourished** – Nazism. Educated and civilized societies can be willing to support extremist ideologies if certain conditions are met. These conditions include **charismatic** leaders, extreme economic situations, perceived

Subject vocabulary

systematic study a careful and disciplined approach to studying
constructing making
explanations answers to questions
Nazism an extreme ideology usually associated with Germany between 1933 and 1945
in poverty the position of being poor; it is usually measured by how much someone earns and if they can buy adequate food and shelter
democracy a system of government whereby people can vote and are represented by people in positions of power
centre ground a term usually used to describe moderate people who want moderate policies from government
architecture the study of building design
philosophy the study of ideas

Synonyms

extremism...... radical beliefs
collapse......... failure
moderate....... reasonable, not extreme
back.............. support
flourished...... prospered
charismatic .... charming, persuasive

General vocabulary

sources people, books, or documents that supply information
chronological arranged according to when things happened
catalyst something which causes a consequence to happen; if the catalyst is absent, the consequence does not happen
savings all the money a person has saved, especially in a bank
through no fault of their own they were not responsible
parliament a place where lawmakers meet to discuss governing the country
outlet a place where goods and services are available
outlawed made illegal
civilized society a society that is well organized and developed, and has fair laws and customs
destructive causing damage to people or things

threats to the country and/or culture, and war. Leaders may create these conditions or create a perception of these conditions to gain support.

Lesson 6: False flag operations can be used to gain support

A false flag operation is an action that is carried out in a **deliberate** way to deceive people into thinking other parties are responsible. Some historians believe the Nazis were responsible for the Reichstag (government building) fire that occurred just before a major election in 1933. The Nazis blamed the Communists, who were their opponents, and used it as an excuse to introduce laws against them.

What makes this area of knowledge important?

History is important for the following reasons.

- It gives people information about politics, economics, culture, human nature, geography, science, and religion, and about how these affect humanity.
- It gives people a sense of identity, a sense of place in the world.
- It provides explanations for past events that still influence human societies today.
- It gives people information about how the forces that influence human nature (e.g. economic, cultural, military, psychological forces such as nationalism) can have certain **outcomes** (e.g. war, **corruption**, national pride, defending the weak). In other words, it is the study of causes and consequences in human affairs.
- It gives people information about how and why powerful people act, and what they might do to less powerful people.
- It gives people information about how and why less powerful people can act, and what they might do to improve their own lives, and hold powerful people **accountable**.
- It allows us to predict possible futures and to take action to determine the future.

What are the current open questions in this area?

Open question 1: To what extent does hindsight bias influence the process of writing about history?

Hindsight bias is the tendency to regard outcomes as **inevitable**. It can be summed up in the following statement.

It was inevitable it was going to happen. How do we know this? Because it happened.

It is also known as retrospective determinism or creeping determinism.

Hindsight bias causes two main problems.

- It can cause memory **distortion** in witnesses who 'knew all along' an event would happen.
- It can cause historians to ignore other evidence and not present a full and accurate picture of the events of the time.

Hindsight bias example 1: The Nazi party's accession to power in 1933 is seen as inevitable

The historical narrative is usually: *The Nazis were swept to power on a wave of popularity.*

Counter claim: Hindsight bias has downplayed an important historical narrative – there is evidence that significant numbers of Germans were growing tired of the Nazis

The counterclaim is supported by the following evidence.

During 1932, support for the Nazis dropped from 37% to 33% between July and November. Hitler was appointed Chancellor in January 1933 and was successful to some extent in **suppressing** his political opponents and their supporters in the press. The Nazis also used the Reichstag fire of February 1933 to suppress their main opponents, the Communists. They created the Reichstag Fire **Decree** which allowed them to imprison communist sympathizers and leaders. As a result, the Nazis were able to increase their electoral support in March 1933 to 43% of the vote. However, it can be noted that despite controlling much of the media, government **institutions**, and the police, the majority of the German population *voted against the Nazis*; even when it had become dangerous to publicly **defy** the Nazis. The Nazis felt they had to move towards a one-party state with **totalitarian** rule because they could not guarantee strong public support. Hitler believed that support for the Nazis would **decline** over time. His personal architect, Albert Speer, explained Hitler wanted the designs for new public buildings to include **barracks** for soldiers. This was because Hitler predicted that the German public might try to rebel against one-party rule in the future.

Hindsight bias example 2: The UK fighting against Nazi Germany

After Germany defeated Poland, Belgium, and France in 1939–1940, Nazi Germany wanted to make a deal with the UK. Germany would have **invaded** the UK if a deal could not be reached.

The historical narrative is usually: *The UK stood alone and defiant against Nazi Germany.*

Counter claim: Hindsight bias has downplayed an important narrative – many British people were in favour of negotiating a peace settlement with Hitler.

The counterclaim is supported by the following evidence.

The May 1940 War **Cabinet** Crisis was a **confrontation** between UK Prime Minister Winston Churchill and a group in the War Cabinet who wanted to **negotiate** with Hitler. There is strong evidence (e.g. diaries, statements, interview extracts) that many of the UK's **ruling classes** wanted to make a deal with Hitler. Churchill called a full cabinet meeting rather than just the smaller War Cabinet meeting, knowing he could **manipulate** a larger group of people with an emotional speech. He then made a speech containing the words: *'If this long island story of ours is to end at last, let it end only when each one of us lies choking in his own blood upon the ground'*. This speech was emotionally received and it convinced all those present that the UK must fight on against Hitler. However, without this speech and without the personality of Churchill to convince doubters, the UK, and Nazi Germany might have made a deal. The deal would probably have allowed Hitler to **dominate** Europe. The history of the modern world would have been radically different.

Source: Quote reproduced with permission of Curtis Brown, London on behalf of the Estate of Winston S. Churchill

Articulation sentence:
Hindsight bias can downplay important historical narratives.

What are the ethical considerations that limit the scope of inquiry?

Ethical consideration 1: Historical ownership

Knowledge question: To what extent can history be 'owned' by one group or government?

How history is taught in schools is often a subject of **controversy**. There are many examples of national governments **banning** history books because they do not show the 'correct' version of history. For example, in 2000, the Japanese **Ministry** of Education approved the *New History Textbook* (Atarashii Rekishi Kyokasho). The book **downplayed** Japanese **atrocities** during the Second World War. Very few schools used the book but it caused widespread **demonstrations** in China and Korea where the Japanese committed their crimes. Japan (as well as other countries) has had many 'textbook controversies' over the years as different political opponents want their versions of the 'truth' taught to school students.

> Articulation sentence:
> **Ethical** considerations surrounding the issue of 'banning history books' have limited the scope of enquiry in the form of information being denied to school students who use the book. However, it has widened the scope of the debate by prompting other historians to bring their complaints to public attention.

Ethical consideration 2: Historical subjectivity

Knowledge question: To what extent is it the ethical responsibility of historians to present a single 'truth'?

Knowledge question: To what extent can history be an objective process?

Even if history is just seen as a collection of facts without any subjective interpretation placed on them, there is still a problem of subjectivity. No collection of facts can be objective as it will have been edited and arranged in a specific way to suit the needs of the author and/or audience. This editing and arranging can occur in a subconscious or a deliberately conscious way. Historians can arrange the same facts in different ways because they see the importance of them differently.

> Articulation sentence:
> Historians can arrange the same facts in different ways because they see the importance of them differently.

Ethical consideration 3: Historical bias

Knowledge question: To what extent should history become more like a predictive science, in order to fulfill an ethical responsibility of presenting an unbiased 'truth'?

Turchin (2008) argues that history should **move away from** subjective interpretations of the past and become a predictive science. As an example, he states there have been more than 200 explanations for the collapse of the Roman Empire. However, there is no agreement on which theories are more realistic and which are not. Turchin argues that history is being **held back** as a subject, and compares it to the natural sciences where such disagreement would not be acceptable.

Knowledge framework: Concepts/language

What role does language play in the accumulation of knowledge in this area?

One question history authors ask themselves is: Who is the **intended audience** for the work? The answer to this question will determine what language is used to present the knowledge. There are two broad **categories** of history writing: academic and mass market. The language used for each is different.

Academic

Academic history has the broad purpose of revealing new evidence or interpretations to other academics. The purpose is to **stimulate** debate as well as check the findings of the writer through a process known as peer review. Peer review is the evaluation of professional work by others working in the same field. The language style used focuses on the efficient delivery of information in the most objective way possible. The work concentrates on the **findings** and the interpretations of the historian, and an explanation of how they arrived at their conclusions. There is no attempt to **appeal to** the feelings of the reader.

Mass market

Mass market history books are not academic and are written for non-historian consumers. Mass market history books sell very well; many authors make a lot of money from selling their work. The language has to be accessible to the ordinary person. The writer may also use techniques commonly used in storytelling so the book reads more like a novel to keep the reader entertained. Such techniques include the following.

- The author may present the narrative with a clear beginning, middle, and end. The story will need action sequences such as battles.
- The author may use interesting characters with clear arcs. This means the emotional lives of the characters need to be explored as the they develop and change. Details about their hopes, relationships, and personal habits are important.
- The author may emphasize interesting characters more than less interesting characters.
- The author may use emotional language to appeal to the feelings of the reader and take them on an emotional journey.

What are the roles of the key concepts and key terms that provide the building blocks for knowledge in this area?

Historians work with concepts of history, place, and people. These concepts will influence how they understand and write about the past. Each of the following can be seen as a **lens**. A lens changes how humans see things. When we place a different lens over historical periods, we change how we view them.

The following are not the only lenses that can be applied. And there may be more than one lens applied at a time – it is possible to view history through multiple lenses, Figure 7.1, opposite.

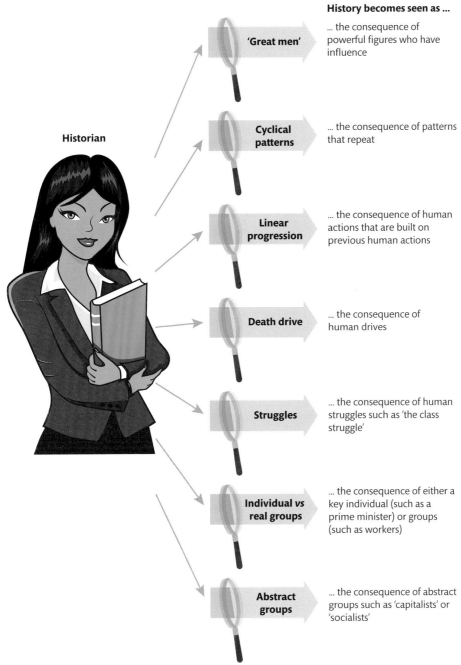

History becomes seen as ...

'Great men' → ... the consequence of powerful figures who have influence

Cyclical patterns → ... the consequence of patterns that repeat

Linear progression → ... the consequence of human actions that are built on previous human actions

Death drive → ... the consequence of human drives

Struggles → ... the consequence of human struggles such as 'the class struggle'

Individual vs real groups → ... the consequence of either a key individual (such as a prime minister) or groups (such as workers)

Abstract groups → ... the consequence of abstract groups such as 'capitalists' or 'socialists'

Historian

Figure 7.1 *Viewing history through various lenses.*

Key Concept 1: The 'great man' theory of history

The 'great man' theory of history explains history by the impact of some highly influential individuals who, due to their intelligence, **charisma**, or political skill were able to shape the course of events. It assumes individual human action can cause significant consequences. The term 'great men' is old-fashioned because it is gender-specific (men) and also can give the impression of greatness that equals 'goodness.' Individuals such as Ghandi, Mandela, Churchill, Kennedy may be seen as supporting the basic assumptions of the theory. However, the theory can also apply to individuals who are not widely regarded as morally great: Hitler, Stalin, Pol Pot.

Synonyms

charisma........ charm, persuasiveness

Key Concept 2: History as a cycle

History can be seen as repeating itself in a **cyclical** pattern, Figure 7.2. This could be supported by analysing the rise and fall of empires. The Aztecs, Romans, Byzantines, Spanish, Ottomans, and British have all been labelled as having the most powerful empire at some point. It is possible citizens living within the various empires thought it was inevitable they would be the greatest empire. Some citizens would also have found it difficult to imagine the **fall** of the empire. Using this way of thinking, it is possible to imagine the present cultural 'empire' of the USA **losing ground to** a Chinese empire. Some writers have predicted the 21st century will be characterized by a non-military conflict between the Americans who want to maintain their position, and the Chinese who want to assume a more powerful world role.

e.g. The rise and fall of empires

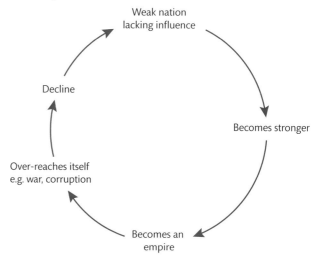

Figure 7.2 *History as a repeating cycle.*

Key Concept 3: History as linear progression

Human development can be seen as progressing along a **linear** timeline, Figure 7.3. This could be supported by the notion of human improvement. In most societies, humans can be said to be living in improved conditions compared to those of their ancestors.

e.g Human rights improve over time

Roman Europe	Enlightenment	Industrial age	Modern era
			Time →
Slaves and gladiators are common	Questions of morality become part of political, artistic, and religious discussions	Slavery abolished, in Europe 'workers' rights'	Women's rights, gay rights, children's rights, ethnic minority rights, animal rights

Figure 7.3 *History as a linear progression.*

Key Concept 4: History as the product of the death drive

Freud saw history as a product of internal human conflict. For example, he argued there existed a basic human drive towards death. The death drive is a hypothetical construct that suggests humans want to return to a state where they do not exist. If seen on a wider scale, the death drive can explain the constant presence of war in human societies.

Key Concept 5: History as the product of struggle or conflict (for example, class struggle)

Karl Marx (1818–1883) saw history as the product of the competing aims of the different socio-economic classes, Figure 7.4. For example, social classes have conflicts over money – the middle classes may **resent** paying higher taxes to help pay for working-class **benefits**. Marx focused on the struggles between the socio-economic classes. He was born in Germany but spent much of his life in London, UK. He is best known for writing about the effects of capitalism on workers.

Figure 7.4 *History as a class struggle.*

Key Concept 6: Human beings as individuals *versus* human beings as social groups

History can be seen as the product of **individual endeavour** or the product of social groups, Figure 7.5. An individual bias can be seen in the great man theory of history. Placing a bias on social groups can be seen in the writings of Karl Marx.

Figure 7.5 *History as individual endeavour.*

Key Concept 7: Societies made up of abstract groups

Historical analysis may use **abstract** groups as a way to analyse periods. For example, societies could be divided into democracies or totalitarian groups. Economic approaches could be divided into **capitalist** and **socialist**; political approaches could be divided into **liberal** and **conservative**.

> Articulation sentence:
> There are many different approaches to studying history. Different approaches will have different assumptions, ask different questions, access different sources, and produce different answers as to why certain events occurred, and what consequences they had.

Subject vocabulary

socio-economic classes groups in society that are usually characterized by their economic income and educational level of the workers

abstract existing in thought as an idea without an actual existence

capitalist an economic approach that favours making money in largely free financial markets

socialist an economic and political approach that believes the state or governmental power should heavily regulate financial markets as well as other areas of life

liberal a political approach that generally favours progress and reform as a constant governmental task

conservative a political approach that generally favours maintaining stability as a constant governmental task

General vocabulary

resent to feel angry or upset about a situation, or about something that someone has done, especially because you think that it is not fair

benefits money provided by the government to people who are sick, unemployed, or have little money

individual endeavour individual action

Knowledge framework: Methodology

What are the methods or procedures used in this area and what is it about these methods that generates knowledge?

The term 'historical method' refers to the techniques and **guidelines** historians use to write 'histories' – these are **narratives** to explain the past. The study of the historical method and the different ways of writing history is known as historiography.

Historical method 1: Source analysis

The historical method consists of questioning the sources from which histories are written. A source is anything which gives information to a historian. It is usually a document, an interview, a speech, a photograph, an observation made by other historians, a poster, a piece of art.

There are many ways to analyse a source. Source analysis produces knowledge because historians are generally asking: What is it about the *origin* and *purpose* of this source that makes it *valuable* or *limited* as a historical document? This is known as OPVL analysis. It allows historians to make decisions as to what extent narratives can be written based on the source. Historians usually do not work with just one source – the process usually considers many sources and they are considered in relation to each other.

Sources are usually **assessed** by questioning the following.

- Origins – Who created it? When and where?
- Purpose – Why did they create it?
- Value – To what extent is it useful?
- Limitation – What are the problems with the source?

These questions have been further extended by Olden-Jørgensen (1998) and Thurén (1997).

- Is the source original or has it been **forged**?
- How many other sources contain the same message? The more sources that confirm an event happened, the more likely it is to have happened.
- How close was the source to the event it describes? For example, **eyewitness testimony** is more reliable than **second-hand testimony**

Historical method 2: Primary evidence/eyewitness testimony

Using eyewitness testimony has problems. Shafer (1974) poses the following questions to evaluate eyewitness testimony.

- Is the real meaning of the statement different from its **literal meaning**? Do the words used have the same meaning today? What did the person literally mean when they said those words? This is a key problem with old documents – it is difficult to fully understand how and why people used certain words because words change meaning over time and place. Historians have to make 'best guesses' about what was most **probable**.
- How well could the eyewitness **observe** the event they are reporting on? For example, how close was the eyewitness to the events they are describing?
- When did the eyewitness write the report?

- What was the intention of the eyewitness in writing the report?
- For whom did the eyewitness write the report?
- Given other evidence, is the statement probable?
- Are there **contradictions** within the source? How serious are they?
- Are there contradictions from other sources?

> Articulation sentence:
> Source analysis produces knowledge because historians are generally asking: What is it about the origin and purpose of this source that makes it valuable or limited as a historical document?

What ethical thinking constrains the methods used to gain knowledge?

Knowledge question: To what extent do ethical considerations hinder **understanding of the past?**

When historians write narratives about past events they are influenced by their own cultural and personal ethical standards.

Ethical Consideration 1: Soviet brutality to Soviet soldiers

It is a standard historical narrative that Soviet leaders killed large numbers of soldiers unnecessarily to achieve their goals.

In the Second World War, there were **approximately** 10 million Soviet military deaths, 382 600 UK military deaths, and 407 000 US military deaths.

Western historians are critical of the methods Soviet military leaders used on the battlefield, which they view as wasting Russian lives. They take this position using a Western view which values the individual and generally has more respect for the human rights of citizens. However, taking this position may limit the scope of understanding as it may ignore or downplay the following.

- Stalin is viewed by many Russians as a strong leader who did what was ethically right to protect Russia. Many Russians accept that he killed large numbers of people but they believe that without Stalin, Russia may have had to **surrender** to the Nazis.
- The Soviet military system was a more brutal system than its Western counterpart. The Soviet soldiers were more brutal because they were raised in a totalitarian system. Generally, they would do things Western soldiers would not do (e.g. mass **rape**; mass killings). The **brutality** of the Russians matched that of the Nazi soldiers and allowed them to kill more enemy soldiers.
- The Soviet military system valued the individual soldier less than its Western **counterpart**. This led to **tactics** that killed large numbers of Soviet soldiers but also large numbers of enemy soldiers. Western leaders were very **reluctant** to waste the lives of their soldiers on the battlefield. The British General, Montgomery, was particularly cautious with his men's lives.
- If Soviet tactics had been applied to Western soldiers, there would have been large-scale **rebellion** at home and on the battlefield. Soviet soldiers were less likely to rebel because of the constant threat of **execution** by their own side and because they had become used to their own system's brutality. Soviet military leaders wasted the lives of their soldiers because they could. Western military leaders did not have that option.

To conclude: Western historians may be critical of the Soviet treatment of Soviet soldiers but there is a historical narrative that many accept: *The Second World War was won by a combination of Russian blood and American money.*

> Articulation sentence:
> Western historians using Western ethical standards have been very critical of Soviet tactics during the Second World War. This may have **constrained** their understanding of how important these tactics were in winning the Second World War for the Allies.

Ethical Consideration 2: Nazi electoral success

The Nazis are often written about through an ethical lens – they are seen as 'evil' by Western historians. But the Nazis would not have been elected if they were universally seen as evil by the people living at the time.

The Nazis were an attractive political option for Germans for a number of reasons.

- They acted as a defence against communism. Communism was seen as a problem by some because it threatened the property rights of the middle classes and was controlled by a foreign power (Russia).
- They represented economic stability which appealed to Germans, who were living through an extreme financial crisis and who had lost much of their savings.
- They represented cultural stability, which appealed to Germans living through the Weimar era. The Weimar era was seen by many as having **deviated** from traditional cultural values.
- They represented German strength and national pride, which appealed to Germans who had seen the **prestige** of their country **diminish** after their defeat in the First World War.

The Nazis were **anti-Semitic** and had a history of street violence. But many people assumed these more extreme characteristics would be **toned down** when they were elected. Hitler changed his message depending on the audience and was able to convince many people who were suspicious of the Nazi extremism to vote for them.

It is the job of historians to understand and then explain events from the point of view of the time. For example, it is easy to condemn the Nazis as 'evil' but once this **label** is applied it undermines the ability of historians to understand why they were elected, and why they were so popular.

> Articulation sentence:
> When historians write narratives about past events they are influenced by their own cultural and personal ethical standards. Interpretations of past events should be considered in the context of the personal and cultural ethical standards of the historians.

Synonyms

constrained.... restricted

deviated .... moved away from

diminish .... reduce

General vocabulary

prestige the respect and admiration that someone or something gets because of their success or important position in society

anti-Semitic prejudiced against the Jewish people and their religion

toned down reduced in effect so that people will not be offended

label a word or phrase which is used to describe a person, group, or thing, but which is unfair or not correct

Knowledge framework: Historical development

What is the significance of the key points in the historical development of this area of knowledge?

Key point 1: History as a way to promote morality

Early historians such as Herodotus (c. 484–425 BCE) partly used the telling of history to **promote** a certain moral outlook. History was used to show how good could **overcome** evil. He is often praised for being among the first to use empirical evidence. However, he is also criticized for using **folk tales** as sources of evidence although this was a traditional and **partially** effective way to gather evidence of events.

Key point 2: History should be studied on its own terms using empirical data

19th century historians such as Leopold von Ranke argued history should be written to explain how the events were interpreted by the people living at the time. Ranke placed a great deal of emphasis on primary sources and built his narratives on their interpretation. He did not use his imagination, as other historians did. The significance of this point is that history moved away from literature and philosophy towards the **stance** of a social science. It was influenced by the progress of science during the 19th century as more empirical methods were developed and the understanding of the natural world increased. History focused on reaching conclusions from data

Key point 3: History has fragmented into diverse disciplines

During the 20th century, history expanded into a greater range of types of history with an overall emphasis on causes and consequences.

- Cultural history – focuses on the causes and consequences of cultural traditions of a particular place and people. For example, a focus on the development of rock and roll (rock 'n' roll) in the North of England in the 1960s.
- Economic history – focuses on the causes and consequences of economies, and economic policies. For example, the introduction of free trade agreements between countries.
- Labour history – focuses on the causes and consequences of the development of the labour movement, and the working class; their rights and needs.
- Social history – studies the experiences of ordinary people in the past.

Key point 4: The influence of revisionism

Historical revisionism is the **re-interpretation** of a **prevailing** historical narrative. Revisionism is a key trait of 20th century history. It may be partly caused by the increasing availability of different kinds of source, different kinds of historian, and a greater interest from history readers in different ideas.

Example of revisionism 1: The Dark Ages

'The Dark Ages' is a label for a period in history usually between the 6th and 13th centuries. The label deliberately uses the word 'dark' to describe the period as being culturally and economically **subdued**. The period is traditionally characterized by religion and superstition slowing the progress of science. It was a popular term during the 19th century because historians wanted to distinguish the period from the Renaissance.

Subject vocabulary

empirical evidence evidence collected by carrying out experiments and observation

disciplines areas of study

revisionism challenging dominant ideas and revising them

narrative explanation of an event

superstition a belief in a supernatural influence on the world

Synonyms

promote .... encourage

overcome .... win against

partially .... partly

prevailing ...... dominant

subdued .... held back

General vocabulary

morality beliefs or ideas about what is right and wrong, and about how people should behave

folk tales traditional and typical stories of the ordinary people who live in a particular area

stance a position an individual or a group can take on something

diverse featuring great differences

re-interpretation understanding and explaining events again

working class a group of people in a society who do not have very much income to spend on goods or services outside what is necessary (e.g. food and shelter); they have little personal freedom in their jobs and are usually manual workers or engage in work that does not need individual intellectual input

middle class a group of people in a society who have some income to spend on goods or services outside what is necessary; they have personal freedom in their jobs and are usually engaged in work that does need individual intellectual input

industrialized countries countries that have an advanced economy and have the means (usually factories) to produce products for their populations, and to produce weaponry for their military

Synonyms

in decline .... less common

insight .... clear understanding

General vocabulary

incompetent not very good at something

indifferent uncaring, not interested

zeitgeist the spirit or trend of the times

social mobility the ability to move easily from one social class to another

warfare the activity of fighting in a war; used especially when talking about particular methods of fighting

How has the label been revised? What is the impact on knowledge creation?

● The Dark Ages as a label has been **in decline**.

● Historians have focused on the achievements of the period. It is now acknowledged that many people who considered themselves very religious were also scientific leaders.

● The power of the church negatively influencing scientific discovery during the period has been questioned.

Example of revisionism 2: 'Lions led by donkeys'

'Lions led by donkeys' is a famous label for the idea that during the First World War, British soldiers were brave and effective (lions), while their leaders were **incompetent** and **indifferent** to their suffering (donkeys). The phrase is originally thought to have come from the title of a book, 'Lions Led by Donkeys' by Captain PA Thompson (1927). However, it was misused by the British historian Alan Clark who claimed two German generals discussed the British soldiers in this way. He later admitted inventing the conversation because he could not find the original source for the phrase. The phrase is thought to have encouraged a simplistic and inaccurate view of how the war was conducted. However, the notion of brave soldiers led by incompetent commanders has remained a popular view of the war.

The book that popularized the phrase was *The Donkeys* by Alan Clark, published in 1961. It thought to have inspired the famous musical *Oh, What a Lovely War!* (1963). The **zeitgeist** (or the spirit of the age) of the 1950s and 1960s in the UK was that this time was a period of rebellion. Traditional values were being questioned. For example, in the 1950s and 1960s:

● automatic respect for one's elders was being questioned

● automatic respect for the upper classes was being questioned

● **social mobility** was being promoted – people no longer had to stay working class, they could become middle class if they wanted

● young people began to develop an identity of their own with their own fashion and music

● there was an influence from other cultures as people travelled more, and more people travelled to the UK.

Clark's book fitted into the *zeitgeist* of the time. *Zeitgeist* refers to dominant fashions or ways of thinking that influence the culture of a particular period in time.

How has this idea been revised? What is the impact on knowledge creation?

● There is now more sympathy for the generals who organized the battles of the First World War. They are now less characterized as incompetent and uncaring. They had developed their military skills during the 19th century, when they fought against less developed enemies. They did not have the training or the **insight** to fight other industrialized countries.

● It is accepted there were many mistakes made by all sides in the early years of the war. The dominant narrative 'lions led by donkeys' has underestimated the improvements that were made by military leaders as they adapted to the new conditions of **warfare** throughout the war – which the British ultimately won.

Articulation sentence:
Historical revisionism is the re-interpretation of a prevailing historical narrative. Revisionism is a key trait of 20th century history. Two examples are a re-assessment of the Dark Ages and the 'lions led by donkeys' narrative.

How has the history of this area led to its current form?

History has **expanded** into very diverse disciplines. For example, economic history, social history, military history. This expansion of history into diverse disciplines may be partly due to the increasing availability of different sources and new technologies such as the following.

- Governments became more professional – evidence was increasingly written down. Ministers, secretaries, and so on left a **paper trail** of their thinking and actions.
- Printing became easier and cheaper. More people in positions of importance began to write their personal histories and publish their personal diaries.
- The 19th and 20th centuries saw the expansion of the school, university, and public library systems. History became a popular academic subject for more people.
- More people were able to read and were generally better educated – not only were more people wanting to study, research, and teach history, but there was more demand for books about history.
- The invention of cameras (photography and moving film) created a primary source for historians to be able to actually see events and people from the past.
- Newspapers became more numerous, allowing historians to access a greater range of primary sources (e.g. interviews, **editorials**, photographs, cartoons, commercials, journalism) from the time they were studying.

With the increasing availability of these different sources and new technologies, history became better researched and more accessible. For example, a historian wanting to study the First World War (1914–1918) in the 1920s would be in a better research position than a historian writing about the Napoleonic Wars (1803–1815) in the 1820s. This is because of the following reasons.

- More individuals at the centre of events published their memoirs (e.g. politicians, military leaders); memoirs were more widely available.
- More individuals who experienced the events were **literate** (e.g. common soldiers). They could write about their own experiences in the form of diaries and letters home. Some of them were published.
- Journalism helped gather diverse evidence from **the front line**.
- The battles had been photographed and filmed, providing a primary source for anyone who wanted to study them after the event had taken place.

> Articulation sentence:
> History has expanded into very diverse disciplines. For example, economic history, social history, military history. This may be partly due to the increasing availability of different sources and new technologies to research the past.

Subject vocabulary

primary source a piece of evidence from the time that is being studied

memoirs the memories of individuals usually written down

Synonyms

expanded....... grown bigger

General vocabulary

paper trail a series of documents providing evidence of actions

editorials writing in newspapers that gives the editor's opinion about something, rather than reporting facts

literate able to read and write

journalism a profession that investigates centres of power (e.g. governments and corporations) and publishes the findings; in the past, this usually took place in newspapers

the front line the soldiers at the front of a battlefield

Knowledge framework: Links to personal knowledge

What is the nature of the contribution of individuals to this area?

Key individual 1: AJP Taylor (1906–1990)

Alan John Percivale Taylor was an English historian who focused on 19th- and 20th-century European political history. He grew up in the North of England (Lancashire) and then attended Oriel College, Oxford. The North of England is a region with many cultural **traits** including **bluntness** or straight talking, **irreverence**, and **non-conformity**. Taylor's parents were left wing; his mother was a **feminist**, a **suffragette** campaigner, a communist, and an advocate of '**free love**'. Taylor saw himself as part of a tradition of **radical dissent**. He saw dissent as a key cultural trait of being English – and a particular trait of the northern English. He became a communist when he was young and visited the Soviet Union. He later broke away from communism but kept his left-wing beliefs. He became a popular historian because of his writing style, which made him more accessible to ordinary readers, and his televised **lectures**.

Taylor wrote a number of books which did not conform to traditional historical narratives. Therefore, he is often referred to as a 'revisionist.' His influential works include: *The Origins of the Second World War* (1961).

Taylor argued the Second World War started by accident rather than being a grand German plan for dominance in Europe. He argued that wars start because of external threats rather than internal political themes. He was writing at a time (the 1950s) when primary sources were not available (e.g. government **memos**) which he later acknowledged was a problem. Two dominant narratives in the 1950s were:

- the appeasement of Nazi Germany had led to the Second World War (this is still an influential narrative)
- the Soviet Union represented a threat and should not be appeased.

Taylor was influenced by two basic personal assumptions.

- He had sympathy for socialist ideas. The Nazis did not plan on war. Therefore, the Western powers should not use their lack of appeasement of the Nazis to justify a **hard stance** against the Soviet Union.
- He supported the Campaign for Nuclear Disarmament (CND). Wars can start by accident. In a nuclear age, this is particularly threatening. Therefore, the Western powers should not use the threat of force to try to prevent war as it may lead to war. The threat of force is the basic assumption behind nuclear weapons.

> Articulation sentence:
> A historian's approach to writing history will be influenced by their cultural background. This has implications for how history is viewed because it can become an exercise in subjectivity more than objectivity.

Subject vocabulary

left wing a position on the political spectrum usually associated with liberal and socialist beliefs

appeasement the act of making someone less angry or stopping them from attacking by giving them what they want

Campaign for Nuclear Disarmament (CND) a political campaign that wants to rid the world of nuclear weapons

Synonyms

traits .... characteristics

lectures .... lessons

memos .... short notes

General vocabulary

bluntness being honest in a way that may seem rude

irreverence being flippant, cheeky, and mischievous

non-conformity not yielding to group pressure

feminist someone who supports the idea that women should have the same rights and opportunities as men

suffragette a woman who tried to gain the right to vote for women especially as a member of a group in the UK or the US in the early 20th century

'free love' not conforming to usual rules associated with love or marriage; for example, allowing one's husband or wife to have other girl- or boyfriends

radical dissent questioning centres of power and accepted truths

hard stance an inflexible position

What responsibilities rest upon the individual knower by virtue of his or her knowledge in this area?

Knowledge claim: The extermination of the Jewish people (collectively known as the Holocaust) is a historical event that provokes emotional reactions in many people.

David Irving is a British historian who has published work widely interpreted as having a pro-Nazi bias. He is a convicted 'Holocaust denier' – he believes the Holocaust did not exist on a large scale and he argues Hitler had no direct knowledge of the Holocaust. During the early stages of his career he was widely respected for having expert knowledge of German military archives. However, the academic community now largely regards him as an anti-Semite who has allowed his beliefs to negatively affect his historical judgement. His work is no longer taken seriously by the mainstream academic community.

Knowledge question: To what extent can controversial historians influence mainstream history writing for the better?

Knowledge question: To what extent is controversy a useful part of the academic process?

Knowledge claim: It could be argued that controversy surrounding Holocaust denial has influenced other historians.

Possible influence 1: Clarification of key terms

It could be argued that previous presentations of the Holocaust may not have been as clear and consistent as they are now. For example, early Holocaust writers were sometimes confused about what **constituted** a *concentration camp* (in German a *Konzentrationslager*) and what constituted an *extermination camp* (in German a *Vernichtungslager*). The lack of historical consistency has arguably helped **fuel** Holocaust denial because it suggests the terms are not properly defined and therefore might have been invented, or exaggerated. Modern history books make it very clear what the differences were between a *concentration camp* and an *extermination camp*. Concentration camps were developed during the 1930s to control political and social opponents of the Nazis. They were built next to major cities. Extermination camps were developed during the 1940s to murder Jews and other 'undesirables', and were built away from cities, partly to hide the crimes.

Possible influence 2: Clarification of key evidence

Irving has consistently argued Hitler had no knowledge of organized plans for the Holocaust. He has therefore presented a challenge to other historians to provide solid arguments for Hitler's involvement in the Holocaust. Irving has used the **absence** of evidence of an order from Hitler as a key support in his argument. Currently, there is no surviving record of Hitler giving an order relating to the Holocaust.

Knowledge question: When should the absence of evidence in history be taken as the evidence of absence?

Knowledge question: If there has been no evidence of an order from Hitler, is it likely that Hitler did not know?

In 2008, 15 original architectural plans (known as blueprints) for the extermination and concentration camp Auschwitz–Birkenau were found in a Berlin apartment. The plans were drawn at different points during 1941 by architects and engineers. They show the deliberate **evolution** of Auschwitz–Birkenau from concentration camp to extermination camp. The blueprints show designs for key elements such as

Synonyms

clarification	explanation
constituted	made up
extermination	murder
fuel	encourage
absence	lack
evolution	change over time

General vocabulary

the Holocaust the killing of millions of Jews and other people by the Nazis during the Second World War

provokes makes a response happen

archives place where a large number of historical records are stored; the records that are stored

anti-Semite someone who hates Jewish people

gas chambers and **crematoria**. They also have the handwritten initials of SS Chief Heinrich Himmler – a key Hitler **ally**. The blueprints are now used as key evidence when challenging Holocaust deniers.

Articulation sentence:
Historians have to make judgements on what is probable. Historians speculate about the level of involvement Hitler had in planning the Holocaust, but no serious historian believes Hitler had no knowledge of the Holocaust because of Hitler's personal and political history of anti-Semitism.

Possible influence 3: Clarification of numbers

Irving has raised some interesting questions about what constitutes the 'Holocaust' and what constitutes a 'Holocaust denier'. For example, he was able to demonstrate how the estimates of the number of Jewish victims killed by the Nazis have been reduced by mainstream historians from about eight million to the now accepted figure of approximately six million. Irving asked: *At what low estimate of Jews killed does a historian become a 'denier?'* Irving argued he was not denying Jews had been killed – he was **contesting** the numbers presented by mainstream historians, and contesting the notion that Jews had been **systematically** killed.

Knowledge question: To what extent is it ethically appropriate to prosecute people for their beliefs?

Irving was labelled a 'Holocaust denier' and someone who had manipulated historical evidence to suit his own **ideological** beliefs. This label has meant he is no longer considered a mainstream historian and he has difficulty being published by mainstream publishing groups.

Articulation sentence:
It could be argued Irving's status as a controversial historian has prompted other historians to correct errors, double check their sources, search for new sources, and focus their arguments.

8 The arts

Knowledge framework: Scope/applications

What is the area of knowledge about?

It is not easy to **define** the arts. Nor is it easy to say what the arts **have in common**. A list of the arts is a helpful starting point:

- music
- dance
- literature
- film.
- theatre
- visual arts
- architecture

Some people believe that cooking, gardening, and creating perfume are art forms. Defining the arts is a difficult task and every definition has its critics. Here are some possible definitions.

- The arts are the **imitation** of nature.
- The arts are the expression of human imagination and creativity.
- The arts are an imaginative **investigation** of sense perception.
- The arts are an expression of the artist's **intention**.
- The arts are what **the art world** decides they are.

> Articulation sentence:
> The arts are the expression of human imagination and creativity, but they may have to be accepted as 'art' by the art world.

Art often involves the **transformation** of experience in one **realm** into a new artistic realm. The ancient Greeks realized that art was something only humans do. Nature does not produce art, but natural products are often included in art. Art offers an escape from the normal **boundaries** of life. Imagination allows the creation of things that do not exist in the world. For example, music does not exist in nature. There are sounds and bird songs in nature, but not real music. Music may use the sounds of nature, but it forms them into new shapes. Realistic painting puts things into frames. The stage and the film screen also create **artificial** frames or space around the art. Real life does not contain these artificial frames. So how do the arts relate to ways of knowing?

- Religious faiths, including Christianity and Hinduism, have used art to tell stories and increase faith.
- Language is a central feature in literature, theatre, film, and often in connection with music. It is also possible to talk about the language of music, the language of dance, and the language of visual representation.
- Imagination is a key way of knowing, both in creating art and in responding to art.
- Memory is an important part of responding to the arts. For example, in film or music, memory **keeps track of** what happened before and what comes after. Memory can also show how one work of art relates to another. The arts also help to keep events alive in our memories.
- Sense perception is a key aspect of all of the arts. Music requires close listening. Painting and sculpture require an increased sense of sight.
- Emotions are expressed with power and beauty through the arts.
- **Reason** plays an important role in making **coherent** forms and in solving the many problems that come with creating works of art.
- Artists often claim that their ideas come from inspiration and **intuition**. Einstein believed his scientific **insight** and intuition came mainly from music.

Subject vocabulary

Christianity the religion that follows the teachings of Jesus Christ

Hinduism main religion of India and parts of Southeast Asia

Synonyms

imitation........ copy

investigation .. study, examination

realm .... region, domain, area

boundaries .... limits

artificial......... not real

General vocabulary

have in common share the same features

define to explain exactly the meaning of a particular word or idea

intention plan or desire to do something

the art world all the people involved in creating, commenting on, preserving, displaying, and selling works of art

transformation significant change

keeps track of pays attention to someone or something, to know where they are or what is happening to them

coherent logical and consistent

reason the ability to think beyond our immediate experiences

intuition the ability to understand or know something because of a feeling rather than by considering the facts

insight clear understanding

What practical problems can be solved through applying this knowledge?

Practical problem 1: Uniting people

- Soldiers **march** together in time, **accompanied** by music.
- Work songs and field **chants** unify a group, and help workers put their work to a rhythm.
- People sing and chant together to express their feelings and beliefs.
- People share their favourite songs and music. They build connections through shared **tastes**.
- People sit together in concerts and share the experience with other members of the audience.
- **National anthems** stir up **patriotic** feelings.
- People come together in choirs and orchestras to make music that no individual can create alone.

Practical Problem 2: Exploring sensitive topics and providing insight into the human condition

- In the 1980s, the British **soap opera** *EastEnders* introduced a **gay** character who suffered from AIDS. This was a deliberate attempt by the BBC to reduce **prejudice** towards gay people and to educate people about the AIDS **epidemic**.
- The film *Blood Diamond*, set in Sierra Leone, explores the effects of the diamond mining industry. It demonstrates how dangerous and **exploitative** the industry can be. It also increases **empathy** for the diamond miners themselves.
- The novel *To Kill a Mockingbird* explores the theme of racism in the American South. The story concerns a black man who is falsely **accused** of raping a white woman. The story explores the nature and effects of racism. It demonstrates that racism affects not only the victim; it also affects the **oppressor**.

The arts can be successful at dealing with **sensitive** topics because they tell **compelling** stories that involve listeners. Film and television allows viewers to imaginatively **identify with** people they would never meet in normal life. Through imagination, people come to understand what it would mean to have AIDS, or to work in a diamond mining camp in Sierra Leone. Understanding through empathy and emotion is critical to social and political change.

What makes this area of knowledge important?

Example 1: The arts examine human relationships

The arts examine human **relationships** through imagination. The human sciences also examine relationships but there is a major difference. The human sciences seek to make broad statements that apply to people in general. Artistic works examine particular people in particular situations. **Adultery** is an issue in every society. Adultery is an essential theme in 19th-century novels, and one of the most famous examples is *Anna Karenina* by Leo Tolstoy. Tolstoy treats his central character, Anna Karenina, with great sympathy and insight. Tolstoy does not say that Anna Karenina is a **universal portrait**. But Tolstoy's description of Anna's relationship with her husband, her lover, and her child says much about love and passion. The novel tells the reader why one woman might have an affair. But, this may give the reader insight into why other women would have an affair.

> Articulation sentence:
> The novel provides deep insights into the thoughts and feelings of characters that would never be available in ordinary life.

Example 2: The arts deepen sense perception

A visual artist learns to see the world in a different way. Artists must pay attention to the effects of lights and shadow. They must learn to see negative space and to perceive colours with great accuracy. They must find ways to re-create the three-dimensional world on a two-dimensional surface. Artists must make decisions about the meaning and the emotional content of their work. Drawing, painting, and sculpting increase the power and accuracy of sight.

Example 3: The arts can engage with politics

Pablo Picasso's painting, *Guernica*, was a protest against the fascist government's bombing of a small town, Photo 8.1. The painting is immense. It shows the suffering of people and animals in a powerful, **abstract** way. Spain was in the midst of a civil war in 1937 when Picasso painted the picture. The fascist government of Spain, led by Franco, asked its political allies, Germany and Italy, to bomb the small village of Guernica. Picasso was opposed to the Fascist government. He supported the opposing Republicans and wanted to gain support for his side. The painting was displayed across Europe and brought attention to the Spanish Civil War.

Source: 123RF.com

Photo 8.1 *Guernica.*

Example 4: Civilizations are remembered for their artworks

Most of the events of the past, such as wars and **reigns** of kings, are of little interest to people today. However, art from the past has a large audience. The cave paintings in Altamira, Spain are some 40 000 years old, but they continue to **fascinate** the public. They demonstrate that art has a very long history and they provide insight into the people of that time.

The **ruined** temples and other artefacts of the Mayan culture in Central America provide links to a civilization that no longer exists. The Mayan temples attract visitors from around the world. Mayan artefacts have real artistic value. People attempt to understand what Mayan art tells us about the Mayan society. It is Mayan art that makes people want to understand the Mayan culture. The quality of the art suggests that the culture was deep and worthy of study.

> Articulation sentence:
> The arts are important because they portray society, human relationships, and political struggles.

Open question 1: What are the criteria for judging works of art?

Criterion 1: The expressive goals of the artist

This could include:

● what the artist intended and felt about the artwork

● what message the artist was trying to convey with the artwork

● the artist's emotional and psychological state, and its relationship to the artwork.

Criterion 2: The aesthetic value of the artwork itself

This critical approach looks at the formal and technical aspects of the artwork. It compares one artwork to other similar artworks. In literature classes, students look at tone, diction, voice, and rhythm. This method of judgement is not concerned with the artist's life. It examines the work of art itself and so the work of art must stand on its own.

Criterion 3: The effect on the audience

Many works of art depend on having an audience. For example, a concert is not a concert without an audience. A play is only a **rehearsal** until the audience arrives. The interaction between the performer and the audience is central. The value and quality of an artwork is related to the response of an audience. For example, Mozart is still considered a great composer because audiences continue to react to his music with pleasure and delight.

Open question 2: Are there objective criteria for artistic greatness?

The reputations of artists rise and fall. Some believe that artistic greatness is merely a popularity contest. People argue that the arts are completely subjective and that there are no clear standards for greatness. Although the standards are partly subjective, there may be strong reasons to **single out** particular artists.

Many musicians regard Johann Sebastian Bach as the greatest composer of all time. What makes this judgement **valid**?

Reason 1: Influence

Bach has had an enormous influence on the composers and musicians who came after him. He profoundly **influenced** Mozart, Beethoven, Mendelssohn, Wagner, and Bartók, among others. Their music would have been different if they had not known the music of Bach. The composer Robert Schumann said that Bach's *Well-Tempered Clavier* should be the **daily bread** of all composers. All classically trained musicians play the music of Bach. Musicians rearrange his music and play it on instruments ranging from marimbas to brass bands and electronic synthesizers.

Reason 2: Technical mastery of composition

Bach completely mastered the art of counterpoint. Counterpoint involves combining two or more musical parts. To be **comprehensible**, these musical parts must relate to one another. Bach wrote musical parts that are very independent. Each musical part has a distinctive melodic character. But the musical parts are also strongly related through harmony and rhythm. For example, in a fugue, one short musical idea serves as the building block for a very strict musical structure, Figure 8.1, opposite. Bach was able to build complex musical structures from very limited materials.

Figure 8.1 *Bach's* Art of the Fugue *is built on this one theme. It is the basis for 14 fugues and four canons.*

Reason 3: Includes many ways of knowing

The music of Bach appeals to a range of ways of knowing. Bach was a great composer of **sacred** music and so he appeals to religious faith. He wrote 60 cantatas a year for a period of five years and consistently came up with unique imaginative solutions to specific musical challenges. Thousands and thousands of musicians have memorized the music of Bach and so it has a major place in the collective musical memory. Bach's music is very complex because each of the musical parts is like an individual melody. This makes great demands on our hearing, as we try to hear several melodies **simultaneously**. Musicians and listeners find Bach's music to be profoundly and deeply emotional. Bach used reason and logic to give his music clear structure, balance, and integrity. His fugues are a striking example of this.

What are the ethical considerations that limit the scope of inquiry?

Knowledge question: To what extent is it possible to separate the arts from ethical considerations?

Ethical consideration 1: The morals of the artist

The great 17th-century Italian painter Caravaggio murdered a man and may have been killed in revenge by that man's family. He fought in public and was constantly in trouble with the law. He may have used a drowned **prostitute** as a model when he painted the death of the mother of Jesus. This raises an interesting knowledge issue: Should an artwork be judged purely on its own merits, or is it important to include the life and character of the artist in the evaluation?

Ethical consideration 2: The politics of the artist

Leni Riefenstahl was an important German film director who worked during the Nazi era. She directed two films at that time which received international praise and attention. The *Triumph of the Will* is important in film history but it was also used as a Nazi propaganda film. *Olympia* celebrated the 1936 Olympics in Berlin, another important event in Nazi history. Riefenstahl's career raises many questions. To what extent is she responsible for the effects of her films? Does she share in the responsibility for Nazi war crimes? Is it possible to separate her work from its political era? Is her work inevitably compromised by her connection to the Nazis?

Ethical consideration 3: Censorship

Governments and the politically powerful try to censor the arts.

- The Chinese government has repeatedly jailed and attempted to censor the artist Ai Weiwei. Ai Weiwei is a strong critic of China's **authoritarian** government.
- The 19th-century opera composer Giuseppe Verdi set his operas in earlier times. He did this so it would not appear to censors that he was criticizing the governments of his time.
- The wealthy American newspaper **publisher** William Randolph Hearst attempted to **ruin** the career of Orson Welles. He did this because of Welles's film *Citizen Kane*. Hearst believed the film **belittled** him. He attempted to stop the film's distribution and success.

Subject vocabulary

cantatas major works of church music for singers and orchestra

collective musical memory the musical memories of a group of people

censor control what is and is not allowed to be published, or seen

Synonyms

sacred .... very important, religious, holy

simultaneously at the same time

ruin .... badly damage

General vocabulary

integrity the quality of being honest and strong about what you believe to be right

prostitute someone, typically a woman, who earns money by having sex with people

authoritarian strictly forcing people to obey a set of rules or laws, especially ones that are wrong or unfair

publisher person or group who make newspapers, magazines and books available

belittled made someone or something seem small, or unimportant

In the long run, great art seems to rise above censorship. But artists often censor themselves, and so the power of governments and the wealthy does affect art.

Knowledge framework: Concepts/language

What role does language play in the accumulation of knowledge in this area?

Role 1: Language is central to artistic expression.

In some art forms, language is central. For example, in poetry, novels, and short stories language itself is the art form. Language also plays a critical role in film, theatre, musicals, opera, and songs.

Poetry often uses language in original and non-standard ways. Poets are often interested in the sounds of words and in the patterns created by joining words together. Many poems follow formal patterns, and have rhyme and **metre**. Poets use language in extreme and unusual ways, for example, *Jabberwocky* by Lewis Carroll.

Jabberwocky
By Lewis Carroll

'Twas brillig, and the slithy toves
Did gyre and gimble in the wabe:
All mimsy were the borogoves,
And the mome raths outgrabe.

Beware the Jabberwock, my son!
The jaws that bite, the claws that catch!
Beware the Jubjub bird, and shun
The frumious Bandersnatch!

This poem by Lewis Carroll is full of words that have no meaning in English. But it follows the **conventions** of the English language and so seems to have meaning. It also uses the conventions of poetry such as rhyme and metre. On the one hand, the poem seems to be **nonsense**. On the other, it is a brilliant investigation of how we understand language.

Role 2: The language of music

In some ways, music is not a language. Music does not have words and does not convey precise meaning. In music there is no way to say something like, 'My uncle called me yesterday to congratulate me.' But, music can be seen as having grammar and structure. For example, in a melody there are reasons why one note follows the next. The movement from one note to the next is not random; it has order. Likewise, there is a logical pattern of **chord** sequences. In music, there are patterns of consonant and dissonant notes. Consonant notes fit together in an agreeable way. Dissonant notes **clash** or conflict. The alternation of dissonance and consonance gives a sense of **tension** and relaxation. By writing and playing specific patterns of music using consonance and dissonance, musicians create emotions in the members of the audience.

Articulation sentence:
In music, there are patterns and logic that can be seen as a form of language.

What are the roles of the key concepts and key terms that provide the building blocks for knowledge in this area?

Key concepts in the arts:

- tradition
- medium
- canon
- performer.
- form
- beauty
- audience

Key concept 1: The role of tradition

Many art forms follow long-established traditions. Artists who follow these traditions work in the same ways and with the same materials as other artists did in the past. Examples of traditions are:

- Javanese gamelan music
- Peking or Beijing opera
- Japanese Noh theatre
- the blues
- Chinese landscape painting.

A person who wants to work in one of these areas must first come to understand the tradition, study with a **master** and then **apply** the skills learned.

Key concept 2: The role of form

Form plays an important role in works of art. Some artistic forms are quite strict but others are looser. Poetic forms include haiku, the sonnet, and the ballad. Musical forms include call and response, variation, and the sonata. Dance forms include jig, waltz, tango, and salsa. Artistic forms provide structure and tradition. These forms can create a kind of language for performers and creators.

Key concept 3: The role of the medium

Artists and performers work with specific materials. These materials influence what artists can and cannot do. Architects work with glass, steel, wood, and stone. Filmmakers work with cameras, lights, and **sets**. Visual artists work with charcoal, pencil, oil paint, and **canvas**. Musicians work with different instruments and different voices. The choice of medium may be the artist's first decision. The medium itself often has specific traditions and conventions.

Key concept 4: The role of 'beauty'

Many artworks try to create beauty. A beautiful subject may come from nature, such as a sunset, or a lovely face, but the artist must reshape this material subject with imagination. The poet John Keats famously said:

Beauty is truth, truth beauty, — that is all
Ye know on earth, and all ye need to know.

The attraction of beauty and the desire for the beautiful seem to be basic human desires. Art may be the area of knowledge most capable of achieving beauty.

Key concept 5: The role of the artistic canon

Many of the arts have a canon. A canon is a group of the greatest works from in that art form. The canon of Western literature includes Homer, the Bible, and the plays of Shakespeare. The idea of an artistic cannon is controversial. Critics say that it leaves out the contributions of women and non-Western artists. Some see the canon as **elitist** and oppressive. People ask if these **distinctions** are based on facts or merely on opinions. Others argue that the canon has **stood the test of time** and that it represents highly influential works.

Subject vocabulary

gamelan traditional music for instruments from Java

Noh traditional Japanese theatre form with dance and song

haiku Japanese poetic form made up of three lines and 17 syllables

sonnet a poem with 14 rhymed lines

sonata a musical piece for an instrument, or instruments having several parts

jig a lively, jumping dance

waltz a social dance in triple time that involves much spinning

charcoal a drawing instrument made from burned wood or bone

Synonyms

apply............. use

elitist............. snobbish, self-important

distinctions .... differences

General vocabulary

master person who has learned a skill or a language so well that they have no difficulty with it

sets places where films or TV programmes are filmed

canvas a piece of cloth for painting on

medium the material in which an artist expresses ideas

stood the test of time still remains relevant today

The concepts of a performer and an audience are tied together. Today, it is common to pay to see **professional performers**. In some traditional cultures, all members of the group are involved in singing, playing, and dancing. Today digital art, the internet, and YouTube are also making the distinction between artist and performer less clear. Today, it is possible to create a work online and have a potential audience of half the world. However, this is very different from a live performance with a live audience.

What metaphors are appropriate to this area of knowledge?

Metaphor Example 1: Colours and Kandinsky

The Russian artist Wassily Kandinsky used several metaphors to describe his paintings.

> Colour is the keyboard,
> the eyes are the hammers,
> the soul is the piano with many strings.
> The artist is the hand that plays,
> touching one key or another purposively,
> to cause vibrations in the soul.

Kandinsky **compares** music, which is an art that uses listening, to painting, which is an art that uses sight. Colours are keyboards and the painter plays on the strings of the soul.

Metaphor Example 2: The fourth wall and Brecht

The fourth wall and breaking the fourth wall are metaphors in theatre. The first three walls are the back and the sides of the **stage**. The fourth wall is an imaginary wall between the stage and the audience. Normally, the actors pretend that the audience is not there. The German playwright Bertolt Brecht wanted to 'break the fourth wall'. In Brecht's approach to theatre, actors come forward and speak directly to the audience. Brecht does not want the audience to identify emotionally with the characters on stage. He wants the audience to be rational and to consider issues like social justice. He does not want audience members to **lose themselves** in the **illusions** of theatre; he wants audiences to continue thinking critically.

What is the role of convention in this area?

Conventions are rules that groups agree to follow. Conventions are a means to solve problems through common agreement. Artists use and **manipulate** conventions.

Convention 1: The willing suspension of disbelief

In a theatre, the audience agrees to pretend that the action on stage is real. The people on stage are not dying or falling in love. But entering into this imaginary world is what makes theatre powerful and convincing. In the days of black-and-white film and television, audiences ignored the lack of colour. People also ignore the fact that film and television are shown on two-dimensional surfaces. In television shows and films, the audience is often invited to forget that the story is not real. Audiences can become fully involved with the emotions of a story. Followers of soap operas may forget that the actors are not the characters. Their fan mail, blogs, and Facebook posts often suggest that they make no distinction between the actors and their fictional characters.

Convention 2: Performance conventions

In Beijing opera, conventions of acting, costume, and make-up are **essential**. Human actions are performed in a **stylized** manner that generations of actors have **passed on** to each other. When an actor walks in a large circle, it shows that he or she is travelling a long distance. When an actor straightens his or her costume or **headdress**, it shows that an important character will speak. These conventions must be learned by both the actors and the audience.

Convention 3: Beauty

The **ideal** of beauty changes over time, particularly female beauty. Female Hollywood stars of the past had fuller **figures** than today's actresses. Marilyn Monroe and Mae West are two examples. The fashions for eyebrow shapes, lip size, and eye shape change frequently. Ideals of beauty change from time to time, place to place, and culture to culture.

Ancient Egyptian artists used a convention in which some parts of the body were **pictured** from the front and some from the side. The goal was to **portray** parts of the body in the most attractive way. The Egyptians considered the profile to be the most attractive view of the head. The body was more attractive seen from the front but the feet were more attractive from the side.

> Articulation sentence:
> Conventions are rules that groups agree to follow. Conventions change over time.

Knowledge framework: Methodology

What are the methods or procedures used in this area and what is it about these methods that generates knowledge?

The arts use many different methods and procedures. These methods are often techniques. The violinist must **master** his instrument. The dancer must master her body. The painter must master control of the brush, paint, and pencil. The sculptor must learn to use clay, bronze, and marble. Creative artists use their techniques to solve problems and create imaginative **illusions**. The problems they face range from creating believable characters in a novel to creating computer-generated **dragons** in a film.

Method 1: Violin technique

Learning to play the violin requires training from early childhood. In violin playing, the right and left hands do very different things. The hands and arms move in different ways, and in different directions. The left hand makes very small, precise movements to produce the correct pitches. The right hand holds and moves the **bow**, which produces the musical tone. The right and the left hand must work together but they have very different jobs. The violinist must learn to read music, to play in tune, and to make a good sound. As many as 16 violinists play the same musical part in a **symphony orchestra**. Therefore, violinists become very good at working together and listening carefully. Until a violinist has learned good technique, he or she is not able to play musically, emotionally, or with beauty. A violinist cannot become a performer without **mastering** the methodology of string technique. Methodology and artistry go hand in hand.

Synonyms

essential .... necessary, basic

portray .... show

General vocabulary

stylized in an artificial style that does not look natural or real, but that is still pleasant to look at

passed on gave someone something that someone else gave to them

headdress something that someone wears on their head, especially for decoration on a special occasion

ideal the best possible model, perfection

figure the shape of a woman's body

pictured shown in a photograph, painting, or drawing

master learn a skill or a language so well that it presents no difficulty

illusions impressions that are not based on reality

dragons large imaginary animals, with wings and a long tail, that can breathe out fire

bow a long, thin piece of wood with a tight string fastened along it, used to play musical instruments such as the violin or cello

symphony orchestra a very large group of musicians who usually play classical music

mastering learning a skill or a language so well that it presents no difficulty

Method 2: Lighting

New technologies can create new methodologies and new possibilities for the arts. The invention of electric lighting created many new possibilities for theatre and film. Before electrical lighting, theatres were illuminated with candles or gas flames. This was both expensive and difficult to control. Electrical lighting allows **illumination** from many directions, the use of different colours, and rapid changes in lighting. This technology created new possibilities for theatre directors and actors. Artificial lighting allows directors to film at night. It means they can overcome the difficulties caused by the constant changes of natural light. Artificial lighting can create the illusion of sunrise in an interior **shot**. The lighting can make an actor seem more, or less attractive. Many film illusions are created through electrical lighting.

> Articulation sentence:
> Each art form has a set of methodologies. These methodologies are often techniques. They link the intention of the artist to the reaction of the audience.

What are the assumptions underlying these methods?

Assumption 1: The arts require the mastery of techniques

Playing in a rock band does not require as much technique as playing in a string quartet. So the arts vary in their technical demands. Even though playing in a rock band is not as technically difficult as playing in a string quartet, there are still good and bad rock guitarists. Therefore, it is safe to assume that the best rock guitarists know things and can do things that less successful rock guitarists cannot. The greatest rock guitarists have a **unique** sound and style that sets them apart from the other guitarists. They may be more creative in their interpretation of other people's material. They are able to **improvise** solos with a clear shape that create tension and release. Technique alone is not enough to create compelling art works. But **intensity**, originality, and creative ideas are also not enough. These ideas can only be **realized** when an artist has the technique required for the art form.

Assumption 2: Art is the expression of emotion

Many people assume that the arts are the expression of emotions. If this were true, a baby **screaming** in an airplane would be a very good artist. The baby is expressing emotions with great **clarity** and intensity. Clearly, a screaming baby is not an artist. Great artworks often convey powerful emotions, but they also do much more. They communicate logic and order through a structure such as theme and variation. Artworks communicate information about the time of their creation. Paintings convey clear information about clothing, hairstyles, furniture, and architecture. Novels and stories may convey important information about the social structure and culture of other places and times.

> Articulation sentence:
> The arts communicate emotion, but they communicate far more than just emotion. They can also communicate logic and order.

What counts as a fact in this area of knowledge?

Understanding and analysing the arts requires facts. These facts may increase understanding, but they may not reveal the *magic* of an artwork.

Example 1: Objectivity **in poetry**

The analysis and interpretation of a poem may include the following aspects.

- Metre is the rhythmic pattern of a poem. Metre can be a specified pattern of strong and weak syllables.
- Rhyme scheme is the pattern of rhyming in a poem.
- Genre is the type of poem, such as sonnet, ballad, epic, or limerick.
- Date of publication.

In most cases, all the above aspects are clear.

Example 2: Subjectivity **in poetry**

The analysis of the poem may go on to include the following aspects.

- Style includes word choice, tone, author's voice.
- Imagery conveys sensory images such as the sights, smells, and sounds.
- Literary influences are poems and poets that inspired the poem.
- Literary devices include metaphor and simile.

These elements are subjective but are supported by the objectivity of metre and rhyme. To recognize style and influence, the reader must know other poems and poets. The reader will have to make a case with arguments and examples. The reader may try to show why the poet uses a certain image or metaphor. This kind of analysis demonstrates greater understanding. Good analysis often moves from objective facts to subjective ideas.

Articulation sentence:
Understanding artworks requires both facts and interpretation.

What role do models play in this area of knowledge?

There are at least two ways to understand models in art. A model can be a person, a landscape, or object that the artist uses for the artwork. A model could also be a formal procedure, like variation in music.

Role 1: Models as an object of study

Nature serves as an important model for some art. 18th-century theorists stated that art was the imitation of nature. On a simple level, this could mean that the artist tries to re-create nature. On a more complex level, the artist tries to understand the **principles** of nature. The beauty and power of nature can be an important model for artists.

Example: Chinese landscape painting

Art often depicts beautiful or striking landscapes. Chinese landscape painting is a high point in Chinese art. These paintings **depict** an ideal natural world. The calm and beauty of this world often contrasts with the **chaos** and **corruption** of the outer real world. These idealized landscapes may also be a reflection of the artist's mind and heart. Therefore, nature serves as a source of **inspiration** but nature is reshaped through art.

Subject vocabulary

objectivity not being influenced by personal feelings or opinions

metre the rhythm pattern of strong and weak syllables

rhyme using words with similar ending sounds

subjectivity being influenced by personal feelings or opinions, which are thought to uncover greater understanding

arguments line of reasoning, claim

Synonyms

depict............ show

General vocabulary

principles the basic ideas that a plan or system is based on

chaos a situation in which everything is happening in a confused way, and nothing is organized, or arranged in order

corruption dishonest, illegal, or immoral behaviour, especially from someone with power

inspiration a person, experience, place, etc. that gives you new ideas

Role 2: Models as a formal procedure

Models help the artist solve a major problem. The problem is how to create structure and order in an artwork. A model provides the artist with a starting point. The artist can then **adapt** or **transform** the model to suit his or her purposes. The following models are examples of formal procedures:

- musical forms such as the fugue or the rondo
- dance forms such as the flamenco, kathakali, or waltz
- poetic forms such as the ode, elegy, sonnet, and haiku.

Example: Dramatic structure

Shakespeare's plays follow a five-act structure. This formal structure is like a **mould** that can be filled with content. The five-part structure was developed in Roman times and **dramatists** continue to use it.

- Act 1: The exposition introduces background information and sets the scene.
- Act 2: The rising action is the series of events that build up to the climax.
- Act 3: The climax is the turning point when things go from bad to good, or from good to bad.
- Act 4: The falling action happens when events come apart and one of the central characters wins or loses.
- Act 5: The resolution is the happy ending or the tragic conclusion.

This model is still used today because it provides structure, tension, release, and resolution.

> Articulation sentence:
> Models in the arts provide materials for artists, and formal techniques to provide structure.

Knowledge framework: Historical development

What is the significance of the key points in the historical development of this area of knowledge?

Key point 1: The arts as a record of history

In the National Museum of Ancient Art in Lisbon there are paintings by 16th century Japanese artists. This art, called Nanban art, is from the time when the Portuguese first went to Japan, Photo 8.2, opposite. The Japanese artists see the Portuguese from their Japanese cultural perspective. The ships, figures, and costumes are neither entirely Japanese nor Portuguese. The *Namban* screens tell us at least two important things:

- that the Portuguese went to Japan (they are an artistic record of history)
- that the Japanese artists adapted new information about the Portuguese in traditional Japanese style.

Art often provides important insights into the past.

> Articulation sentence:
> Art can be used as an historical resource and as a means to record history. It can be used to study how people in the past thought, felt, and behaved.

Photo 8.2 *An example of Nanban art: how Japanese artists interpreted Portuguese style.*

Key point 2: The arts as revolutionary ideas

Stravinsky's ballet, the *Rite of Spring*, caused a riot in Paris on 29 May 1913. The audience was shocked by the power, **brutality**, and **novelty** of the music. The ballet showed **primitive** rituals with the dancers **stomping** across the stage. This was in complete contrast to the ideal of beauty and **grace** that the audience expected. The *Rite of Spring* is one of the first great works of Modernism. It came one year before the beginning of the First World War. Musically and artistically, it marks a great break with the past. In some ways, its power and brutality **prophesy** the horror of the First World War.

Knowledge framework: Links to personal knowledge

Why is this area significant to the individual?

How does art contribute to a person's sense of self?

For many people, art has a **profoundly** important personal meaning. Some people are passionately involved with doing some kind of art. Other people are passionate members of the audience. For most people, particular songs, films, or novels have a special meaning and significance. People often **idolize** musicians and actors. Why is this?

A great novel may go deep into another person's life. Although the character is fictional, the reader may identify with the person deeply. The reader has information about the character's thoughts and life that would never be available about a real person. Readers may ask themselves what they would have done in that situation. A novel can take readers to distant times and places, or to cultures they will never visit. The reader can live another life, even the life of an animal, through the imagination.

Source: © Heritage Image Partnership Ltd/Alamy stock photo

What is the nature of the contribution of individuals to this area?

Great artistic geniuses have shaped the history of the arts. Mozart is one classic example. The history of Western music would be very different without Bach, Mozart, and Beethoven. The history of Western painting would be different without Michelangelo, Rembrandt, and Picasso.

Key individual 1: Richard Wagner (1813–1883)

The German composer Richard Wagner created the largest and **grandest** opera of all time: *The Ring of the* Nibelungen. It is actually a cycle of four very long operas; it ends with the destruction of the gods. The story follows the struggles, battles, and loves of gods, heroes, and mythical creatures. The **settings** range from the bottom of the River Rhine to the palace of the gods, Valhalla. The themes include passion, the struggle for power, greed, betrayal, and heroism. Wagner created the idea of the *Gesamtkunstwerk* or total artwork. His combination of music, drama, and stage design **revolutionized** opera. Singers, conductors, and directors still struggle to make his epic ideas a reality. But the music is so **overwhelming** that opera houses around the world continue to stage the *Ring*.

Key individual 2: Akira Kurosawa (1910–1998)

The Japanese film director Akira Kurosawa brought the world of the Samurai into the Western imagination. Kurosawa combines elements from Hollywood with Japanese theatrical traditions. His films capture a world that is completely foreign and yet utterly compelling. The film *Seven Samurai* influenced the *Magnificent Seven*. George Lucas drew inspiration from Kurosawa for his *Star Wars* films. The film *Rashomon* tells the story of a **rape** from four radically different perspectives. It perfectly demonstrates the problem of finding the truth among **competing** stories. *Throne of Blood* is Kurosawa's film **adaptation** of Shakespeare's *Macbeth*. He radically transforms the story drawing on the tradition of Noh theatre. Like Shakespeare, Kurosawa was able to combine **comic** elements in a violent tragedy. His influence can be seen in the work of film directors such as Robert Altman and Quentin Tarantino.

What responsibilities rest upon the individual knower by virtue of his or her knowledge in this area?

The arts can be used for good or bad purposes, but they are not morally neutral. The Nazis used the arts extensively in their propaganda. Hitler was a failure as a young artist, but he took his artistic ambitions into the realm of politics. He was a great lover of the operas of Wagner. He created political theatre with his ability to speak and **stir** the emotions of his listeners. The Nazis **consciously** used all of the arts to support their rise to power. Hitler's Minister of propaganda, Joseph Goebbels, wanted to combine the arts and politics. Hitler enthusiastically embraced this combination. The Nazis supported painters and architects, and made hundreds of films. Most of the films were popular and relatively low quality, but *The Triumph of Will* is a part of film history. In the film, Hitler appears as a godlike figure in the middle of an **adoring** crowd. The Nazis supported some artists but they also **persecuted** many artists, especially Jewish artists. They also persecuted artists who were interested in Modernism. The use of the arts was central to the success of the Nazis.

Knowledge framework: Scope/applications

What is the area of knowledge about?

At the most basic level, ethics is about right and wrong. What should be done? What should not be done? What rights do people have? What obligations do people have? These are typical questions about ethics.

Many actions have consequences for others. It is possible to act in ways which improve the lives of others. However, it is also possible to act in ways which harm the lives of others. In short, it is possible to help and to harm. Imagination and empathy can help us understand how words and actions can both help and harm. But people may be mistaken about the consequences of their actions. They may intend to help someone but actually cause harm. Morality is concerned with praise and blame. People praise others for their good actions and also blame others for their bad actions.

Moral rules are a key area to discuss in ethics. Some ethical systems involve following rules. Is following rules enough to make a person moral? Are there actually moral rules? People also debate whether or not moral rules may be broken. If moral rules are not absolute, then when could they be broken? A key question is whether or not humans are basically selfish, or altruistic. Another key question is whether moral judgement should be based on actions, the reasons for actions, or the results of actions.

Branches of ethics

- Normative ethics assumes that there are right and wrong answers as well as right and wrong actions.
- Applied ethics looks at what to do in specific situations. It looks at such things as the ethics of medicine, environmental ethics, and the ethics of business.
- Meta-ethics asks broader philosophical questions about the nature of ethics. For example: What does it mean to say something is right or wrong? Are there moral truths? Where do rights come from? Is ethics independent of human beings? In other words, do ethics exist in the universe like light and gravity?

> Articulation sentence:
> At the simplest level, ethics is about right and wrong.

What practical problems can be solved through applying this knowledge?

Ethics is very much concerned with what should be done and what should not be done. Ethics is therefore constantly looking at both the large and small problems that occur in daily life.

Everyday ethical questions include the following.
- Is downloading a movie without paying for it unethical?
- Should you tell a friend that her boyfriend is cheating on her?
- Is giving money to beggars a good thing to do?

Practical problem 1: Decision-making

A particular moral system may offer rules or guidelines for making moral decisions. For example, the Roman Catholic Church is opposed to abortion. A Roman Catholic thus has a clear rule to follow. A Roman Catholic may decide to break this rule, but the rule itself is clear.

Subject vocabulary

utilitarian approach to ethics that focuses on the results of actions

illegal against the law

responsibility duty, obligation

Synonyms

poses............ presents, gives

decreased ...... reduced

General vocabulary

shame regret and embarrassment after doing something wrong

slavery being forced to work for no money

obligations duties, responsibilities

brothels houses where men pay to have sex with prostitutes

sneaking going somewhere secretly and quietly in order to avoid being seen, or heard

A **utilitarian** approaches ethics very differently. A utilitarian looks at the consequences or results of actions. A utilitarian asks if an abortion will result in a more positive outcome. A utilitarian may decide that an abortion is the right thing to do. Perhaps the mother will not be able to provide a good life for the child. The guideline for a utilitarian is not based on abortion itself. A utilitarian asks if the results of an abortion are positive or negative.

In both cases, the woman or girl is facing an unwanted pregnancy. The decision about what to do may be very difficult. Ethics is often concerned with such difficult questions. Having an abortion may lead to guilt and **shame**. Having an unwanted child may create financial, educational, and practical problems for the mother. The decision may also have an impact on other people. Ethics is not just a private matter. Ethical decisions affect other people.

> Articulation sentence:
> A particular moral system may offer rules or guidelines for making moral decisions.

Practical problem 2: Dividing limited resources

The 'tragedy of the commons' describes the conflict between what is good for the individual and what is good for the group. One example is fishing. If one company or one country catches a very large number of fish, they make large profits and provide high-quality food. However, if many companies or countries catch large quantities of fish, there will soon be no more fish. Many areas of the ocean are already overfished. This is both an economical and an ethical question. The ethical question concerns the fairest way to divide limited resources. If the different groups cannot cooperate and act fairly, the results are bad for everyone.

What makes this area of knowledge important?

Ethics is important because it looks at what is good and bad, or right and wrong. Ethical principles affect politics, law, and education. Ethics is critical in resolving conflicts between individuals and groups. Ethics is the basis for determining rights and **obligations**.

Example 1

Today 20–30 million people live and work in **slavery**. Slavery is not legal in any country, but it continues to exist. This is a shocking problem. Slaves work in farms, factories, homes, and **brothels**. People are bought and sold for as little as $90. Making slavery **illegal** in the United States, Brazil, Russia, and in many other countries around the world was a great moral victory. But the problem of slavery remains today and **poses** a great ethical challenge. Knowing about slavery may give a person reasons to take action.

Knowledge question: To what extent does knowledge also bring responsibility to act?

Example 2

Many people illegally download music, television shows, and movies. Many believe that everything on the internet should be free. But it takes a lot of money to make music, television shows, and movies. Therefore, the people who make these products are not being fully paid. People who illegally download do not believe that they are stealing, but they are not paying for what they are getting. The internet may lead to a **decreased** sense of **responsibility**. **Sneaking** into a cinema without paying feels like a small immoral action but downloading a movie without paying feels different. This intuition may be wrong. Intuition plays an important role in moral decisions and so moral intuition has consequences.

> Articulation sentence:
> Ethics is critical in resolving conflicts between individuals and groups.

What are the current open questions in this area?

Open Question 1: What are rights and what is the ethical foundation of rights?

Rights play an important role in many ethical and legal systems. But what is the basis of these rights? Where did they come from? The Declaration of Independence of the United States includes the following text: 'We hold these truths to be self-evident, that all men are created equal, that they are endowed by their Creator with certain unalienable Rights, that among these are Life, Liberty, and the pursuit of Happiness.' The document states that the Creator gives rights that cannot be taken away. It is not entirely clear what or who the Creator is, and it is not entirely clear why people have such rights. One possibility is that people agree that they have rights. Human rights may be like mathematical axioms or rules: they are there because people have agreed that they are there.

The Universal Declaration of Human Rights was adopted in 1948. It gives individuals protection against tyranny and oppression. Most countries signed this declaration, even though they did not all truly respect human rights. Nevertheless, this had a big effect on how people think.

Open Question 2: Is happiness the best basis for ethics?

Utilitarian ethics focuses on reducing pain and increasing happiness for as many people as possible. Jeremy Bentham, the founder of utilitarianism, stated: 'Create all the happiness you are able to create: remove all the misery you are able to remove.' Both of these goals seem to be very good, but important things may be left out of the equation. For religious believers, their religious beliefs may be the true basis for ethics. Meaning and purpose are also possible bases for ethics. The philosopher Immanuel Kant argues that morality should be based on reason and duty; he stated that duty was the basis for ethics. Serving humanity could be another basis for ethics. One advantage of choosing happiness is that it seems like an easy starting point. But happiness may not be easy to measure. Happiness is a bad measure for ethics if it involves the suffering of others. If happiness is only bodily pleasure, this also seems to be too narrow. Each concept for the foundation of ethics has problems. This is why ethics continues to have major open questions.

Knowledge framework: Concepts/language

What role does language play in the accumulation of knowledge in this area?

Role 1: Defining moral concepts

One role of language is to define what ethics is about. The language of ethics often uses common words. But it can be very difficult to precisely define these words. *Good, bad, right, wrong, should, ought, rights, justice, duty, consequence,* and *obligation* are words commonly used in ethics. These words are fundamental in discussing morality but they are not quite like axioms in mathematics.

Mathematicians accept axioms as the agreed rules, and then continue their work. But moral philosophers have difficulty agreeing on what these ethical 'axioms' mean. What makes something a duty? What is a good act? What makes something right? The approach to defining the question can influence the ethical outcome. For example:

● a Christian might search in the Bible to define right and wrong

● a Confucian might consult Chinese traditions to define right and wrong

● a humanist might consider fairness, justice, equality, and freedom to define right and wrong.

In each of these cases, the actions taken will lead to a different definition. The definition of the word also affects the reasons for saying something is right or wrong.

Role 2: To describe what people should do

Moral language is different from the language of the human sciences. The human sciences try to describe what people *actually* do. Ethics describes what people *should* do. This means that ethics includes a call to action. Researchers in the human sciences could observe that people drive when they are **drunk** and try to discover the reasons why they do this. Ethics **typically** states that this is bad and wrong. People shouldn't drive when they are drunk. An **anthropologist** might try to discover why people are still kept in slavery. But slavery is **condemned** in ethics. An ethical statement says that no human ought to be held in slavery. Therefore the **purpose** of language in ethics can be very different from the purpose of language in the human sciences.

Articulation sentence:
The purpose of language in ethics can be very different from the purpose of language in the human sciences.

What are the roles of the key concepts and key terms that provide the building blocks for knowledge in this area?

Key concept 1: Universalizability

Universality means an ethical concept applies in all situations. The Universal Declaration of Human Rights is a good example. This document was adopted by the United Nations 1948. Here is the first article:

All human beings are born free and equal in dignity and rights. They are endowed with reason and conscience and should act towards one another in a spirit of brotherhood.

This is a clear example of universalizability. The statement applies to all human beings. It does not make differences according to class, place of birth, or religion.

Key concept 2: Relativism

Relativism expects that different groups will have different ethical systems. Ethical relativism does not claim that there is only one correct moral system. Ethical relativism states that there is no objective standard for right and wrong. Right and wrong depend on a particular culture, or historical **era**. All points of view are equally **valid**. People determine what is true for them. Ethical relativism rejects universal moral statements. It is clear that different cultures and religions have different ethical systems. Some societies view suicide as an honourable way to save face. Other societies view suicide as a crime, a **sin**, or a mental illness. Relativism argues

Subject vocabulary

anthropologist a person who studies the wider cultural and historical influences on humankind

universalizability applicability in all situations (of an ethical concept)

relativism the idea that there are no absolute universal standards for morality

objective standard a rule or guideline that has no bias or subjective element

universal can be applied to all situations at all times

suicide killing oneself, taking one's own life

Synonyms

typically .... usually

era .... time

valid .... acceptable

General vocabulary

drunk unable to control behaviour, speech, etc. because of alcohol

condemned censured, declared bad, or evil

purpose reason, intention

dignity pride, self-respect

save face avoid embarrassment

sin an action that is against religious rules and is considered to be an offence against God

that the values and morality of others should be accepted. It argues against universal ideas of right and wrong. However, ethical relativism does not provide good ways of settling **disputes** in **multicultural** societies.

> Articulation sentence:
> Universality means that an ethical system applies everywhere. Relativism means that an ethical system varies from place to place.

Key concept 3: Sin

Some people define sin as an action that is against religious rules and is considered to be an offence against God. If this definition is correct, it means that sin depends on believing in God. Therefore, sin may be a religious concept and not an ethical concept. This is another example that demonstrates why ethical decisions are difficult. Disagreement about the basic terms can easily lead to conflict.

Key concept 4: Distributive justice

Distributive justice looks at how rights, power, and **privileges** are divided up in society. Distributive justice often looks at the balance between the rich and the poor. Should we have systems that help the poor, the sick, and other **worse-off** people? Distributive justice can also look at the balance between humans and non-humans. Should we make sacrifices to help animals or **ecosystems**?

What metaphors are appropriate to this area of knowledge?

Ethics contains a range of metaphors. Metaphors often connect abstract ideas to feelings and sensations. Metaphors are more than just words and phrases. Metaphors can be connected to the body, to emotions, and to feelings.

Example 1: Metaphors for evil

When people find something immoral they may say it is low, disgusting, rotten, sickening, or dirty. An evil act is disgusting and **repulsive**, like **rotten** food, or **vomit**. An evil person is **loathsome**, a snake, a disgusting insect, or a beast. A bad person is rotten to the core, a bad apple. Sin and evil are an **abyss**. There are moral **swamps** and moral **minefields**. Death and evil are dark and shadowy. Hell is below.

Example 2: Metaphors for good

Heaven is above. Good is upwards and high minded. A good person takes the high road and is **upstanding**. Goodness is clear and filled with light. A good person is an **angel**, a heavenly creature.

Example 3: The path

The path of goodness is straight and narrow. The path of evil is **crooked**. The good path is the moral high road. Leaving the path is bad or dangerous. Psalm 23 from the Bible speaks of the 'paths of righteousness' and the 'valley of the shadow of death'. A person can choose the path of good or the path of evil.

> Articulation sentence:
> Metaphors often connect abstract ideas to feelings and sensations.

What is the role of convention in this area?

Ethics contains a variety of conventions. These include religious, legal, and social conventions. A country must decide whether cars should drive on the left or right side of the road. There is nothing ethical about driving on the left or right side of the road. However, driving on the wrong side of the road is dangerous and probably unethical.

Convention 1: Dress

Most societies have **customs** regarding what parts of the body can be shown in public.

Example 1

In many countries, it is considered immoral if a woman does not cover her upper body in public. However, on some European beaches it is acceptable for women to show their upper bodies.

Example 2

In parts of Sierra Leone, there was a clash of customs when Christian **missionaries** arrived. Many local women did not cover their upper bodies and the Christian missionaries thought this was immoral. This conflict of customs created difficulties for many women in Sierra Leone. Clothing is largely a matter of convention. However, many people treat it as an ethical issue.

Convention 2: Treatment of the dead

Societies have widely varying ways of respecting the dead.

- Orthodox Jews bury their dead within 24 hours.
- In the United States, bodies may be **embalmed** and put on display for several days.
- In Islamic tradition, the body is bathed, covered with a cloth, and buried in a simple grave.
- **Cremation** is forbidden in Islamic tradition.
- In the Hindu tradition, cremation is the usual procedure.
- The Fore people of Papua New Guinea ate the bodies of the dead to capture the person's **life force**.
- In modern, multi-ethnic cities, hospitals may face great difficulties in dealing with the dead. For example, some UK cities have as many as 30 or 40 different religious and ethnic groups. Their practices of treating the dead may vary greatly.

There does seem to be a **unifying thread** in all of these traditions: the dead must be **honoured**. But the **interpretation** of how the dead should be honoured varies widely. Conflicts and misunderstanding can **arise** from these varying conventions.

> Articulation sentence:
> Ethical conventions very greatly but they may share a common justification.

Knowledge framework: Methodology

What are the methods or procedures used in this area and what is it about these methods that generates knowledge?

Every society must find methods that balance the needs of individuals and the needs of the group. Every society faces conflict and every society must deal with immoral or criminal acts. There are many methods or procedures to reach moral decisions. These methods include monotheism, utilitarianism, and deontology.

Method 1: Monotheism

Monotheism is an important example of divine command theory. In the monotheistic religions, God is the source of ethics. It is the task of the believer to interpret, understand, and follow the rules given by God. Morality is based on God's command. God determines what is good or bad. God's commands say what is obligatory, allowed, or not allowed. God's message is communicated in a sacred text such as the Bible or the Qur'an. The challenge for the believer is to interpret the text.

One of the Ten Commandments states that people should honour their fathers and mothers. The question is: What does this mean in practice? This could mean strict obedience to the wishes of the parents. It could also mean simply respect. It is often difficult to interpret sacred texts from the perspective of today's world. There is often great disagreement among believers about how to interpret sacred texts. People who do not follow a monotheistic religion may not accept a sacred text. They may see no reason to follow such a text.

Method 2: Utilitarianism

> Articulation sentence:
> Utilitarianism is an important ethical theory which looks at the results of actions.

What are the consequences of a particular action? Something is good if it produces good consequences. Something is bad if it results in bad consequences. Different systems of utilitarianism give different ways of measuring consequences. Happiness is one measure of good results. Avoiding pain and suffering is another measure of results. Ideals and preferences can also be the goals of utilitarianism. According to utilitarianism, the broader purpose of morality is to produce a better world. Measuring happiness or preferences can be very difficult. Choosing between competing claims can also cause problems. Utilitarianism also lacks a clear place for rights. Every ethical system must balance the needs of the group with the needs of the individual. These needs may be in conflict. Utilitarians may speak of the greatest good for the greatest number. This favours groups. An example of this was China's one-child policy, which limited a couple to having a single child. This policy was very good for controlling China's population but it violated the right of a couple to decide what kind of family they would like to have.

Method 3: Deontology

> Articulation sentence:
> Deontology focuses on rules. Is the action intrinsically right or wrong? What is the intention behind the act?

Subject vocabulary

care ethics ethics based on care and intuition

feminist the idea that women should have the same rights and opportunities as men

utilitarian ethics increasing happiness for the many and avoiding pain

General vocabulary

emphasized placed importance on

frameworks structures to help thought

cold unfriendly or lacking normal human feelings such as sympathy, pity, humour, etc.

What is the right thing to do? Deontology is based on the thinking of Immanuel Kant. Kant **emphasized** logic and reason. He created a kind of test for a moral rule. He asked, what if everybody did something? What if everybody cheated on tests? That would be a bad idea. Tests would have no meaning. What if doctors cheated on their medical tests? This would be a bad idea. It would not be possible to believe in their medical abilities. What if everybody killed? This is clearly not a good universal law. It would create a world of chaos and violence. What if everybody kept promises? This would be an excellent universal law. Kant tried to discover what was good and bad through logic.

Each of these ethical **frameworks** begins with general principles and tries to discover what to do in a specific situation. Deontology, utilitarianism, and monotheism work in this logical manner. Recently some thinkers have suggested that ethics should be based on care and intuition. This system can be called care ethics. Carol Gilligan, a moral philosopher who looks at ethics and communities from a **feminist** perspective, argues that ethics should be based on the needs of others. She says that ethics should be based on caring and relationships, not on **cold**, abstract principles.

What are the assumptions underlying these methods?

Assumption 1: The basis for ethics

- Monotheism states that a sacred text such as the Bible or the Qur'an is the basis for ethics.
- Care ethics assumes that intuition and emotion provide the best basis for ethics.
- Ethical relativism allows each culture to make decisions about what is ethical.
- Utilitarian ethics assumes that ethics should be judged by results.
- Deontology assumes that ethics should be judged by duties and reasons for actions. Reason and not emotion is the proper basis for ethical decisions.

Assumption 2: Universalizability

Deontology, utilitarianism, and monotheism contain the idea of universalizability. Each system seeks to find universal ways to solve ethical problems. Each tries to be a system that will work in all situations.

Assumption 3: Rules

Deontology, monotheism, and utilitarianism use rules and the interpretation of rules to make moral decisions.

- Monotheism includes the Ten Commandments, and the Seven Laws of Noah (Genesis 9:5–6): 'Blessed are the peacemakers: for they will be called children of God.' (Matthew 5:9)
- Deontology is based on a clear rule: 'Act only according to that maxim whereby you can, at the same time, will that it should become a universal law.' This means that an action is good if it could be turned into a universal law. 'Cheat on your next test' is not a good universal law. 'Treat people with dignity' is a good universal law.
- Rule utilitarianism is a version of utilitarianism that uses rules to guide decisions. A rule is good if it leads to actions that lead to the greatest good. Act utilitarianism is another version. It looks at individual cases to decide if an action is good. Rule utilitarianism supports the use of traffic lights and stop signs because they reduce traffic accidents and deaths. This benefits more people and does not require drivers to make a decision in every case.

What counts as a fact in this area of knowledge?

Perspective 1: The Ten Commandments

If the ethical system is based on a set of rules such as the Ten Commandments, then it is clear what the facts are. However, even when the facts are clear, as in the Ten Commandments, there are still problems of interpretation. 'Do not kill' is one of the Ten Commandments. Does this mean it is immoral to kill anything? Are there situations when killing is acceptable? This has certainly been the case in the Christian, Jewish, and Islamic traditions. For example, the Catholic Church has an official doctrine of a just war. This allows for war in certain circumstances. Therefore killing is sometimes allowed, which shows that sacred texts must be interpreted.

Perspective 2: Euthanasia

It may be possible to establish the facts about a particular ethical dilemma. Suppose a person has a terminal illness, is in great pain, and the doctors have no cure. The person may wish to die because of the pain and suffering. Euthanasia is the painless killing of a patient in such a situation. Most countries have laws that **prevent** doctors from practising euthanasia. Many religions **oppose** euthanasia. These are facts. What is not a fact is whether euthanasia is moral or immoral. Here, it is not possible to speak of facts. There are no empirical facts that make euthanasia right or wrong. Instead, there are laws, **traditions**, and beliefs that support or oppose euthanasia.

What role do models play in this area of knowledge?

Models play an important role in determining moral judgement. Two kinds of model are particularly important. The first are models of human nature. The second are models of human society. These two models are often closely connected.

Model 1: Human nature

Thomas Hobbes was an important English philosopher known for his work in political philosophy. He thought of humans as selfish and often at war with each other. He describes human life as 'solitary, poor, nasty, **brutish**, and short.' Humans are sophisticated machines. They have desires and wants that they must satisfy. Hobbes emphasizes the animal nature of mankind. He believes that humans have free will but that they live independently and compete with one another. Hobbes does not believe in an immortal soul.

John Locke was an English philosopher known for his work on learning and politics. Locke has a very different idea of human nature. Locke said that babies come into the world as **blank slates**. They learn from sense perception and through their families and cultures. Locke believes that humans in their natural state are mostly good, peaceful, and **cooperative**. People mostly know what is good and understand what is theirs, and what belongs to others. Locke believes that people can and should live together in peace. Locke's ideas about human nature and society influenced the American **Founding Fathers.**

Model 2: Society

Hobbes says that without a strong government, society would be in **perpetual** conflict. He spoke of a 'war of all against all.' People would live in fear of death, and fear of losing their property and family. People give up power to the government in order to have safety and security. People also give up some rights and freedoms. Hobbes called this the social contract. Hobbes has a negative view of human nature and thinks that the government has to be strong to control

Subject vocabulary

doctrine of a just war belief that war is acceptable in certain circumstances

euthanasia painless killing of a patient (usually one who is terminally ill)

immortal soul the concept that a human has a soul that does not die when the body dies

social contract what makes states legitimate, it is what gives governments the right to rule

Synonyms

prevent.......... stop

oppose .... disagree with

traditions....... customs

brutish .... cruel, insensitive

perpetual....... constant

General vocabulary

blank slates innocents, with no prejudice, or experience

cooperative working together without conflicts or warfare

Founding Fathers political leaders who were part of the American Revolution and the founding of the new nation after independence was won

Subject vocabulary

authoritarian governments governments which concentrate power in the hands of one ruler or a small group; people are not given freedom and rights

general welfare the overall state of a society, how well people are doing

tyrannical ruling by power and force

democracy a system of government in which the leaders are chosen by people through free elections

Hammurabi king of ancient Babylonia from 1792–1750 BCE

Babylon Noah's city in Iraq; in the ancient world, it was the capital of an empire

Confucian Analects a set of sayings and ideas by the Chinese philosopher Confucius

Dialogues of Plato writings of the Greek philosopher Plato which include Socrates as a character; a cornerstone of Western philosophy

Ottoman Empire the great Turkish Empire (1299–1918) with a capital in Constantinople (now Istanbul)

Synonyms

go back.......... date from

by word of mouth .... by speaking

significance.... importance

General vocabulary

punish to make someone suffer because they have done something wrong

passed on gave someone something that someone else gave to them

stable steady and not likely to move or change

back and forth going in one direction and then the other, and repeating this several times

unity agreement, harmony, as one

immigration migration or movement of people into a new country, or area

---

people. If people are nasty and brutish, then governments must be ready to **punish** them. Therefore, Hobbes's ideas about human nature and society support authoritarian governments.

Locke has a much more positive view of human nature. People should to be able to pursue happiness and pleasure. Locke says that individual happiness is connected to the general welfare of society. People also have basic rights, including the right to choose religion. One job of society is to educate people to become moral. In Locke's view, political authority is based on the consent of people. It should not be based on the power of a tyrannical leader. Therefore, Locke's ideas about human nature and society support democracy.

Knowledge famework: Historical development

What is the significance of the key points in the historical development of this area of knowledge?

Key point 1: The development of writing

Written sources dealing with morality **go back** 4000 years. Writing itself is about 5000 years old. Before that time, knowledge was **passed on** **by word of mouth**.

- The *Story of Sinuhe* is an ancient Egyptian text dated about 1800 BCE. It is a work of literature that is not concerned only with ethics, but it does raise ethical questions.
- The *Code of* Hammurabi is a text from ancient Babylon. It is concerned with contracts and relationships. It uses normative ethics because it tells people what to do.
- The Confucian Analects was concerned with getting people to do the right things in order to have a **stable** society. The *Analects* looks at obligations, duties, and the structure of society.
- The Dialogues of Plato from around 350 BCE introduce a more modern way of thinking. The *Dialogues* argue ideas **back and forth**. They use questioning and reasoning to arrive at answers to moral questions.

> Articulation sentence:
> The Code of Hammurabi and the Confucian Analects tell people what to do. They provide rules, laws and guidelines.

Key point 2: The historical expansion of religions

The world's largest religions, Christianity, Islam, Buddhism, and Hinduism have all had great historical importance. They continue to have great **significance** today. Christianity and Islam have spread far beyond where they began. For example, the Muslim empire grew very rapidly from 622 until 750. Islam spread from the Arabic peninsula across North Africa into Spain. It also expanded throughout the Middle East into present day Iran. Later, through trade and the growth of the Ottoman Empire, Islam spread further still across Turkey, parts of Europe, India, and across Southeast Asia. This expansion is one of the key points in modern history. It gave religious **unity** to diverse peoples. It introduced a common sacred language, namely Arabic. The **immigration** of Islamic peoples into Europe and North America is one of the great issues of the 21st century.

Key point 3: Changes in ethical thinking

Ethical thinking is not **static** over time. For example, ethical views about the following have changed quickly in the recent past:

- homosexuality and same-sex marriage
- the role of women
- obligations to protect the environment.

Monotheism is based on ancient texts. Some of these are over 2000 years old. Although the texts are old, the process of interpreting them continues. Slavery is not condemned in the Bible. Slavery was a part of the cultural tradition in the time of the Old and New Testaments. Slavery is not condemned in the New Testament but a slave may become a Christian. In 19th-century America, both opponents of slavery and supporters of slavery called themselves Christians. Both sides used quotations from the Bible to support their views. Therefore, changes and ethical thinking were both supported by and opposed by Christians.

Knowledge framework: Links to personal knowledge

Why is this area significant to the individual?

Each person must make moral decisions. Each person has needs and **desires** that may conflict with the needs or desires of others. These conflicts sometimes force a person to make moral decisions. These moral decisions are an important part of a person's character. People often judge others on their moral character. Moral decisions may require **sacrifice**. Moral dilemmas may demand painful decisions.

If ethics were simply emotion and intuition, it would not be a separate area of knowledge. It would be a good topic for psychology or cognitive science. Understanding ethics would be like understanding how the brain processes visual information. But ethics is a separate area of knowledge and it is connected to many other ways of knowing, and areas of knowledge. Ethical decisions can be some of the most difficult decisions people make. The following questions can be very significant in an individual's life.

- Are there times when it is acceptable to lie?
- Is it always right to tell the truth?
- What are a person's duties to family?
- Which people deserve help?
- Should children always do what their parents tell them to do?
- What should a person say to a friend who is acting immorally?

What is the nature of the contribution of individuals to this area?

Here are examples of types of contributors to ethics:

- spiritual leaders such as Jesus and the Buddha
- moral leaders who changed their societies such as Mahatma Gandhi, Martin Luther King Jr, and Nelson Mandela
- moral philosophers such as Aristotle, Kant, Mill, and Rawls.

Individual 1: The Buddha

The teachings of the Buddha have had a great effect on the ethics of many Asian countries. Buddhism has a large numbers of followers in countries such as China,

Subject vocabulary

cultural tradition the habits and practices of a group of people, often established over a long period of time

moral character the stable or constant ethical qualities of a person over time

psychology the study of what people think and how they relate to other people

cognitive science the study of the human mind using psychology, numerology, linguistics, and computer science

spiritual leaders religious leaders

Nelson Mandela moral and political leader who led the fight against apartheid and white supremacy in South Africa; he later became president of South Africa

Synonyms

desires........... wants

General vocabulary

static constant or unchanging

sacrifice giving up something valuable or important

Japan, Thailand, Myanmar, and Cambodia. Buddhist ethics focus on avoiding harm to others and to oneself. One goal of Buddhism is to develop a **skilful** mind that avoids actions which cause suffering. Buddhism has five precepts. These are guiding rules as opposed to laws like the Ten Commandments. A Buddhist who follows the five precepts avoids killing, stealing, lying, sexual **misconduct**, and the use of **intoxicants**. Buddhist ethics focuses on **intent** more than action. In this way, Buddhism is like deontology. It differs from utilitarianism, which focuses on the consequences of actions. Different ethical systems produce different ways of viewing ethical problems.

Individual 2: Gandhi

Mahatma Gandhi was both a political and a spiritual leader. He is most famous for leading India to independence from the UK in 1948. Gandhi worked to end poverty, to end caste **discrimination**, and to promote brotherhood among differing religions and peoples. One of his greatest contributions to ethics is the concept of **civil disobedience**. The concept actually goes back to the American writer, philospher, and naturalist, Henry David Thoreau. Civil disobedience is deliberately disobeying laws that are **oppressive** and immoral. Gandhi's use of peaceful civil disobedience influenced the great American civil rights leader Martin Luther King, Jr. Many ethical systems focus on following rules or laws. Civil disobedience asserts that people should not follow laws that are oppressive, unfair, or evil. Martin Luther King, Jr opposed the Jim Crow laws that made racial **segregation** legal in the American South. Gandhi opposed laws that allowed the UK to rule India. Leaders like Gandhi and King are important because they put their ethical ideas into political and social practice.

Individual 3: John Rawls

John Rawls was an American political and moral philosopher who taught at Harvard. He gave an important modern example of ethical philosophy in his *Theory of Social Justice*. Rawls believed that social justice is based on fairness. He asks us to imagine that birth is a kind of **lottery**. People have no control over what society they are born into. A person could be born in a rich, developed country. A person could also be among the 2 billion people on Earth who must live on two dollars per day. If people had control over the kind of society they would be born into, what society would they choose? Rawls argues that people would choose a society that did not have large inequalities. He argues that people would choose a society that offered freedom and opportunities. Rawls argues that justice and fairness are the best ways to judge a society's ethics. Rawls is concerned with the social, political, and economic organization of a society. His ethics look at society's choices more than the choices of individuals. The ideas of Rawls are very powerful and influence current debates about social justice.

What responsibilities rest upon the individual knower by virtue of his or her knowledge in this area?

Responsibility 1: Moderating emotions

Morals often start as **gut feelings**. Morality has a strong relationship to emotion. People often use reason to justify emotion. Morality is sometimes about purity. Clean is good, dirty is bad. The holy is associated with purity. Mary, the mother of Jesus, is called the **spotless** virgin. Pork is **forbidden** to Jews and Muslims because the pig is an 'unclean' animal. Like emotions, moral reactions are quick and filled with strong feelings. Emotions often have powerful reasons, as do moral reactions. It is **appropriate** to be disgusted by a **child molester**. **Cold-blooded** murder is horrifying. If someone does not have these powerful gut feelings people say, 'he just doesn't understand.' If someone does not understand what is wrong with randomly torturing children, then they are morally deficient. But it is not enough to approach all ethical questions from an emotional or gut level. Racial, political, and religious prejudices have strong emotional appeal. People have strong 'tribal' instincts. People are quick to organize into groups of 'us' against 'them'. This can lead to a strong bias for the 'right' group and a strong bias against the 'wrong' group. This is an important part of ethics, but empathy may require a leap of imagination. Through imagination, it is possible to understand the difficulties of a child living on the other side of the world. Emotion and intuition may be the driving force of ethics, but knowledge and reasoning are also critical. Good ethical decisions come from drawing together many ways of knowing and areas of knowledge.

Responsibility 2: Obligations to others

People live together and depend on each other. Actions and words affect other people. There is no way to avoid ethical choice. Perhaps there is something like a moral 'muscle.' If there is, it requires use and exercise.

Peter Singer is a moral philosopher who uses a strong version of utilitarianism. He offers a situation that shows the problem of moral decision-making. A child is drowning in a shallow pond. Someone hears the child's screams. They will not have to swim to save the child but the muddy water will ruin their clothes. Do they have an obligation to save the child? Almost everyone answers yes. What then is the difference between this small child who is near and the small child who is dying halfway around the world? If the cost of replacing the clothes is $200, then why not give $200 to save a child in a very poor country? This question is very difficult to answer. Perhaps people have an instinct to save the child who is near. But is this just an accident? Why does being near the child matter? Clearly there is a limitation to any person's moral obligations. One task of ethics is to determine where those obligations begin and end.

> Articulation sentence:
> Emotion plays an important role in ethics, but emotion has limitations.

What are the implications of this area of knowledge for one's own individual perspective?

A moral perspective or theory can affect political, financial, and social decisions. Ethical perspectives have major implications for people and for the world they live in.

Perspective 1: Group

Identity politics is a powerful idea in today's world. Identity politics means that a person strongly identifies with one group. That group might be a religious group or a minority group, such as homosexuals. In identity politics, people think of themselves as belonging primarily to a group. A strong sense of belonging to a particular group influences thinking and decisions. Common ideas and opinions about moral questions can bind a group together. In a world of 7 billion people, a person may feel lost. The group can provide a sense of identity and a sense of belonging. But many people have multiple identities. A person could be a devout Southern Baptist, a skateboarder, a medical researcher, and gay. Identification with only one group may diminish a person's diversity and individuality. Identity politics can also lead to greater conflicts between groups. Individuals can make serious ethical mistakes, but so can groups. Seeing people from only one perspective can mean seeing stereotypes. Seeing a person with a range of identities and interests can mean seeing that person from many sides.

Subject vocabulary

morally deficient lacking in normal moral, ethical qualities

moral obligations the things that one is required to do ethically

minority group a smaller group within the larger society, often identified by race, religion, or sexuality

Southern Baptist member of a large Protestant Church in the United States with a fundamentalist and evangelical approach

diminish lessen

stereotypes simplified and often common views of people, or things

Synonyms

drawing together .... combining

depend on ..... rely on

shallow .... not deep

muddy .... dirty

ruin .... badly damage

gay .... homosexual

General vocabulary

prejudices unreasonable dislike and distrust of people who are different in some way

tribal relating to a tribe or tribes

driving force the impetus, power, or energy behind something

pond a small pool of water

instinct a natural tendency to behave in a particular way or a natural ability to know something, which is not learned

implications the indirect results of an action or a thought

bind a group together unite a group of people

Perspective 2: Virtue

The Greek philosopher Aristotle greatly influenced Western thought. He argues that the point of ethics is not to follow rules or achieve useful results. The point of ethics is to develop certain qualities or virtues. Aristotle's list of qualities or virtues includes:

- courage
- high-mindedness
- gentleness
- wit
- modesty
- friendliness
- justice.

Aristotle says one goal of life is to use reason to achieve excellence in these qualities. The implication of virtue ethics is that if we develop these qualities, we will become ethical people. A virtuous person does not make ethical choices based on rules or utilitarian calculations. A virtuous person focuses on building a good character. The assumption is that good character leads to good ethical decisions.

Perspective 3: Moral relativism

Ethical relativism is a moral theory. It states that each culture or society has a set of ethical beliefs and rules. The traditions and beliefs vary from culture to culture. No culture has the right to impose its beliefs on another culture. Therefore there are no universal ethical standards. Ethical relativism comes from two sources. One source is anthropology, which demonstrates the wide range of customs around the world. Differing burial customs are one example. Different sexual and marriage practices are another example. History is another source of ethical relativism. History includes examples of wars, genocide, imperialism, and the oppression of peoples. These examples show that evil can happen when one culture imposes itself on another culture. Moral relativism seems to be more open and tolerant. It seems to be a philosophy of live and let live.

But there are negative implications with choosing moral relativism. One such implication is that the ethical system of each culture is correct. The examples from history, such as genocide, show that this is not true. Cultural practices may include oppressing minority groups. Cultural practices may include preferring men over women. A culture may be intolerant. It may choose not to live and let live. A person who chooses moral relativism also abandons the idea of universal human rights. If a culture chooses to violate human rights, then it is correct for that culture. Moral relativism also makes it more difficult to bring about change and reform. The larger implications of moral relativism are problematic.

Scope/applications

What is the area of knowledge about?

Religious knowledge systems give answers to basic questions about human life. Religious knowledge systems contain a great range of beliefs and practices. Some people believe that there is only one true religion but others think that the different religions look at the same basic truths. Religious knowledge includes shared and personal knowledge.

Religion can be difficult to talk about. People have strong feelings and beliefs about religion. Religion has a big impact on how many people understand the world and this influences how they see other areas of knowledge, especially ethics.

The following are some perspectives on religion. Religion is a broad term, so not every element below applies in all cases.

- A religion is a group of beliefs, customs, and worldviews that relate humans to some higher order.
- Religions try to explain the meaning and purpose of life.
- Religions are made up of people who share a group of beliefs and practices.
- Religions include symbols and **sacred** histories.
- Religions have ethics, laws, sacred places, and ways of life.
- Religions have special practices, **clergy**, holy places, and scriptures.
- Religions have rituals, sermons, festivals, special services, meditation, prayer, and art.
- Religions usually have a god or gods (but Buddhism does not).
- Religions include belief in spiritual beings and sacred things.

There are over 4000 religions in the world so no single definition will fit all religions. Many people define religion on the basis of one or two religions. This gives a narrow view of a very wide range of beliefs and practices. So it is good to be aware of some problems that occur in defining religion.

- Not all languages have words that can be translated as 'religion.'
- Judaism does not make a difference between religious **identity** and ethnic identity.
- Some critics say that religion is a modern concept that does not apply well to the past or to some non-Western cultures.
- Religion includes monotheisms which have one god. Judaism, Christianity, and Islam are examples of monotheisms and these religions share common **roots**.
- Religion also includes polytheisms which have several gods. Hinduism can be seen as polytheistic, although this is a debate within Hinduism.
- Pantheism is a kind of polytheism that recognizes a **unity** between God and nature, or God and the universe. Taoism is an example of this.
- Many indigenous groups have religions that are unique to their cultures and small geographic spaces. Their religious beliefs and practices may be a part of their knowledge system.
- Many religions such as those of ancient Greece and Rome no longer exist. But the gods and goddesses of ancient Greece and Rome **live on** in art – particularly in the painting and sculpture of Western Europe during the **Renaissance**.

Subject vocabulary

worldviews global ways of looking at things, larger concepts of how the world works

scriptures sacred books, sacred texts

rituals ceremonies or behaviours that are always performed in the same way and have deep significance for the individual

sermons religious speeches or talks

meditation quiet inner reflection, sitting still and emptying the mind

Buddhism a major religion of Asia founded in the 5th century BCE by Siddhartha Gautama

Judaism religion of the Jews or the Jewish way of life

Taoism a Chinese religious or philosophical system that focuses on living in harmony with the Tao (the source of all things)

indigenous belonging to the people or the culture native to a particular area

Synonyms

sacred .... very important, religious, holy

roots .... beginnings

unity .... agreement, harmony, as one

General vocabulary

clergy priesthood, people who conduct religious services

identity individuality, the essential self

live on continue to exist

Renaissance cultural movement in Europe between the Middle Ages and modern history; approximately the 14th to 17th centuries

Even within one religion there is huge variety. Here are two examples.

● There are some 40 000 different denominations of Christianity.

● Hinduism contains a very wide range of beliefs and practices. It is a religious category containing dozens of separate philosophies.

These problems make it very difficult to generalize about religion. In the United States, religious organizations do not have to pay taxes. Therefore the question of whether a group is a religious group is also a legal question.

Religion and ontology

Religions have ontologies. Ontology is the philosophical study of the nature of being. This means religions state what exists. A religious ontology often includes the supernatural. The supernatural is about things that cannot be perceived by normal means. Religious ontologies include God, gods, angels, evil spirits, souls, heaven, hell, and ghosts. Religions tell us what will happen after death. Religions tell us how the world or the universe was created. They tell us how to live on Earth and which rules to follow. They may tell believers how to eat and dress, or when to work, and when to pray. Religions include special practices like prayer, meditation, sacrifice, fasting, and worship. Religions often include a sacred text and stories, as well as duties, and obligations.

> Articulation sentence:
> Religions have ontologies. Ontology is the philosophical study of the nature of being. This means religions state what exists.

Knowledge question: To what extent is there unity among religions?

Some thinkers see unity among religions. Religions often speak of compassion, which means pity and concern for the suffering of others. Religions call people to action. Religions often have a version of the Golden Rule: you should act towards other people as you would want them to act towards you.

Some thinkers say that there is no unity among religions. They think different religions solve different problems. For example, Christianity solves the problem of sin with salvation. Islam solves the problem of pride with submission. Buddhism solves the problem of suffering with awakening.

Criticism of religion

Critics of religion see religions as failed science or sets of ancient beliefs that do not fit the modern world. They note the extreme variation in beliefs across religions as opposed to the greater unity in science and mathematics. Critics note the lack of empirical support for religion. They note that many passages in texts like the Qur'an and the Bible support practices like killing adulterers by stoning to death.

What practical problems can be solved through applying this knowledge?

What kinds of problem do different religions try to solve?

Practical problem 1: What happens at death?

Humans come to understand that they will die. Many people fear death. For some, this is the central tragedy of life. Many Christians believe that the soul leaves the body at death and possibly goes to heaven.

Solution 1: Life after death

To reach heaven, a Christian must believe in Christ and follow his teachings. Within Christianity, there is much discussion about what it means to believe in Christ and follow his teachings. Some argue that faith is more important than action. Others argue that good actions or following the practices of a particular church are more important. The idea of heaven is often paired with the idea of hell. In heaven, the soul will have **eternal** life. In hell, the soul will suffer for all time.

Solution 2: Reincarnation

Reincarnation is another solution to the problem of death. Reincarnation is the belief that the soul or spirit can leave one body at death and go into another body. Reincarnation is central to Hinduism and Buddhism. The form the spirit takes in the next life is based on *karma*. Good intentions and good actions make good *karma*. Bad intentions and bad actions make bad *karma*. Therefore, the present life strongly influences the next life.

These **traditions** offer hope for a better future. But they also offer the possibility that the future could be worse. They encourage a person to lead a better life now and warn of the dangers of leading a bad life. In the end, the believer must have faith in these knowledge claims. As Hamlet said, 'death [is] the undiscovered country from [which] no traveller returns.' There is no ultimate way to know if there is a heaven or hell. The claims for heaven and hell are based on faith, belief, and **revelation**. Critics see these as weak ways to justify knowledge.

Practical problem 2: Why is there suffering?

This problem takes many forms.

- Why do people suffer mental, emotional, and physical pain?
- Why do terrible things like earthquakes, floods, and **plagues** happen?
- Why do people cause terrible suffering to other people?

Solution 1: Free choice

Christians believe that God gives us the ability to choose between good and bad. They believe that sin causes suffering and that Christ's death brings salvation. Some Christians also believe that suffering redeems us; it makes people better. But people who believe in an all-powerful, all-good God face a problem. Why does God allow suffering and evil? This is known in theology as the *problem of evil*.

Solution 2: Buddhism

For Buddhists, suffering is the central problem for **humanity**. Suffering can be physical, such as sickness and injury. Suffering can also be mental or emotional, such as depression, or **jealousy**. According to Buddhism, **desire**, ignorance, and hatred are the causes of mental suffering. People desire pleasure, things, or even life without death. Ignorance results from an untrained mind and leads to greed, envy, hatred, and anger. To end suffering, a Buddhist must achieve Nirvana, a state free from suffering. To achieve Nirvana, a person must follow a path of good moral action, meditation, and wisdom.

Subject vocabulary

Christ Jesus Christ, the Messiah

Christianity the religion that follows the teachings of Jesus Christ

Hinduism the main religion of India and parts of Southeast Asia

Hamlet main character in the play of the same name by Shakespeare

redeems frees from captivity or sin

Synonyms

eternal .... everlasting

traditions .... customs

jealousy .... envy, resentment

desire .... want

General vocabulary

revelation religious experience that is considered to be a message from God

plagues epidemics, large outbreaks of a contagious disease

humanity all human beings

What makes this area of knowledge important?

Knowledge claim: Religion is important because large numbers of people claim to be religious.

- About 4.3 billion people (about 60% of the world's population) claim to be religious, Figure 10.1.
- About 2.2 billion people are Christian.
- About 1.6 billion people are Muslim.
- About 1 billion people are Hindu.

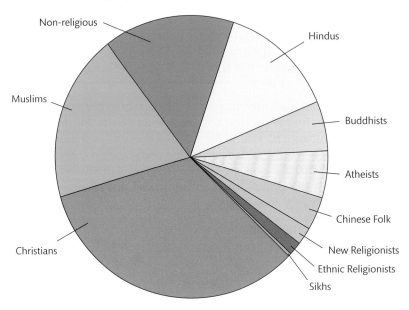

Figure 10.1 *How the world's religions are divided up.*

Religions are important because they **shape** personal and shared identities. Religion can give a group of people a sense of unity because they share common beliefs.

Example 1: Shared beliefs

Shared beliefs in Sikhism, a religion from India founded in the 16th century.

- Sikhs believe in one God, Waheguru.
- Sikhism teaches equality of all humans.
- Sikhism rejects worship of idols, pilgrimages, fasting, and superstition.
- Sikhism teaches freedom of religion.

> Articulation sentence:
> Religions are important because they create unity through shared practices, which gives people a shared identity.

Example 2: Rules concerning food

- Pork is forbidden in Islam and Judaism.
- 20–30 per cent of Hindus are **vegetarians**.

Example 3: Religious clothing customs

- Women must **cover their heads** in many parts of the Islamic world.
- The Amish in America wear plain clothing that is based on clothes from the 19th century. They do not use modern materials such as **zips** and **Velcro**. In the Amish tradition, clothing should not **stand out** or follow fashion.

Subject vocabulary

idols objects that are worshiped as gods

pilgrimages religious journeys, trips to important religious destinations

superstition a belief in a supernatural influence on the world

Amish a Christian group living in old-fashioned ways in Pennsylvania and Ohio

Synonyms

shape .... influence

stand out .... be noticeable

General vocabulary

vegetarians people who do not eat meat or fish

cover their heads wear a headscarf, so hair cannot be seen

zip two lines of small metal or plastic pieces that slide together to fasten a piece of clothing

Velcro a material used to fasten clothes; consists of two pieces of material which stick to each other when pressed together

Example 4: Religious holidays

- At Christmas, Christians celebrates the birth of Jesus Christ.
- Buddha's birthday is known as *Vesak*.
- Ramadan is one of the **five pillars** of Islam. It is a time when Muslims **fast** from dawn until sunset.
- Diwali is a major Hindu festival that takes place in the autumn. It celebrates the victory of light over darkness.

Example 5: Systems of government

Religions offer **ethical systems** and sometimes laws. They play an important role in the governments of many countries. The spread of Christianity and Islam are central historical events in the last 2000 years.

- England has an official state church: The Church of England.
- Iran and Pakistan are Islamic Republics.
- The Indian People's Party (BJP) is a right-wing Hindu party in India. It is the country's largest political party.

> Articulation sentence:
> Religion is important because it enables people to form groups, but it can also be the source of conflict and even war between different groups.

Religion is important because one religion can make knowledge claims that conflict with other religions.

Religions are often intolerant of each other and throughout history there have been great conflicts between religious groups. For example:

- conflicts between Protestants and Catholics continue to this day in places like Northern Ireland
- conflicts between Shiites and Sunnis in the Islamic world continue to shape politics, culture, and history
- conflict between Christians and Muslims has raged for centuries.

Religion does not play a role in the lives of many people.

Atheists and agnostics may oppose religious teachings. Many people find that religion is simply not important. Church attendance in Europe continues to **decline**. The importance of religion varies greatly from person to person and place to place.

> Articulation sentence:
> Religions both unite and divide people.

What are the current open questions in this area?

Open question 1: What is the relationship between science and religion?

The question of how the universe was created is important both to religion and science. Many religious knowledge systems, as well as many indigenous knowledge systems, have stories about the beginning of the world. According to the first book in the Bible (Genesis) God created the world in six days. In this tradition, the world is roughly 6000 years old. Astrophysicists believe that the universe is approximately 13.6 billion years old and was created in what is called the Big Bang. These very different **timelines** point to an important difference. Some believers take the account of Genesis as **literal** truth. Other believers understand Genesis as a metaphorical interpretation.

Subject vocabulary

fast go without food

right-wing the conservative part of the political system

intolerant not accepting views, behaviours, or beliefs that are different

Protestants members of the Christian Church that separated from the Roman Catholic Church (e.g. Lutherans, Presbyterians, and Baptists)

Shiites members of the Shi'a branch of Islam

Sunnis members of the Sunni branch (the more orthodox branch) of Islam

atheists people who do not believe in God or deities

agnostics people who doubt that there is a God

indigenous knowledge systems knowledge belonging to the native people of a country or geographical area

astrophysicists people who study the physics of stars and other objects in outer space

metaphorical interpretation understanding an idea or a text as a metaphor rather than as literally stated

Synonyms

ethical systems moral rules

decline .... decrease

literal .... actual

General vocabulary

five pillars core Islamic beliefs

timelines lines showing the order in which events happened

Open question 2: Do ethics and morality depend on religions?

The great 19th-century Russian novelist Dostoevsky is often credited with writing: 'If there is no God, then everything is **permitted**.' This statement implies that ethics depends on religion. For example, shari'a law is the legal framework in many Islamic countries. It is based on the Qur'an and on tradition. Religious leaders are expected to be experts in morality. They are often **consulted on** moral questions. However, many modern ethical systems do not rely on religion. For example, utilitarianism does not require religion or a belief in God. In utilitarianism, something is moral because it will bring happiness and reduce suffering. Utilitarianism seeks to bring the greatest good to the greatest number of people. Utilitarianism uses reason and emotion to decide what is good and what is bad. Decisions about right and wrong do not have to be based on religious ideas.

What are the ethical considerations that limit the scope of inquiry?

Knowledge question: How does one live an ethical life?

How to live an ethical life is a difficult question hiding other questions such as the following.

- Should a person follow a religious tradition?
- Should a person follow a sacred text?
- Should a person follow a religious leader?
- Should a person follow some inner spirit?

With each choice, a person must ask: What makes this choice ethical? Following a sacred text, or a religious tradition, or a religious leader involves knowledge by authority. This means that a person accepts the rightness or correctness of a source without direct personal experience.

Ethics asks what makes something good. Is something good because it is morally good or because a religion says it is good? The Greek philosopher Plato challenges the idea that ethics comes from a divine source. If something is good simply because it is morally good, then it does not depend on a religion. If something is good simply because a religion says it is, then what if a religion says that rape or murder is good? Rape or murder being bad does not seem to depend on religion. Plato is saying that being good does not come from a divine source. Something is not good because a religion says it is good. Something being good depends on other things.

So, how does a person live an ethical life? Does a religious knowledge system make something ethical? This question remains open. What are the ethical considerations that limit the scope of inquiry? The main consideration is the basis for ethics. If the basis for ethics is not religious, then religious ethics are limited by other forces.

Knowledge framework: Concepts/language

What role does language play in the accumulation of knowledge in this area?

Language plays a central role in religion. Many religions have sacred texts or scriptures. Scripture usually has a divine or holy source. Scripture includes (among many others):

- the Vedas in Hinduism
- the Pyramid texts of Ancient Egypt
- the New Testament in Christianity.

Before the invention of writing, sacred texts were spoken. Some sacred texts seem to have been written down over periods of many centuries. The Torah of Judaism is one such example.

Example 1: The Vedas

The Vedas are the oldest and most basic texts of Hinduism, Photo 10.1. The Vedas are very old religious texts and have a great spiritual value to Hindus. They have influenced other religions such as Buddhism and Sikhism. They also give **insight** into life in ancient India and are important in the study of languages.

Photo 10.1 *The Vedas are written in the ancient language, Sanskrit.*

Example 2: The Bible

In the monotheistic traditions, the sacred texts play an extremely important role. In Judaism, Islam, and Christianity the sacred text is believed to be the direct transmission of God's words. For example, the Gospel of John from the Christian New Testament begins, 'In the beginning was the Word, and the Word was with God, and the Word was God', Photo 10.2.

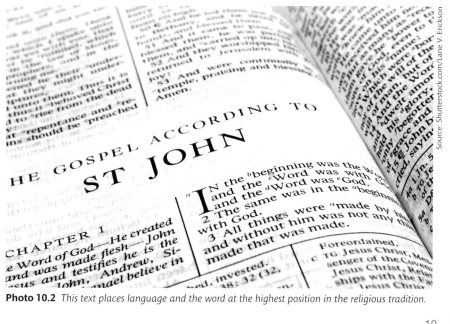

Photo 10.2 *This text places language and the word at the highest position in the religious tradition.*

Subject vocabulary

Torah the major Jewish teachings

monotheistic believing in one god; examples are Judaism, Christianity, and Islam

transmission method of spreading or broadcasting something

Synonyms

insight .... clear understanding

Example 3: The Qur'an

The Bible has been translated into hundreds of languages but the Qur'an only exists in Arabic, photo 10.3. A translation of the Qur'an into another language is not really the Qur'an. The Qur'an is said to preserve the exact language that the angel Gabriel spoke to the prophet Muhammad.

Photo 10.3 *The Qur'an is written in Arabic.*

In all three monotheistic traditions, tremendous importance is placed on understanding and interpreting sacred texts. Clearly, language plays a central role in these religious traditions.

What are the roles of the key concepts and key terms that provide the building blocks for knowledge in this area?

Key concept 1: Miracles

A miracle is an event that cannot be explained by scientific laws. There are miracles by God or gods, saints, and religious leaders. The Catholic Church recognizes miracles as works of God. The Church thinks of some miracles as the direct work of God, such as the **parting of the Red Sea** when Moses leads the Israelites out of Egypt. Christ's ascent to heaven after his death on the cross is another central miracle. Saints also perform miracles. The Catholic Church believes that St Francis of Assisi, a 12th-century Italian preacher and saint, healed a **crippled** boy, a **paralysed** man, and a blind woman. Buddhists go to see **relics** in Sri Lanka due to reports about miraculous rays of light, **apparitions**, and legends. Muslims believe that Muhammad travelled from Mecca to Jerusalem, and also to heaven in one night.

The Bible and the Qur'an do not use the word 'miracle.' Instead they speak of wonder, power, and sign. Many people believe in a personal God. They believe that miracles demonstrate that God can affect normal life. Believers say that miracles show the sacred in the everyday world. They claim that miracles can strengthen belief and faith. However, believers of one religion **seldom** accept the miracles of other religions. Sceptics doubt the truth of miracles and look for alternative explanations. Many miracles took place in the past so it is difficult if not impossible to **establish** their **validity**.

Key concept 2: Revelations

Revelation is the direct communication of truth or knowledge from God, or the gods to humans. Some religions have religious texts that they believe come directly from God. Orthodox Jews believe the Torah comes from God. Muslims believe the Qur'an was revealed to Muhammad word by word. In Hinduism, some Vedas are supposed to have been directly revealed. Most Christians believe that God inspired the Old and New Testaments. Mormons believe in the modern revelations of their founder

Joseph Smith in the 19th century. Revelation also refers to human knowledge about God and prophecy. Revelation is not important in Taoism and Confucianism.

Revelation may be a reason to follow an ethical system. In the monotheistic tradition, God speaks to Moses who brings the Ten Commandments to the Israelites. For many monotheistic believers, the Ten Commandments are the word of God. They argue that divine knowledge is far greater than human knowledge.

Believers note that human reason is flawed. Therefore, they argue that systems like utilitarianism are not as valid as God's word. Utilitarian judgements are made by people, not by God. People decide what will make the greatest number of people happy and reduce suffering. This kind of human judgement seems much weaker to monotheistic believers who accept the idea of revelation from God.

> Articulation sentence:
> Revelation is the direct communication of truth or knowledge from God, or the gods to humans.

What metaphors are appropriate to this area of knowledge?

Example metaphor 1: The Lord is my shepherd

This metaphor comes from the Bible and is a part of the monotheistic tradition. The ancient Hebrews were pastoral people, meaning that they kept animals like sheep and goats. A good shepherd was crucial to maintaining the safety and wellbeing of the sheep. Hence this metaphor was clear to people of that time who compared God to a shepherd and themselves to his flock. This metaphor comes from Psalm 23 and is one of the most loved in the Bible. However, it makes no sense to people from New Guinea who have no sheep. Their most important animal is the pig. The metaphor of God as a swineherd is problematic.

Example metaphor 2: From sleep to awakening

Buddha means the 'Awakened One.' Buddhist awakening is a sudden insight into some deeper truths. This awakening leads to an understanding of reality. In 1 Corinthians 15:51 of the New Testament, death is compared to sleep. 'Behold, I tell you a mystery; we will not all sleep, but we will all be changed.' In Christian belief the soul may go to heaven after the body has died or 'gone to sleep' in a metaphorical sense.

Example metaphor 3: Life is a journey

Tao, one of the basic ideas in Chinese religious thought, can mean 'the way', 'the track', or 'the proper way', Photo 10.4. People who are trying to understand the meaning of life may set out on a journey. They could set out alone, or go with the guidance of a teacher, or guru. The journey may contain many hardships and challenges, but it may lead to new understanding, or even enlightenment.

Source: Interfoto/Sammlung Rauch/Mary Evans

Lao tze. Nach M. G. Pauthier, „La China." I (Paris o. J.). Typisches Bild aus der Tang-Zeit.

Photo 10.4 *The legendary 6th century Chinese author and founder of Taoism, Lao-Tze, journeyed west to live life as a hermit.*

What is the role of convention in this area?

Convention 1: Use of ceremonies and worship services

A believer builds up a series of practices and habits. Worshipers may experience emotions such as love, **awe**, fear, and wonder. They may also feel a strong emotional and moral connection to fellow believers. Many places of worship have significant artistic qualities. Music, visual art, incense, and sacred foods may be involved in a worship service. Therefore, sense perception may play a key role in acquiring religious knowledge. There are strong ties to memory and faith. Language plays a central role in many religions, especially those with sacred scripture. This scripture is often seen as the word of God and so it has an authority that no other text can have. Attempts to understand and experience the supernatural may involve intuition.

Convention 2: Use of stories

Religious knowledge is often conveyed through stories because stories grab our attention. These stories can often be interpreted in different ways. In a literal interpretation, people understand the story as it is. They do not look for secondary meanings. In the Old Testament, God created the world in six days. Jonah, a prophet of ancient Israel, is swallowed by a whale and stays there three days and three nights. Many fundamentalist believers accept these stories **literally**. Other believers interpret these stories metaphorically.

The Greek myths with their gods and goddesses were once part of a religious system. Today, people call these stories myths. In common usage today, a myth is something that is not true. But originally myths were stories that explained something in the world and often involved the supernatural. In the Greek myths, Hades, the god of the underworld, kidnaps the beautiful Persephone who is the daughter of Demeter. Demeter is the goddess of agriculture. Demeter **mourns** the loss of her daughter, and so the plants and trees begin to die. In the end, Hades releases Persephone for part of the year, and the plants and trees grow and bloom. This myth is a way to understand why the Earth 'dies' each year in winter and why it is 'reborn' in spring.

The question of how to interpret religious stories is a central question in religion and a source of much conflict. Splits within a religion are sometimes about conflicts concerning how to interpret these texts. In the United States, Creationists oppose the teaching of evolution because they feel it opposes the biblical creation story.

Knowledge question: Why are stories, ceremonies, and rituals key conventions for religion?

Throughout history, the vast majority of people have not been able to read or write. Interesting stories are easy to remember and retell. Most of the first believers in Christianity were poor. Much of their knowledge of the world was contained in stories. The story of the crucifixion and resurrection of Jesus is very dramatic. Shared stories **bind** people together in groups. Rituals and ceremonies also create a strong sense of group identity. They include movement, **gestures**, actions, and responses. Rituals and ceremonies often have a long history that can give a group shared memories.

Knowledge framework: Methodology

What are the methods or procedures used in this area and what is it about these methods that generates knowledge?

Methodology example: Use of rituals

Religious practices are often built around traditions such as rituals and ceremonies. Ritual practices involve knowing by doing. The following are examples of religious rituals and ceremonies; many of them may seem unfamiliar or even strange to outsiders.

- Hindu worship is often carried out at home. Worshippers repeat the names of their favourite gods and goddesses. They offer water, fruit, flowers, and incense. Pilgrimages to holy places are also a part of Hindu life.
- Devout Muslims pray five times a day. This is the second most important of Islam's five pillars of faith. Each prayer includes movements and speaking memorized text from the Qur'an.
- Devout Catholics worship weekly or even daily. A Catholic child must learn when to sit, stand, kneel, pray, repeat a memorized text, and sing.
- Pentecostalism is a form of Christianity. Pentecostal worship may include people raising their hands, dancing, waving flags, speaking in tongues, and healing by faith.

What are the assumptions underlying these methods?

Assumption 1: Special people are needed to lead and interpret

Many religions have a priest, minister, or other officially recognized figure. This person often has special moral and even political authority. The religious leader often interprets sacred texts or traditions.

Example 1: The role of the imam

An imam is a leader in a Muslim community. The community selects an imam for his knowledge and wisdom. His most important job is to lead the community in prayer. An imam does not have to have special training and there is not a **governing body** that supervises imams. The imam should have a good knowledge of the Qur'an and may serve as a **counsellor** and spiritual advisor. Muslims believe that each person has a direct connection to Allah so it is not necessary to have a clergy between the believer and **the Almighty**.

Example 2: The role of the shaman

Many cultures and tribes have a shaman. A shaman is a person who can enter the world of good and evil spirits. The shaman often uses trance and ritual to enter this realm of the spirits. The shaman may also be a medicine man/woman and a guide to the community. Many cultures that have a shaman do not have a religion in the formal sense. But they certainly have beliefs about the supernatural realm. The role of the shaman varies greatly from culture to culture so it is difficult to make generalizations. But clearly, shamans play an important role in their communities and serve religious functions.

Assumption 2: There are spiritual forces that guide or rule the universe

Many people believe that science and other materialistic explanations are not enough to explain how the universe works. Such explanations do not provide meaning and significance. These people believe there is a spiritual world in addition to the material world that we see. Religions offer insight into the spiritual world as well

Subject vocabulary

worshippers people who take part in religious services

speaking in tongues automatic or unconscious speaking said to come from the Holy Spirit; it is not easily understood and must be interpreted

healing by faith using faith or belief rather than medicine to try to make someone healthy

Allah the Muslim name for God

trance a state in which a person behaves as if asleep but is still able to hear and understand what is said to them

medicine man/woman a person in a Native American tribe who is considered to have the ability to cure illness and disease

materialistic explanations explanations with no spiritual elements

Synonyms

counsellor...... advisor

the Almighty .. God, Allah

General vocabulary

incense a substance which has a pleasant smell when burned

devout very religious

governing body a group of people with legal or religious authority

Subject vocabulary

fate a power that is believed to control what happens in people's lives

karma actions that determine what will happen in the future

Brahman the ultimate reality in the Hindu tradition

harmony togetherness

Synonyms

headquarters.. main office

General vocabulary

the damned the people who God or Allah will send to hell when they die because they have been so bad

as guidance. Scientific explanations use matter and forces, such as gravity, to explain the world. A spiritual perspective sees other forces such as God, fate, or *karma* as fundamental aspects of the universe. For example:

● in some forms of Hinduism, Brahman is the only truth and the world is an illusion

● Jesus told his disciples not to be concerned about food or clothing but to seek the kingdom of God

● in the monotheistic tradition, God is the creator of the world and the ruler of the universe.

What counts as a fact in this area of knowledge?

There are at least two classes of facts about religions. There is one class of facts that is widely accepted. There is another class of facts that require religious belief.

Example of widely accepted facts

The Jehovah's Witnesses are a religious group that began in the United States. The present organization was founded in 1931 and its **headquarters** are now in Brooklyn, New York.

Example of facts that require specific religious belief

The Jehovah's Witnesses believe that 144 000 Christians will go to heaven to rule with Christ in the kingdom of God. This belief is based on their reading of Revelation 14:1-4, which is a chapter in the New Testament of the Bible. This belief is a fact within the knowledge system of the Jehovah's Witnesses. Other religious groups do not view this knowledge claim as a fact.

The above examples demonstrate one of the central problems in studying religious knowledge systems: How should religious knowledge claims be judged? TOK examines knowledge claims but believers may be offended by challenges to and questions about their knowledge claims. Knowing something often starts with knowing facts. Establishing facts about religious knowledge systems is often difficult. If the facts are unclear, this makes knowledge less certain.

What role do models play in this area of knowledge?

Example of a model 1: Heaven and hell

In Christianity and Islam, heaven, or Jannah (paradise), and hell, or Jahannam, are the destinations for souls after death. Heaven is the place where good souls will live for all time with God. Hell is the place where evil souls are punished after death. In Christian ideas, heaven is often seen as being in the sky and hell is beneath the Earth. Hell is ruled by the Devil or Satan. It is commonly understood that people are rewarded or punished for the life they lead on Earth. On the Day of Judgement, God or Allah will separate the saved from **the damned**. This model of the afterlife answers two great human questions: What will happen after death? If there is life after death, how does life on Earth affect the next life?

Example of a model 2: Confucianism and the family

Confucian philosophy was the traditional basis for government and society in China. Confucianism is built on ancient Chinese religious traditions. Confucian philosophy states that there is a basic order in the universe. A natural harmony connects humans, nature, and the heavens. Humans are social beings, and human relations should be like the order of the universe. The family unit is the basic social unit and there are five model relationships:

- ruler to **subject**
- husband to wife
- parent to child
- elder brother to younger brother
- friend to friend.

Each role has **defined duties**. Each person has duties and responsibilities to the other. The **devotion** of a child to its parents is the foundation for all others. The highest **virtue** is **humaneness** and the sense of being related to other people. This model connects the family unit with the broader social and spiritual order. The well-ordered family is a model for the well-ordered society.

What ethical thinking constrains the methods used to gain knowledge?

Example 1: Sacred texts

Studying a sacred text like the Bible or the Qur'an is an important method used to gain knowledge of the monotheistic traditions. These texts inform believers about a range of practices and beliefs. Classic religious texts such as the Bible have not changed over time but human understanding of ethics has changed greatly. For example, the Bible does not seem to **condemn** slavery but today people do. In 19th century America, many churches supported slavery. This is no longer true. Today, many people are **rapidly** changing their minds on the question of same-sex marriage. The Bible does not seem to support same-sex marriage. If the Bible is **timeless**, then its meaning should not change. However, it is clear that interpretations of the Bible and other sacred texts do change over time.

Knowledge question: To what extent is it ethical to interpret sacred texts according to changing times and ideas?

> Articulation sentence:
> Classic religious texts such as the Bible have not changed over time but human understanding of ethics has changed greatly.

Example 2: Tradition

Tradition is an important method used to gain knowledge in many religious knowledge systems. Religions often live through traditions passed from one generation to the next. Some religious groups **oppose** education for girls. Some religious groups allow basic education for girls, but oppose higher education. Many more religious groups oppose allowing women to become members of the clergy. In all these cases, tradition plays an important role. Believers who rely on tradition face difficult decisions when changing ethical views clash with tradition. Ethical **considerations** can be more **convincing** than tradition, but tradition is an important method of acquiring knowledge.

Knowledge question: To what extent do ethical considerations clash with traditional religious beliefs?

> Articulation sentence:
> Believers who rely on tradition face difficult decisions when changing ethical views clash with tradition.

Subject vocabulary

monotheistic traditions customs of those religions believing in a single god

Synonyms

defined .... clear
duties .... obligations
devotion .... strong love
virtue .... good quality
rapidly .... quickly
timeless .... always relevant
convincing ..... persuasive

General vocabulary

subject someone born in a country that has a king or queen, or someone who has a right to live there

humane treating people or animals in a way that is not cruel and causes them as little suffering as possible

condemn censure, to declare that something is bad or evil

oppose disagree with

considerations careful thought

Knowledge framework: Historical development

What is the significance of the key points in the historical development of this area of knowledge?

Key point 1: The Protestant Reformation

Until about 1500, the Roman Catholic Church dominated Western Europe. The Protestant Reformation, which began in Germany in 1517, split the European church. The German religious and theological leader Martin Luther, and his followers led one group, the Lutherans. And the influential Frenchman John Calvin, and his followers led another important group, the Calvinists. The Protestants criticized the practices of the Catholic Church. Various Protestant movements spread across Northern Europe, as far as Hungary in the east and England in the west. The Protestant Reformation transformed not only the religion of Europe, it also changed the politics and government of Europe. It led to many wars and contributed to the rise of nationalism. The influence of the Protestant Reformation continued into the Americas. Latin America is predominantly Catholic, while the US and Canada are predominantly Protestant.

Key point 2: The schism in Islam

There is also a great split or schism in Islam. This is the split between the Sunnis, who make up 85–90% of Muslims, and the Shi'as. This split occurred after the death of the prophet Muhammad. The conflict was over who should lead the Islamic community. The two groups share many religious beliefs, but there are also large differences in their political and social history. The split between Shi'as and Sunnis continues to cause conflict today.

> Articulation sentence:
> Key points in the historical development of religious knowledge systems led to new religions emerging, as well as political and social conflicts.

Knowledge framework: Links to personal knowledge

Why are religious knowledge systems significant to the individual?

Perspective 1: Religious knowledge systems are significant to the individual because both personal and shared knowledge play a profound role in religion

It can be very difficult to determine where shared knowledge ends and personal knowledge begins. A religious person shares in the knowledge and practices of the group. But religion can also be a powerful part of individual identity. Most religions have services, rituals, or practices that involve the individual in a group. However, many practices are personal. These include prayer, meditation, and reciting sacred text. For example:

- in Christianity, the believer is encouraged to have a personal relationship with God and Jesus Christ
- the daily practice of a Hindu might include worship at the home shrine, reading from the Vedas, and contemplating the life of holy men and women
- the devout Muslim must pray five times a day facing Mecca.

Perspective 2: Religious knowledge systems are significant to the individual because religions appeal to powerful human needs such as community, family, and love

- Buddhists, Hare Krishnas, and Roman Catholics have special communities such as monasteries.
- The Prophet Muhammad stressed these meanings when he said: 'The best among you are those who are best to their families'. The family is the **cornerstone** of culture in the Muslim tradition. Traditionally, the family has several generations living together.
- The New Testament of the Bible has many passages on love. Corinthians Chapter 13 is a particular favourite: 'Love **bears** all things, believes all things, hopes all things, endures all things. Love never ends.'

Perspective 3: Religious knowledge systems are significant to the individual because personal identity is often linked to religious identity

This link can be even stronger when a person is a member of a **minority** religion. Many religious groups suffer persecution. Majority groups and majority religions often oppress religious minorities. This oppression can lead to a strong sense of identity for members of the religious minority. A religion may require its followers to make a **distinction** between insiders and outsiders. This can lead to a stronger sense of identity but it can also lead to oppression and discrimination against other groups.

Perspective 4: Religious knowledge systems are significant to the individual because they use arts such as music, architecture, painting, and poetry to appeal to believers

Example 1: Music in the Christian church

Music has played a central role in Christian worship. This tradition begins with Gregorian chant in the 9th century and continues into music written for churches today. Almost all of the greatest composers in the Western tradition have composed for the Church. The list of composers includes Machaut, Palestrina, Mozart, Beethoven, Brahms, Stravinsky, and Messiaen. Solo and choral singing of the sacred texts is a particularly important part of the tradition. Unlike painting, **drama**, and poetry, music does not represent anything directly. Music can be at once both very emotional and very spiritual. Music can take listeners to new psychological and spiritual places. Singing together can create strong bonds between groups of people. Music can strengthen and deepen the meaning of words.

Example 2: Sacred architecture in Southeast Asia

Art and architecture have played a major role in Buddhism and Hinduism. Buddhism grew out of Hinduism and there are important connections between these two religions. They both spread outwards from India into Southeast Asia, China, and Japan. They continue to be important religions today. The spread of Hinduism and Buddhism throughout Asia is also **reflected** in the arts. Hindu architecture links humans, gods, and the universe. Hindu temples often include colourful statues **depicting** the gods. The Great Temple of Angkor Wat in Cambodia is an example of Hindu architecture, Photo 10.5, overleaf.

Subject vocabulary

Hare Krishnas a modern religious group that takes some of its practices from Hinduism

Corinthians a chapter in the New Testament; it is a letter from the apostle Paul to believers in Corinth

persecution oppression or harsh treatment

oppression domination, tyranny over a group of people

discrimination treating one person or group differently from another in an unfair way

Gregorian chant plainsong, single flowing line of music with a free rhythm

choral singing many singers singing together, often in different musical parts

Synonyms

drama .... stage plays

reflected .... shown in

depicting .... showing

General vocabulary

cornerstone something that is extremely important because everything else depends on it

bear to bravely accept or deal with a painful, difficult, or upsetting situation

minority a small group of people or things within a much larger group

distinction difference between two things

Source: Shutterstock.com/Stewart Smith Photography

Photo 10.5 *Buddhist monks at Angkor Wat.*

The pagoda in Japan comes out of the Buddhist tradition. Missionaries from China brought Buddhism to Japan around the 6th century. They also brought Buddhist art and architecture to Japan. Art and architecture are powerful ways to depict religious ideas, particularly to illiterate people.

Articulation sentence:
Religious knowledge systems are significant to the individual because personal identity is often linked to religious identity. This link can be even stronger when a person is a member of a minority religion.

What is the nature of the contribution of individuals to this area?

Key Individual 1: Martin Luther (1483–1546)

The Protestant Reformation occurred when Martin Luther and John Calvin broke away from the Roman Catholic Church. This split was one of the major events in European history. Martin Luther opposed many ideas and practices of the Catholic Church. He **disputed** the idea that freedom from the punishment of God could be bought with money. He also stated that salvation comes not from action but from faith. Luther translated the Bible into German. This was very important because the Bible had only been available in Latin until then. Only highly educated people could read Latin. Luther's translation of the Bible made the text available to ordinary people. The **printing press** meant that many more people had direct access to the Bible. It was no longer necessary for a priest to interpret the Bible. This gave the individual more power and a greater sense of **equality**. The Protestant churches challenged the hierarchy of the Catholic Church. Luther also wrote hymns or church songs in German with rhyming texts and strong rhythms. These hymns spread across Europe and inspired followers because they were catchier and easier to sing than traditional Catholic chants. Luther also married, which broke the tradition of Catholic priests who do not marry. The Protestant Reformation also brought war and conflict to Europe including the **Thirty Years War** in Germany.

Key individual 2: The Buddha

Siddhartha Gautama was born over 2500 years ago. He became known as the Buddha, which means the *awakened one*. His life and teachings are the foundations of Buddhism, a religion with some 375 million followers today. Siddhartha led a life of luxury until he went out into the world and **encountered** suffering and death. He then took up the life of a poor **monk**, but rejected that for a middle way between poverty and luxury. Buddhists believe that Siddhartha obtained enlightenment through meditation. Enlightenment is the goal of Buddhism. In the state of enlightenment, a person no longer experiences suffering and desire. Buddhism spread from India into China, Southeast Asia, Tibet, and Japan.

What responsibilities rest upon the individual knower by virtue of his or her knowledge in this area?

Because there are so many different religions in the world, it is difficult to make a statement about individual responsibility that applies **universally**. There is also an important difference between the **demands** of a religion and the responsibilities of a person. Some religions make great demands on their participants.

- In the United States many churches ask their members to **donate** 10% of their incomes to the church. Some religions ask their members to become **missionaries**.

- Muslims are traditionally expected to donate 2.5% of their total assets to charity.

- Conflicts can arise when people oppose the ethical positions of their religion. Many churches in 19th-century America supported **slavery**. The members of those churches who opposed slavery found themselves in a very difficult position.

- Belonging to a religion also often means belonging to a social or cultural group. The perspective of a group can have profound effects on the members of that group. Many religions make strong claims to **exclusivity**. Jesus said,' I am the way, the truth, and the life. No one comes to the father except through me.' Islam states that, 'There is no God except Allah; Muhammad is the Messenger of Allah.'

- People living in a **multicultural** society may find it difficult to cope with such competing claims. Religious people find themselves **torn between** the knowledge claims of their religion and the knowledge claims of other groups they belong to. As TOK often demonstrates, important decisions are complicated.

Subject vocabulary

multicultural containing many ethnic and religious groups

Synonyms

encountered... met with

demands........ needs

donate........... to give

General vocabulary

monk a member of an all-male religious group that lives in a monastery

universally everywhere

missionaries people who go to a different place or country and attempt to convert people to a religion

slavery enforced work for no money

exclusivity uniqueness and desirability

torn between unable to decide which is more important or correct

11 Indigenous knowledge systems

Knowledge framework: Scope/applications

What is the area of knowledge about?

There is not a universal definition of what makes a group indigenous. However, the United Nations and the International Labour Organization have **outlined** the following **characteristics.**

- People who are **descended from** the pre-colonial/pre-**invasion inhabitants** of a region.
- People who maintain a close **tie** to the land in their cultural and economic practices.
- People who suffer from economic and political **marginalization** as a **minority** group.
- People who consider themselves indigenous.

The United Nations has estimated:

- there are **approximately** 400 million indigenous people worldwide
- there are approximately 5000 **distinct tribes** in over 90 countries.

> Articulation sentence:
> For political and academic purposes, indigenous people are often grouped together as one group. They are considered one of the largest minority groups in the world.

For the IB TOK course, the term 'indigenous knowledge system' usually refers to knowledge **constructed** by a particular group of people. Examples of such people include the following.

- The Nama people of Southern Africa.
  Many of the Nama tribes live in Central Namibia. The other smaller groups live in Namaqualand, which is on the Namibian border with South Africa.
- The Secoya people of Ecuador and Peru.
  The Secoya people traditionally inhabited a very large territory between the Putumayo and Napo rivers in Ecuador, Colombia, and Peru. They are known for their knowledge of **medicinal plants**.
- The Ryukyuan people of Japan.
  The Ryukyuan people are the indigenous people of the Ryukyu Islands between the islands of Kyushu and Taiwan.
- The Wopkaimin people of Papua New Guinea.
  The Wopkaimin people are aboriginal people who live in the remote Star Mountains in western Papua New Guinea.

Other terms which cover the same material as 'indigenous knowledge systems' are: native knowledge, community knowledge, folk knowledge.

The IB approach to indigenous knowledge systems assumes indigenous people share enough in common to be grouped into an area of knowledge.

This chapter:

- assumes indigenous knowledge systems have enough characteristics **in common** to be studied as a group (e.g. use of **oral tradition**, the role of music, holistic view of the world)
- considers what impact the shared characteristics have on knowledge creation

---

- explores local knowledge which is considered **unique** to a particular culture or society (e.g. specific gender roles)
- considers what impact those unique characteristics have on knowledge creation (e.g. specific gender roles)
- considers how indigenous knowledge systems are studied by Western researchers using the **tools** of Western science
- considers what impact Western researchers using the tools of Western science to study indigenous knowledge systems have on knowledge creation.

An important feature of indigenous knowledge systems is that they are not static. They are **dynamic** as a result of both internal and external influences. The Maori (the native people of New Zealand) knowledge system today, for example, is a mixture of traditional knowledge and knowledge inherited over time from exposure to European culture.

Figure 11.1 shows characteristics associated with indigenous knowledge systems and Western science.

Source: Alaska Native Knowledge Network with permission

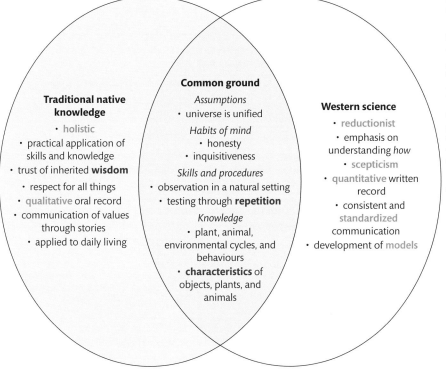

Figure 11.1 *Common ground between traditional native knowledge and Western science.*

What practical problems can be solved through applying this knowledge?

The aims of studying indigenous knowledge systems are to:

- explain the nature and existence of humanity for a particular group of human beings
- consider if any explanations from specific examples can be applied to other people.

Practical problem 1: Explain the nature and existence of humanity in a particular group of people

The Ryukyuan people of Japan are the indigenous peoples of the Ryukyu Islands between the islands of Kyushu and Taiwan. They believe in onarigami. This is the spiritual superiority of women. This belief is particularly **significant** because it differs from the Japanese Shinto tradition whereby men are generally seen as superior because they are the most '**pure**'.

Native Ryukyuan religion has clear roles for men and women. It places great significance on the role of women in the community. Women are seen as **guardians** of the *inside* of the family home. Men are seen as guardians of the *outside* of the family home.

Practical problem 2: Understanding gender roles

An example of an explanation that may be taken from studying indigenous knowledge systems is that concerning the origins and social development of gender roles.

Like most indigenous peoples, the Ryukyuan people of Japan have clear roles for the different genders. This causes social scientists to ask: To what extent are gender roles universal? To what extent are they caused by nature and nurture?

When considering to what extent behaviours are caused by nature and nurture, students are advised to consider the following.

- Behaviours that have greater social construction influence (nurture) show greater variation across cultures. Examples include languages and food.
- Behaviours that have greater biological influence (nature) show less variation across cultures. Examples include gender roles and **sexuality**.
- Social science has a leaning towards *social* explanations for human behaviour. Students should not **dismiss** natural science explanations for human behaviour just because they are not common in social science texts.

Example 1: An indigenous group that demonstrates great gender role variation is the Aka Pygmy people of Central Africa

The total population of Aka Pygmy people is around 20 000. In this group, male and female gender roles are **partially interchangeable**.

- Women **hunt** and take their babies with them. They do this despite the fact that their **prey**, the duiker (a type of antelope), is dangerous.
- Women decide on the location of camps.
- Aka fathers are within reach of their small children 47% of the time – more than fathers in any other cultural group. To calm the children if the mother is not there, the men 'breastfeed'. This involves using a **nipple** to calm the children but not actually feeding them.
- Men cook while the women hunt.

Knowledge question: To what extent can explanations in one culture be applied to other cultures?

Knowledge claim: A social constructionist position argues social forces cause human behaviour. An example of a social force is a stigma.

The Aka Pygmy people of Central Africa demonstrate how gender roles become more interchangeable when stigmas are **downplayed** or are **absent**. For example, there is no negative social consequence for male 'breastfeeding' as the men do not **lose status** when they do this. Therefore, male 'breastfeeding' to calm children is an acceptable activity for men. Studying the Aka Pygmy people causes Western researchers to ask how and why gender norms are constructed, and to what extent gender is from nature or nurture.

Articulation sentence:
The Aka Pygmy people of Central Africa support the notion that gender is partially socially constructed because the male and female gender roles are partially interchangeable.

What makes this area of knowledge important?

Knowledge claim: Indigenous knowledge systems are important because social scientists apply their understanding of them to other cultural groups.

Example 1: The study of gender roles of indigenous tribes of Papua New Guinea by Margaret Mead (1935)

Mead claimed to find the Tchambuli tribe where men showed some feminine behaviour (being passive), and women showed some masculine behaviour (being dominant, shaving their heads, taking control of trading relationships).

Mead's work with the indigenous knowledge systems of the Tchambuli became well known and was important because:

- it argued gender differences are culturally constructed
- it had a noble cause – to promote the notion of freedom and choice in gender roles
- it influenced the sexual revolution of the 1960s (this was a social movement that challenged traditional gender and sexuality norms in the West).

However, Mead's gender role interpretations with the Tchambuli have been heavily criticized and largely dismissed by modern anthropologists. For example, Gewertz (1984) studied the Tchambuli in 1974–1975.

Knowledge question: To what extent can we apply understanding of the Tchambuli tribe gender roles to Western society?

Some points to note:

- Mead admitted she wanted to make her gender findings relevant to a Western audience.
- Mead observed aggressive women. Gewertz observed women who socialized in female groups, laughed and joked about men behind their backs, and who were independent of men in some areas of their lives. For example, they would organize dances at night without the permission of men. These shaven-headed women engaging in dancing at night may have appeared aggressive to a Western woman living in the 1930s but were not considered aggressive to the Tchambuli.
- During Mead's 1930s research, 52% of Tchambuli men were away working. Those who remained were busy rebuilding houses that had been destroyed during a recent war with a rival tribe. These men took little part in the research. Women had adopted roles traditionally performed by men (e.g. management of trade) because of the shortage of male labour. Therefore, the masculine gender roles Mead saw women adopting were not being permanently adopted through choice. They were temporarily adopted because of necessity.
- Mead correctly reported how Tchambuli men were warlike and territorial. However, these findings have been largely forgotten by Western writers.

Articulation sentence:
Indigenous knowledge systems are important because social scientists apply their understanding of them to other cultural groups. For example, Mead's studies of gender.

Subject vocabulary

feminine thoughts, feelings, and behaviours usually associated with women; these are influenced by biology (nature) and society/culture (nurture)

masculine thoughts, feelings, and behaviours usually associated with men; these are influenced by biology (nature) and society/culture (nurture)

culturally constructed created by groups of people in a particular culture who implicitly agree to norms and realities

Synonyms

trading .... business

noble .... worthy, decent

rival .... competitor

shortage .... lack

General vocabulary

notion idea

passive tending to accept things that happen or things that people say, without taking any action

dominant primary, most influential

shaving cutting off hair very close to the skin, especially from the face, using a razor

socialized spent time together

joked about men behind their backs laughed at men without them knowing

adopted taken over

traditionally carried out in the same way over many years and generations

warlike wanting to make war

territorial protective over certain territory

Knowledge framework: Concepts/language

What role does language play in the accumulation of knowledge in this area?

Researcher language

Knowledge claim: Researcher language is often different from indigenous language. Indigenous people will not use language in the same way as Western researchers.

Example 1: Cole and Scribner (1974) investigated memory in different cultures

These researchers wanted to compare the **recall** of US participants with the Kpelle people of rural Liberia. They would do this by asking the participants to remember lists of words. The researchers were aware of how language use may influence their results.

Therefore:

- they did not use the same list of words in the two countries
- they **employed** local college-educated people who spoke the Kpelle language
- they spent time observing everyday activities of the Kpelle so they could create culturally appropriate memory tasks with appropriate words
- they made sure that the words used in the memory tasks were familiar to the participants.

In spite of these precautions, Cole and Scribner found Kpelle children were not very good at remembering lists of words.

Being a rural tribe, the Kpelle **pass down** important information using story telling. So, Cole and Scribner changed their method and presented the words in a meaningful way as part of a story. This is called a narrative. The Kpelle children recalled the words easily. The results have been supported in other cross-cultural studies on children's memory skills. For example, Rogoff and Wadell (1982) found that Mayan children could easily recall objects if they were related in a meaningful way to the local scenery.

> Articulation sentence:
> Researchers of indigenous knowledge systems need to consider how their own understanding of language can limit the accumulation of knowledge when researching indigenous knowledge systems.

Language influences understanding

Knowledge question: To what extent is human perception influenced by language? For example: To what extent can humans perceive a colour if they do not have a word for it?

Knowledge claim: Researchers of indigenous knowledge systems need to consider how language differences influence different understandings of the world.

Example 2: The Himba tribe and the colour blue

The Himba tribe in Namibia do not have a word for blue, or have a **distinction** between blue and green (Davidoff, 2015). When they are shown a 11 green squares and 1 blue square, most cannot pick out which square is different from the others. Those Himba who could see a difference, took much longer and made many

Subject vocabulary

culturally appropriate suitable for the culture

Synonyms

recall............ memory retrieval

employed ...... used

General vocabulary

pass down pass from one generation to the next

distinction difference between two things

mistakes. However, the Himba have more words for types of green than the English language. For example, when they are shown lots of green squares with only one that has a very small **variation**, they can immediately spot the different square.

Example 3: Colours through history (based on Davidoff, 2015)

Gladstone (a future British Prime Minister in the late 19th century) noticed the **ancient** Greek poem *The Odyssey* by Homer contained accurate details about clothing, **armour**, weaponry, facial features, and animals. However, his colour references are not accurate to a modern **Western eye**. For example, iron and sheep are violet; honey is green; there was no reference to blue. Gladstone suggested that Homer might be colour-blind.

The German linguist Geiger argued that in most cultures, words for colours come into existence in a universal way. He argued words for black and white, or dark and light come into existence first; then red (which is the colour of blood and wine); then yellow; green, and then blue.

> Articulation sentence:
> Words allow **subtle variations** to be described to the self and others. When variations are described, they are more likely to be noticed.

Example 4: The role of oral tradition

Oral tradition refers to the practice of verbally passing on information through generations. The information is **transmitted** by speaking. Examples include: folktales (stories), **sayings**, jokes, songs, or **chants**. In this way, it is possible for a culture to transmit information across generations without a writing system.

> Articulation sentence:
> Many indigenous knowledge systems rely on oral tradition to pass on information through generations.

Example 5: The use of symbols

Symbols are often used by indigenous people instead of writing. Symbols have a decorative function but also represent objects. They can describe the environment, **convey wisdom**, or pass on instructions. An example is the use of Adinkra symbols used by the Ashanti of Ghana, Figure 11.2.

	AKOKO NAN	**Akoko nan tia ba, na ennkum no.** *The hen treads upon its chicks but does not intend to kill them.*	Parenthood Care Tenderness Protection
	ODENKYEM	**Odenkyem da nsuo, mu, nso onnhome nsuo, ohome nframa.** *The crocodile lives in water but breathes air.*	Adaptability Prudence
	ADWERA	**Adwera nsuo, wo ne nkwansuo, nsu korogyenn a wohuru nso wonhye.** *Water of life – you are the crystal clean water that boils but does not burn.*	Purity Sanctity Chastity Cleanliness
	OSRAM	**Osram mmfiti preko nntwareman.** *It takes the Moon some time to go around the Earth.*	Patience Understanding
	SANKOFA	**Se wo were fin a wo sankofa a yennkye.** *It is not a taboo to return to fetch something you forgot earlier.*	Wisdom Learning from the past

Figure 11.2 *Adinkra symbols and their meanings.*

Such symbols are used to decorate **pottery**, walls, and **fabrics**.

Subject vocabulary

universal can be applied to all situations at all times

Synonyms

variation........ difference

Western eye ... Western perspective

symbols......... signs

fabrics........... cloth, clothing, curtains

General vocabulary

ancient from a past time

armour metal or leather clothing worn for protection by soldiers in battles in past times

come into existence begin to exist

subtle variations small differences

transmitted communicated

sayings well-known short statements that express ideas most people believe are true and wise

chants regularly repeated tunes, often with many words sung on one note

convey communicate

wisdom cleverness and knowledge

pottery plates, dishes, cups

What are the roles of the key concepts and key terms that provide the building blocks for knowledge in this area?

Knowledge claim: Indigenous knowledge systems often produce useful knowledge. This is because any knowledge produced and communicated is usually essential to survival.

Key concept 1: Enthnobiology

Enthnobiology is:

● the scientific study of the way plants and animals are treated or used by different indigenous people

● the use of local indigenous biological knowledge to study the natural world.

Knowledge question: To what extent should Western scientists consult indigenous people when conducting scientific investigations?

Knowledge question: Should it always be assumed local people have superior knowledge about local biology?

Knowledge question: How can local knowledge be uncovered?

Knowledge question: How can the claims of local knowledge be tested? How can scientists verify or falsify local claims?

If local people are consulted before research is conducted in their local environment:

● it may produce useful knowledge that provides new insights into local biology

● it may also produce misleading knowledge that would take time and money to verify or falsify.

If local people are *not* consulted before research is conducted in their local environment:

● it may cause resentment that would take time and money to address

● it may mean useful local insights into biology are ignored.

The following examples demonstrate how local knowledge has been useful to Western researchers.

Example 1 of Ethnobiology: The Tzeltal people of Mexico and their knowledge of butterflies

The Tzeltal people possess a **sophisticated** vocabulary for describing differences in two-barred flasher butterflies. They base their classification on the **observable** traits of larvae. The larvae are of interest to the Tzeltal because they have a negative impact on **crops**. Western taxonomists claimed two-barred flasher butterflies could be grouped as one **species**. However, the Tzeltal argued there are at least 10 subgroups of the butterfly. DNA analysis demonstrated the Tzeltal were logical in their classification system.

Example 2 of Ethnobiology: The Kayapo people of Brazil and their knowledge of bees

According to Posey (1983), the Kayapo people have a complex taxonomy for different types of bee. Their classification system is 90% the same as that of local field biologists.

They classify the bees by:

- behaviour – **stinging**, biting, or **docile**
- location – forest or mountain, trees, earth, or **vines**
- appearance – colour, **markings**, and size.

> Articulation sentence:
> Enthnobiology is the scientific study of the way plants and animals are treated or used by different indigenous people, or the use of local indigenous biological knowledge to study the natural world.

Key concept 2: Holism

Holism refers to the notions that:

- an object of study has parts that are **interconnected**
- an object cannot be understood by studying its individual parts
- an object of study is greater than the **sum** of its parts
- individual parts must always be considered as part of the whole
- categories of study remove an essential element from the object of study.

Holism can be contrasted with reductionism. Reductionism refers to the notions that:

- an object can be understood by studying the individual parts
- the world can be **broken down** into categories to study
- an object of study is not greater than the sum of its parts.

Knowledge claim: A holistic approach to understanding the world assumes objects must be studied as a whole. If an object is reduced, the object of study no longer exists in a meaningful form.

Generally, indigenous people take a holistic approach to their understanding of the world.

The assumptions that support holism within indigenous knowledge systems are:

- human beings are placed within the world as part of its processes
- the world does not provide resources for humans to use **exclusively** for themselves
- animals occupy a similar place to humans in the world
- the physical world is considered alive and **conscious** – it should be respected.

> Articulation sentence:
> Indigenous knowledge systems can be contrasted with natural sciences in their approach to understanding the world.

Natural sciences assume:

- an **objective** stance to studying the world
- categorization/reductionism is an effective way to understand the world.

However, it should be noted: Western science can adopt holistic approaches to studying the world. For example, the Gaia hypothesis and the increasing influence of environmental awareness.

Subject vocabulary

objective not influenced by personal feelings or opinions

Synonyms

docile .... calm

sum .... total

broken down .. separated

exclusively ..... only

General vocabulary

stinging a defence mechanism whereby a bee makes a very small hole in an animal's skin and injects a poisonous substance

vines plants with long thin stems that attach themselves to other plants, trees, buildings, etc.

markings the coloured patterns and shapes on an animal's fur, on leaves, etc.

interconnected interrelated and with an influence on each other

conscious awake and able to understand what is happening

Subject vocabulary

colonialism control of areas by a foreign power; usually land but it can also refer to culture, economics, and politics

Synonyms

thrive .... be successful

rally around ... support

sincere........... earnest

gullible.......... easily persuaded

traits .... characteristics

General vocabulary

interact with have a relationship with

self-regulating can correct itself

prophecies statements that something will happen in the future

imminent about to happen

cargo goods that are being transported

scam a ruse or plot to deceive people

superficial brief, not in depth

parachute a piece of equipment fastened to people who jump out of planes, which makes them fall slowly and safely to the ground; also used for goods delivery

jeep a type of car made for travelling over rough ground

Example of Holism: The Gaia hypothesis

The Gaia hypothesis/Gaia theory assumes organisms **interact with** their non-living surroundings on Earth to form a single self-regulating system that can maintain itself over time. The theory was developed by James Lovelock and Lynn Margulis in the 1960s and 1970s.

An example of how the Earth can be seen as a single **self-regulating** system is temperature regulation. According to Owen et al. (1979), the Sun has become at least 25% more powerful since life started on Earth. However, the surface temperature of the planet has remained within the levels that allow life to survive and **thrive**.

> Articulation sentence:
> The Gaia hypothesis is an example of how Western science can adopt holistic approaches to studying the world. Viewing the Earth as one single organism is similar to how indigenous knowledge systems view their local environments.

Key concept 3: Millenarianism

Millenarianism is a belief system often found within indigenous knowledge systems whereby:

● people **rally around** religious **prophecies** or leaders who predict a return to power

● people believe the defeat of enemies is **imminent**

● people believe the accumulation of wealth is imminent.

Millenarianism is common among indigenous people who have lived under **colonialism** and had their social, cultural, and military arrangements challenged or disrupted.

Example 1 of millenarianism: Cargo cults

Cargo cults believe that ancestral spirits will arrive in non-indigenous transport machines (usually ships or aircraft), bringing with them cargoes of food, and non-indigenous goods. Cargo cults were typically created by individual and charismatic leaders. It is still not clear if these leaders were **sincere** in their beliefs or were simply running a complex **scam** to control more **gullible** people.

Cargo cults occurred within indigenous knowledge systems because:

● interaction with Western products was often **superficial**

● details of Western product manufacture and use were not explained

● Western products arrived by means never seen before by indigenous people (e.g. by aircraft, **parachute**, ship, **jeep**)

● Western products were seen in the hands of colonizers, who were considered powerful and disruptive

● indigenous people do not have knowledge of Western manufacturing processes and apply a spiritual explanation to Western products.

The biologist Richard Dawkins has argued in his book *The God Delusion* (2006) that cargo cults show enough similarities between them to suggest they are a product of universal human psychological **traits**.

An example of a cargo cult within an indigenous knowledge system is seen among the Melanesian islanders in the years during and after the Second World War.

The Melanesian islands are in the South Pacific, northeast of Australia. During the Second World War, the islanders witnessed the build-up of military equipment from the Japanese and the Allies who both **occupied** the islands. The military **equipment** was dropped using parachutes and aircraft. Examples included: manufactured clothing, medicine, canned food, vehicles, tents, weapons, radios, **compasses**, etc.

Foreigners (in the form of soldiers) inhabited the islands and built airbases. They shared some of their equipment with the islanders who were their hosts.

At the end of the Second World War, the military left the islands, **abandoned** their airbases, and stopped dropping cargo. They took a lot of the equipment with them. This caused **anxiety** among some islanders who did not understand where the foreigners had come from or whether they would return.

The following behaviours developed.

- **Charismatic** individuals promised deliveries of more Western equipment (cargo). It was explained the cargo would be a gift from **ancestors**.
- Islanders **mimicked** the day-to-day activities and dress styles of US soldiers. For example, they performed parade ground **drills** with wooden or old **rifles**.
- Islanders imitated behaviours they had seen the soldiers, sailors, and airmen use. It was thought they were trying to get cargo to fall by parachute, or land in planes, or ships again.
  - Some islanders **carved** headphones from wood and wore them while sitting in **fake** control towers.
  - Some waved landing signals while standing on the old **runways**.
  - Some built life-size **replicas** of airplanes out of straw.
  - Some cut new runways out of the jungle.

The cult members thought that the foreigners had some special connection to the gods and ancestors of the natives. This is because they believed the gods and ancestors were the only beings powerful enough to produce such complex products/gadgets.

Knowledge question: To what extent can communism be considered a cargo cult?

Knowledge question: To what extent can liberal economic capitalism be considered a cargo cult?

Example 2 of millenarianism: The Prince Philip Movement

The Prince Philip Movement is a religious group. It is centered on the Kastom people around Yaohnanen village on the southern island of Tanna in Vanuatu (off the northeast coast of Australia). According to Shears (2009) they can be considered a cargo cult. Their basic belief is: Prince Philip, Duke of Edinburgh who is married to Queen Elizabeth II, is a divine being.

> Articulation sentence:
> Cargo cults and The Prince Phillip Movement are examples of the key concept of millenarianism. People rally around religious prophecies or leaders who predict a return to power. People also believe the defeat of their enemies is imminent and the accumulation of wealth is imminent.

What is the role of convention in this area?

Example of convention: monomyth

Joseph Campbell wrote *The Hero with a Thousand Faces* (published in 1949).

Subject vocabulary

communism an ideology associated with complete state ownership of many aspects of society such as industry

capitalism a theory whereby money should be created in largely free financial markets with little government interference

divine being a god

monomyth a myth shared by many cultures in various forms

Synonyms

occupied .... inhabited

equipment ..... material

abandoned .... left

anxiety .... worry

ancestors .... forebears

mimicked .... copied

rifles .... guns

fake .... not real

replicas .... models

General vocabulary

compasses instruments that show directions and have a needle that always points North

charismatic charming and persuasive

drills military training in which soldiers practise marching, using weapons, etc.

carved cut out of wood

runways long, specially prepared hard surfaces like roads on which aircraft land and take off

conventions agreed methods or ways of doing things

illiterate unable to read or write

courtship dance a special dance to attract a partner of the opposite sex

Campbell argued human societies had similar conventions:

- there are similarities in the *content* of stories across different indigenous cultures
- there are similarities in the *structure* of stories across different indigenous cultures.

Campbell called the phenomenon a monomyth. The film writer and director George Lucas acknowledged the influence of Campbell's monomyth on *Star Wars*.

An example of a monomyth is The Hero's Journey, which has been identified across many cultures, Figure 11.3.

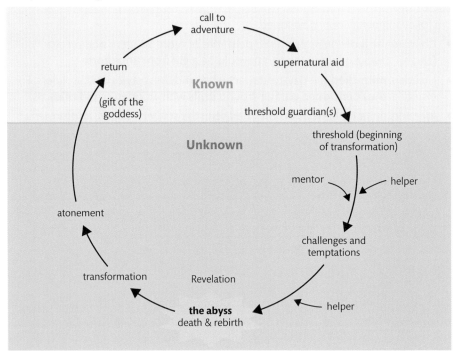

Figure 11.3 *The Hero's Journey.*

> Articulation sentence:
> A monomyth is an example of how human cultures have similar conventions. The Hero's Journey is an example of a monomyth.

Knowledge framework: Methodology

What are the methods or procedures used in this area and what is it about these methods that generates knowledge?

Method Example: The role of music for the Nama people of Southern Africa

Many of the Nama tribes live in Central Namibia and the other smaller groups live in Namaqualand, which is on the Namibian border with South Africa.

Like many illiterate people, the Nama consider music, dance, and story-telling very important. These have been passed down orally from one generation to the next. An example of using music to communicate meaning would be a Nama traditional courtship dance. The males and females line up and take turns to perform in front of each other.

What is the assumption underlying music in knowledge creation for the Nama?

Music allows knowledge to be communicated across generations and geographical spaces without the need for writing. The **melodies** and simple **lyrics** allow complex information to be stored and then repeated when necessary. Music also acts as a **cohesive force** on a tribe, promoting unity and identity through shared tradition.

What role do models play in this area of knowledge?

Knowledge claim: A model is a tool to allow for complex concepts to be understood in a more simple form.

Example: The Mabui of the Ryukyuan people of Japan

The Ryukyuan people of Japan are the indigenous people of the Ryukyu Islands between the islands of Kyushu and Taiwan. They believe in the notion of a *mabui*, or spirit. It can be compared with the Christian notion of a soul.

- The mabui is the **essence** of the self.
- The mabui is **immortal** and unique to the individual.
- The mabui of a dead person may **attach** itself to a living person, requiring a ritual of separation (*mabui-wakashi*).
- The Ryukyuan people believe that if there is a sudden death, the mabui may **cling** to the body of the dead person because it might not accept that it has to move on. They believe a ritual has to take place so it can find peace.
- The mabui is **transferable** through touching. For example, through a piece of jewellery that belonged to the dead person. It is believed objects can contain the mabui of dead people.
- Pictures or photographs can also contain one's mabui.
- The Ryukyuan people believe the mabui of children is not as attached to their physical body as it is in old people, due to their young age.

> Articulation sentence:
> The concept of the mabui acts as a **mechanism** to allow for the existence of an independent self.

What is the assumption underlying the mabui in knowledge creation?

The Ryukyuan people believe the mabui is a defining characteristic of the self. It can be seen as way to explain the complex and abstract notion of the self. The Ryukyuan people use it to explain problems people may have.

For example:

- The mabui can leave the body, resulting in lost mabui (*mabui-utushi*) with **various** physical results, such as a physical illness, or an unwillingness to engage with the world and perform tasks (**lethargy**).
- The mabui can be lost as the result of stress, loneliness, being suddenly frightened, or helplessness.
- The mabui can be lost due to unhappy relationships. The person becomes **depressed**.
- Rituals can be performed to bring back a lost mabui or protect one that may be about to leave.

> Articulation sentence:
> The mabui is a model that helps the Ryukyuan people understand why they are ill and how they can be helped.

Subject vocabulary

ritual ceremony or behaviour that is always performed in the same way and has deep significance for the individual

mechanism the means by which a cause produces an effect

Synonyms

melodies .... tunes

various .... diverse

depressed ...... extremely sad

General vocabulary

lyrics the words of a song

cohesive force something that brings people closer together

essence the most basic and important quality of something

immortal unable to die

attach connect to

cling hold on, especially when feeling unsafe

transferable able to move from one place to another

lethargy a feeling of having no energy and no interest in doing anything

trading routes pathways that allow people to trade goods

closed market places an economic notion whereby other countries do not have access to a market place/country; this allows the colonizer to control prices

labour the workforce

military dominance the superiority of one military force over others

naval relating to navies

navigational aids devices that help with finding routes; for example, maps and compasses; knowledge of the stars

agricultural purposes related to farming

racial extermination killing a particular group of people in an systematic way because they belong to a certain race

collective punishment punishing individual people because they belong to a particular group even though they themselves have not committed a crime

Synonyms

imposes......... forces

enrich............ make richer

bounty .... wealth, treasure

General vocabulary

secure make something safe

telegraph an old-fashioned method of sending messages using radio or electrical signals

off limits out of range; forbidden

scramble chase a particular goal in a disorderly way

nomadic constantly travelling from place to place and not living in any one place for very long

confiscated removed from a person

mining digging large holes in the ground in order to remove coal, gold, diamonds, etc.

genocide mass killing of a group of people because of such things as religion, race, or ethnicity

precursor something that happened or existed before something else and influenced its development

Knowledge framework: Historical development

What is the significance of the key points in the historical development of this area of knowledge?

Key point 1: The impact of colonization

Colonization is the process whereby a non-indigenous population **imposes** itself on an indigenous group. This usually involves political, cultural, military, and economic imposition – although it does not have to involve all of these to be considered colonization. Human beings are somewhat territorial creatures. Therefore, colonization is likely to have occurred among different tribes on some level throughout human history. Europeans initiated a period of intense colonization beginning in the 16th century. European powers began extending their influence overseas in an attempt to **secure** trading routes, closed market places, cheap labour, and military dominance.

Indigenous land became accessible because there were:

- improvements in naval technology (ship design and navigational aids)
- improvements in military technology (cannon and rifles)
- improvements in communication technology (the **telegraph**) that would allow European powers to dominate new lands
- improvements in medical technology (the treatment and cure of tropical diseases) that would allow Europeans to survive and thrive in lands that were previously **off limits** to them.

Often colonization was carried out with the encouragement of the Christian Church which saw the process of colonization as a way to save non-Christian souls and then **enrich** itself with foreign **bounty** such as gold. The late 19th century was a particularly intense time for colonization. European powers focused on Africa as this was a relatively uncolonized area of the Earth. It happened very quickly. In 1870 only 10% of Africa was under European control; by 1914 it was 90%. The short time period in which it happened has given rise to the phrase 'Scramble for Africa'.

Example of the impact of colonization: The Nama of South Africa

Before colonization, the Nama people of Southern Africa had a **nomadic** way of life. The Germans waged war with many tribes in the region from 1904 to 1907. They wanted to control the land and use it for agricultural purposes. The Germans **confiscated** large herds of cattle and the Nama were either forced into the desert, imprisoned in concentration camps (where many died of disease), or became slave labourers – **mining** for diamonds, or building railways.

The actions of the Germans led to what has become known as the Herero and Nama **Genocide** (the Herero were another indigenous group affected). This refers to the German campaign of racial extermination and collective punishment. In total, 24 000–100 000 Herero and 10 000 Nama died (e.g. Friedrichsmeyer et al. 1999).

Why is the Herero and Nama Genocide significant?

The Herero and Nama Genocide was the deliberate killing by Germans of a racial group simply because they belonged to that particular racial group. It is now seen by many historians as a **precursor** to the Nazi extermination of the Jews – usually referred to as the Holocaust.

The Herero and Nama Genocide can be seen as precursor to the Nazi extermination of the Jews because:

- ideas of racial **supremacy** of one group of people over another group of people were established
- organizational practices were established (for example, concentration camps and how to **run** them)
- the norm of conducting medical experiments on an 'inferior' group of people was established
- individuals gained expertise and experience of how to conduct a genocide; this knowledge was then passed on to others.

> Articulation sentence:
> The Herero and Nama Genocide is significant because it shows the impact of colonization. It can be seen as precursor to the Nazi extermination of the Jews. It established the idea of racial supremacy with the German colonizers. It also established norms of thoughts, feelings, and behaviours, which the colonizers then implemented elsewhere.

Key point 2: The impact of globalization

Globalization is the process of international integration. It usually refers to cultural and economic integration.

- Cultural integration: coming from the interaction of people with products (such as films, music, clothes, food) and ideas (such as gender and sexual equality; animal welfare).
- Economic integration: coming from the increasing interdependence of national economies and the increasing cross-border movement of goods, services, technologies, and money.

The integration is usually seen as being Western led and Western dominated.

Example 1: The Achuar and Secoya of Ecuador and Peru

The Achuar are an Amazonian community. They number about 18 500 individuals along either side of the border in between Ecuador and Peru. The Secoya occupy the same region and number about 1100.

What is the impact of globalization on the Achuar and Secoya?

- Major oil pipelines run above rivers used for bathing and drinking. When these oil pipelines leak, they **pollute** the water. Occidental Petroleum Corporation (Oxy) is a US-based oil and gas company. In 2012, they were fined an **undisclosed** sum for the rate of birth **defects** and early deaths caused by oil leaks polluting local water supplies.
- Industrial activity (such as rubber extraction, palm oil production, and oil activity) has significantly reduced the indigenous people's territory.
- Traditional food and water activities have changed due to contamination. For example, the Secoya can no longer trust the fish they catch because of heavy oil pollution.
- New diseases including **sexually transmitted infections (STIs)** have been introduced, as local people interact with non-indigenous workers.
- Western business practices have been introduced as local people interact with non-indigenous workers.
- Violent interactions have increased as the Achuar and Secoya try to protect what they see as **rightfully** theirs.

Subject vocabulary

concentration camps prisons where large numbers of people can be held for a long periods of time

Synonyms

supremacy ..... superiority

run .... organize

pollute .... poison

undisclosed .... not revealed

defects .... faults

rightfully .... correctly

General vocabulary

integration groups becoming closer together

sexually transmitted infections (STIs) diseases that are passed on via sexual activity

Articulation sentence:

Globalization has had an impact on the Achuar and Secoya because non-indigenous people use their territory and bring diseases, pollution, the potential for conflict, and Western habits and norms.

Example 2: The Wopkaimin tribe of western Papua New Guinea

The Wopkaimin are a small aboriginal tribe. Their traditional land is within the Star Mountains in western Papua New Guinea.

What is the impact of globalization on the Wopkaimin?

- The third largest open-pit copper and gold **mine** in the world is located in the traditional territory of the Wopkaimin (Hyndman, 1994). The mine is known as the Ok Tedi Mine. The mine owners built a modern town next to the mine to serve the miners.
  - The mine has brought a large number of non-indigenous people into the region. These people have introduced new ways of life. For example, paid jobs are available to the Wopkaimin, who can then buy Western products such as food, cigarettes, and beer. However, the jobs are low-paid and low-skilled.
  - The mine has polluted water and agricultural areas.

General vocabulary

mine an area of land that is dug up for minerals, gold, oil, etc.

Articulation sentence:

Globalization has had an impact on indigenous knowledge systems by importing non-indigenous products, business practices, and ways of thinking and behaving.

Rules and guidelines

Each student must write an essay and submit it to the IB for external assessment.

- This essay counts as $\frac{2}{3}$ of the TOK grade.
- The essay must be in a standard 12-point font, double-spaced, and include the word count.
- The IB gives out six essay titles for each session. These are called the prescribed titles.
- The student must use one of the prescribed titles EXACTLY. The student may not change the prescribed title in any way.
- The essay should be focused on answering the prescribed title.
- The essay should include two or three new knowledge questions.
- The essay must include claims and counterclaims.
- The essay must use real-life examples to support its claims.
- The essay should link the knowledge question to areas of knowledge and ways of knowing.

> Articulation sentence:
> The essay should be focused on answering the prescribed title.

Subject vocabulary

external assessment examination of written materials that are sent to examiners outside the school

claims arguments or statements

counterclaims arguments or statements that oppose a claim

real-life examples examples taken from academic sources, schoolwork, or actual experience

thesis proposition, statement of the main idea

implications the indirect results of an action or a thought

The essay-planning document

The student should meet with the teacher three times during the essay-writing process. The teacher and the student must keep a record of these meetings. This record must be sent with the final essay.

Meeting 1

The student and the teacher discuss what the essay title means.

Meeting 2

The student discusses their ideas and plans for their essay with the teacher. The following items should be in the discussion:

- thesis or point of view
- areas of knowledge used in the essay
- ways of knowing used in the essay
- new knowledge questions
- real-life examples
- claims and counterclaims
- connections
- different perspectives
- implications.

Meeting 3

The student gives the teacher a full draft of the essay. The teacher may write general comments on the draft. The students can ask the teacher questions later, but the teacher is not allowed to write more comments after the third meeting.

> Articulation sentence:
> The essay must use real-life examples to support its claims.

Academic honesty

The IB is strict about plagiarism. The student must be careful to cite any work that is not original. The student must be sure to include all quotations, and to note the work and ideas of other people. The student should use a standard reference style. In most cases, the students can use the school's style for referencing and bibliography. This is very important: an essay that does not have correct **citation** can cause a student to lose the IB diploma.

Essay length

The maximum length of the essay is 1600 words. There is a **penalty** of one point (out of 10) for going over 1600 words. The word count includes quotations. It does not include footnotes, references, graphs, or images.

Bibliography/reference list

The bibliography or works cited list should show:

- the author, title, date, and the place of publication
- the name of the publisher or web address
- if a website is used, the citation must include the web address and date of access.

> Articulation sentence:
> The student must be careful to cite any work that is not original.

Understanding the rubric

The TOK essay examiner gives a score between 0 and 10. The examiner bases the score on how the essay corresponds to the following rubric: *Does the student present an appropriate and cogent analysis of knowledge questions in discussing the title?*

The rubric can be considered in three sections:

- understanding knowledge questions
- quality of analysis of knowledge questions
- a list of words that gives a good overall description of the essay.

First section: Understanding knowledge questions

To score highly, the essay should:

- very carefully study the essay prompt, which is often a knowledge question
- find at least one more knowledge question which must clearly connect to the essay prompt
- focus on the knowledge questions throughout
- examine different perspectives
- make strong links to relevant areas of knowledge and ways of knowing.

Second section: Quality of analysis of knowledge questions

To score highly, the essay should:

- make clear arguments
- find appropriate real-life examples
- evaluate these real-life examples
- find counterclaims
- explore the counterclaims
- find implications.

Third section: Some possible characteristics

To score highly, the essay should be:

- cogent
- accomplished
- discerning
- individual

- lucid
- insightful
- compelling.

The essential elements of the TOK essay

The two main jobs of the TOK essay are:

- to identify knowledge questions from the prescribed title
- to answer these knowledge questions using TOK analysis.

The knowledge questions must relate to the IB prescribed essay question. The examples in the essay must be selected and used in order to address the knowledge questions.

Below is a discussion of the essential elements of the TOK essay. The student must understand what each of these elements is. A strong essay will include all of these elements.

Articulation sentence:
The examples in the essay must be selected and used in order to address the knowledge questions.

Knowledge questions

It is critical to understand what knowledge questions are. Here are five example knowledge questions.

Knowledge question: How is knowledge produced, obtained, or achieved?

Knowledge question: How and why is knowledge renewed or reshaped?

Knowledge question: How do people acquire and search for knowledge?

Knowledge question: How do people produce knowledge?

Knowledge question: How do people shape knowledge and cause it to become accepted?

There are several important things to note about these knowledge questions. First, they are general. They are not about a specific way of knowing or area of knowledge. A good knowledge question can be applied to different examples and situations. Knowledge questions are about *how* human beings gain knowledge. Knowledge questions are not about specific subjects such as physics or economics. Knowledge questions would be about the methods that physicists and economists use. They are about things like **uncertainty**, **hypothesis**, theory, experimental method, and bias. Knowledge questions look at the similarities, and differences, in the methods that physicists and economists use. For example, they both use mathematics, models, and make **predictions**. Physicists and economists attempt to be scientific and **systematic**. But they study very different kinds of systems and so they encounter different kinds of problems.

Articulation sentence:
Knowledge questions are about how human beings gain knowledge.

The essay should show understanding of and analyse knowledge questions. Students must find additional knowledge questions. These knowledge questions must clearly connect with the prescribed title from the IB.

Perspectives

The essay must look at different perspectives. Perspectives are viewpoints, or ways of looking at an issue. For example, inflation is an important concept in economics. The essay could look at inflation from the perspective of a professional economist. But the essay could also look at inflation from the perspective of the government, or of consumers, or of poor people who can no longer afford a basic item.

Areas of knowledge and ways of knowing

The essay must include several areas of knowledge and ways of knowing. A typical essay might include two areas of knowledge and two ways of knowing. The areas of knowledge and ways of knowing must link to the prescribed essay question and to the real-life examples. An essay using an example from natural science might look at reason and imagination. An essay using an example from human science might look at memory and language. The knowledge questions may help to make links between different areas of knowledge and ways of knowing. A strong TOK essay constantly goes back and forth between real-life examples and knowledge questions.

Clear arguments

The essay must take a clear stand. The essay must try to convince the reader of a particular position. For example, a prescribed essay question might ask how models help and hinder the pursuit of knowledge. The student might show three ways in which a model helps people understand and two ways in which it hinders understanding. Every area of knowledge has models. Each of these models has strengths and weaknesses. The essay might show why the models are important and why the models also have limitations.

Real-life examples

The examples in the essay must be real-life examples. They must not be hypothetical examples that the student has made up. The real-life example can be local, regional, national, international, or global. The real-life example could be a chemistry experiment, an orchestral piece, a controversy about appropriate clothing for school, or a question of the basis for human gender. A good real-life example is sometimes about a controversy. The real-life example must relate to the knowledge question. The student should describe the real-life example briefly. If the real-life example requires a long explanation, it is not a good example for a TOK essay.

Counterclaims

Counterclaims are ideas or arguments that oppose the main idea, or argument.

Implications

The implications are conclusions that can be drawn from the argument. The implications may be more indirect. The implications may also suggest consequences or results.

Analysis in the TOK essay

The IB asks students to explore and evaluate in the TOK essay. What does this mean? What does it mean to analyse? Below are some key techniques or terms that the IB uses in TOK and in other subjects. The essay should use some of these techniques. Although the essay uses examples from subjects like economics, chemistry, and theatre, it is not an essay about economics, chemistry, or theatre. It mainly is an essay about the nature of knowledge. The essay should focus on how knowledge is acquired and evaluated in these subjects. Therefore, most of the essay will be analytical. The description of the example should always be short. The emphasis is on the analysis.

> Articulation sentence:
> The essay should focus on how knowledge is acquired and evaluated.

Analyse

To analyse means to study closely and to break into parts. The goal is to find what is essential or to show the structure.

Compare and contrast

To compare and contrast means to show what is similar and what is different.

Contrast

To contrast means to look for what is different.

Define

To define means to give a precise meaning to a word or a concept. Dictionary definitions are seldom enough. The student should look for several definitions of the key term or word. The student should then combine these definitions to create one that serves the essay well.

Evaluate

To evaluate means to look for strengths and weaknesses.

Examine

To examine means to look for assumptions and connections.

Explain or justify

To explain or justify means to show reasons and causes.

To what extent ...

Many knowledge questions begin with the phrase, *To what extent* ... This suggests that a range of answers is possible. This kind of question invites the student to look for a variety of perspectives, and to look for claims and counterclaims.

> Articulation sentence:
> A strong TOK essay is based on clear examples and relevant knowledge questions.

Choosing knowledge questions and real-life examples

A strong TOK essay is based on clear examples and relevant knowledge questions. The TOK essay is not a research paper. Students should find real-life examples from their IB courses and from their own knowledge. The essay must be based on strong examples. Students should describe their real-life examples as briefly as possible. Therefore, long, **complicated** examples are not good for the essay.

IB Prescribed title 1

Using one or more examples, demonstrate how models help and hinder the search for knowledge in science.

Here are some real-life examples.

- A globe puts the Earth into human-size dimensions. It shows relationships and shapes, but it is highly **simplified**.
- A fashion model displays clothing. The emphasis is on the clothing, not the person.
- Sound waves are like ocean waves. It is possible to observe what ocean waves look like and what they do. It is not possible to see sound waves and therefore a visible model is very helpful.
- A model airplane is quite simple in comparison to a real airplane. A model airplane can range from a child's small plastic toy, to a radio-controlled model, to a piece of the wing that engineers test in a wind tunnel.

> Articulation sentence:
> Students should find real-life examples from their IB courses and from their own knowledge.

Additional knowledge questions are 'secondary knowledge' questions that have been extracted from the main knowledge question of the prescribed title.

Knowledge question: Why are models and simplified representations necessary to understand complex systems?

Knowledge question: Which factors make one model better than another?

Knowledge question: How does the choice of a model influence understanding, research, and experimentation?

IB Prescribed title 2

That which is accepted as knowledge today is sometimes discarded tomorrow.

Here are some real-life examples.

- The Oedipus complex is the idea developed by the psychologist Sigmund Freud that young children have an unconscious sexual desire for the parent of the opposite sex. This idea was a central part of Freudian analysis. The idea is no longer important in psychology, but it had a major effect on the development of the subject.
- Einstein revolutionized physics with his general theory of relativity. Einstein demonstrated that Newton's ideas about gravity were not correct. However, despite Einstein's revolution, much of Newtonian physics continues to be useful.

- Until the middle of the 19th century, doctors thought that cholera was caused by something in the air. This was known as the miasma theory of disease. In 1854, the English physician John Snow showed that an outbreak of cholera in London was due to bad water from a pump. This was an important development that led to the germ theory of disease. Nonetheless, some diseases such as chicken pox and tuberculosis are airborne.

- The economic ideas of the German philosopher and economist Karl Marx were extremely influential in the 20th century. For example, Marxist economics was the basis of the Soviet Union economic system. Marxist economics includes a criticism of capitalism, and an emphasis on labour and class struggle. Very few countries still use Marxist economics, but the system is still an important intellectual concept.

Here are some knowledge questions related to the prescribed title.

Knowledge question: How and why is knowledge renewed or reshaped?

Knowledge question: Why do certain ideas or concepts become influential?

Knowledge question: At what point is knowledge so changed or altered that it becomes new knowledge?

Knowledge question: What kinds of proof are necessary to show that knowledge is no longer valid?

IB Prescribed title 3

The possession of knowledge carries an ethical responsibility.

Here are some real-life examples.

- Modern media communicates information about natural disasters such as earthquakes, floods, and tsunamis very rapidly. Do people then have the obligation to send money or help out with disaster relief in some way?

- In her book, *Dead Aid*, the Zambian economist Dambisa Moyo states that aid to Africa is a humanitarian and economic disaster. This is a troubling claim and suggests that efforts to help are not always successful.

- Companies such as Google and Facebook now possess immense amounts of data. This data includes sensitive personal information about individuals. Clearly these companies have great responsibilities. But who controls them? Who sets the limits on their ethical responsibilities?

Here are some knowledge questions related to the prescribed title.

Knowledge question: How does knowledge lead to further thought and action?

Knowledge question: To what degree should we limit the pursuit of knowledge?

Knowledge question: Are people responsible for the unintended consequences of their actions?

Knowledge question: What are the proper limits of ethical responsibility?

Articulation sentence:
A strong TOK essay develops and examines new knowledge questions.

Subject vocabulary

cholera an infectious bacterial disease that is carried by water and affects the small intestines

tuberculosis an infectious bacterial disease that affects the lungs

Synonyms

influential ...... authoritative

General vocabulary

airborne something that is carried on the air

Subject vocabulary

responsibility duty, obligation

obligation duty, responsibility

pursuit of knowledge looking for knowledge, trying to discover knowledge

unintended consequences the results of actions that were not seen in advance

General vocabulary

tsunami huge wave caused by an undersea earthquake

humanitarian caring for people

immense extremely large

sensitive personal information information about health, finances, and other very personal matters

The TOK essay outline

Students may use the following outline or template as a way of organizing their essay. The template includes starter sentences that can be used to introduce ideas and parts of the essay. The template is useful for organization and to **ensure** that the essay includes all the necessary elements.

INTRODUCTION

Restatement of question

Rewrite the prescribed title to show understanding.

I understand the prescribed title to be ...

Definitions

Define significant terms in the prescribed title.

I have identified the following words in the prescribed title as important and in need of clear definitions.

They are ... and they can be defined as ...

Knowledge questions

Identify the new knowledge questions.

I have identified the following relevant knowledge questions ...

Areas of knowledge and ways of knowing

Identify the areas of knowledge and ways of knowing.

The following AOK's and WOK's are relevant to this prescribed title ...

Plan of action

Take a position on the prescribed title.

My position on this question is ... / I will show in this essay that ...

THE MAIN PARAGRAPHS

Topic sentence

The topic sentence introduces the reader to the main idea of the paragraph.

Real-life example

Introduce the real-life example to support, illustrate, and justify arguments.

My real-life example is ...

Links

Link the real-life example to the prescribed title in more detail.

My real-life example has links to the prescribed title because ...

Related knowledge questions

Students introduce new knowledge questions. These new knowledge questions must link to the prescribed title and the real-life example. These new knowledge questions are more specific to the real-life example. The student probably only needs to introduce two or three new knowledge questions in the essay.

This raises the following knowledge question ...

Areas of knowledge and ways of knowing

Analyse areas of knowledge and ways of knowing that relate to the prescribed title or the related knowledge questions.

A relevant way of knowing for my example is ... because ...

A relevant area of knowledge for my example is ... because ...

Perspective

A good essay should explore the knowledge questions or the real-life examples from more than one perspective.

My example could be viewed from the perspective of ...

Assumption

An assumption could be an unproven starting point or a knowledge claim.

The assumptions supporting this argument are ...

This example assumes that ...

Counterclaims

It is important to identify counterclaims. Counterclaims are ideas or arguments that oppose the main idea, or argument.

The counterclaims to this argument are ...

Concluding sentence

The concluding sentence ties this paragraph to the essay question.

The previous examples and arguments demonstrate that ...

In conclusion, it is possible to argue that ...

CONCLUSION

The conclusion demonstrates why the arguments in the essay are good. The conclusion shows why the original position of the essay is valid.

In conclusion, the arguments in my essay demonstrate that ...

Implications

Determine the implications of the argument. The implications are conclusions that can be drawn from the argument. The implications may be more indirect. The implications may also suggest consequences or results.

The implications of my argument are ...

Subject vocabulary

conclusion the part of the essay that summarizes the main ideas and arguments

consequences results, the effects of an idea, or action

General rules for the presentation

- Students must make one or more individual and/or small group presentations to the class during the course. This means students can give **multiple** presentations throughout the course.
- If a student makes more than one presentation, the teacher should choose the best one (or the best group presentation in which the student participated) for the purposes of assessment.

Students are **not** permitted to offer presentations on the same specific subject matter more than once.

- Presentations must be delivered in a language accessible to all members of the class.
- Each real-life situation and knowledge question should be treated only once in a particular teaching group.
- The maximum group size is three.
- Approximately 10 minutes per presenter should be allowed, up to a maximum of approximately 30 minutes per group.
- Presentations should be **scheduled** to allow time for class discussion afterwards.
- Interaction and **audience participation** are allowed during the presentation. However, there must be a clearly identifiable input from the presenter(s) that can be assessed.
- The presentation should take place towards the end of the course, as otherwise students may not have had the chance to develop key skills such as formulating knowledge questions which are key to this task.
- Presentations may take many forms, such as **lectures**, **interviews**, or **debates**. Students may use **multimedia**, costumes, or **props** to support their presentations.
- While pre-recorded inserts within a presentation are permissible, the presentation itself must be a live experience and not a recording of the presentation.
- Under no circumstances should the presentation be simply an essay read aloud to the class.

What the teacher should do

- Provide the students with a paper copy and a digital copy of the Presentation Planning document.
- Give the presenter(s) opportunities to develop their presentation during lessons.
- Help the students advance the aims of the TOK course by guiding them towards suitable approaches.
- Provide **sufficient** time for the students to prepare their material.
- Encourage and support the student(s) in the preparation of the presentation.
- Provide guidance on presentation skills.
- Assess the presentation using the presentation assessment **instrument**.

What students should do

- Refer to and update the Presentation Planning document either on paper or digitally.
- Make use of class time that has been given to them.
- Use their **initiative** to seek advice from the teacher either in person or by email.
- Identify and explore a knowledge question raised by a real-life situation that is of interest to them. The selected real-life situation may arise from their personal life, from school, or may have local cultural relevance. Or it can arise from wider national, international, or global contexts.
- Treat the academic knowledge of others the same way as they would in an essay. Therefore, students should be careful to cite and reference correctly the ideas of other people that appear in the presentation.
- Extract a knowledge question from a real-life situation. The knowledge question should be addressed using the concepts and ideas the student has learned in the TOK course.
- Make sure the knowledge question is general enough to apply to other real-life situations.

The Presentation Planning document

Students are strongly encouraged to have three meetings with the teacher. During these meetings the Presentation Planning document is completed by the students. The completed Presentation Planning document should be given to the teacher before the presentation begins.

Meeting 1

The aim of this meeting is to select a real-life situation and an initial knowledge question. The students can bring a choice selection and the teacher can advise on these, but the final decisions belong with the student(s). By the end of the meeting, the students should have chosen a real-life situation and a knowledge question.

Meeting 2

The aim of this meeting is for the students to explain the connections between their real-life situation and their central knowledge question. From these connections further knowledge questions will be formulated.

Meeting 3

The aim of this meeting is for students to explain how the further knowledge questions will be addressed. The teacher will check the examples used to support the further knowledge questions and will check the appropriateness of the further real-life situations.

Subject vocabulary

cite to mention something as an example, especially one that supports, proves, or explains an idea, or situation; the example must be identified in the presentation and the original source identified

reference to mention another book, article, etc. that contains information connected with the main subject of an essay or presentation; the full source of the information or quotation must be given

concepts ideas of how something is, or how something should be done

Synonyms

initiative .... drive, action

How to choose real-life situations and knowledge questions

Real-life situations

Real-life situations should come from the real world. They do not have to be controversial but if they have caused controversy, forming a knowledge question can be more **straightforward**. They can come from a variety of local or global sources including:

- statements by politicians, artists, cultural leaders, etc. that create controversy
- art, religious texts *
- major advancements in science or art
- cultural norms that create controversy in other cultures
- new laws that create controversy.

Knowledge questions

Knowledge questions can be about (but are not limited to):

- what impact a real-life situation has had on knowledge creation
- what impact a real-life situation has had on an ethical perspective
- what impact a real-life situation has had on a cultural perspective
- what impact a real-life situation has had on an academic subject (an area of knowledge).

Knowledge questions are usually introduced by one of the phrases:

- *To what extent ...*
- *How can ...*
- *What is the role of ...*

Prefixing knowledge questions with these phrases ensures the questions assess:

- how far a real-life situation has influenced knowledge creation
- how far a real-life situation can be seen as ethical or unethical, from different cultural perspectives
- how far a real-life situation may change a cultural perspective.

TOK Presentation Assessment instrument

What students are expected to do

- **Focus on a well-formulated knowledge question**
  This means the question should be one sentence. For example, it could focus on an ethical perspective, a cultural perspective, and/or relate to an academic subject (an area of knowledge).

  > Articulation sentence:
  > The knowledge question we have chosen is ...

- **Clearly connect to a specified real-life situation**
  This means real-life situations can come from a variety of local or global sources. There should be a clear identification of what the situation is. For example, if a politician appears on a news programme and makes a controversial statement,

Subject vocabulary

real world anything that has really happened and been commented on; this can include works of fiction published in a real book by a real author (but not products of the student's imagination)

controversial producing different opinions that cause arguments

religious texts religious books or documents*

ethical about moral principles and practices

well-formulated clear and relating to a cultural, ethical, or political question

Synonyms

straightforward
.... simple

General vocabulary

prefixing attaching at the beginning

* (REMEMBER: some cultural groups take offence if their religious texts are not treated as expected; students are strongly encouraged to check with teachers and/or cultural experts and to think about local cultural norms before using religious texts or imagery)

the student should make clear what the situation is. What is the controversy? Is it the statement made by the politician, or the appearance and **airtime** given to the politician on the news programme? Students should brainstorm the potential real-life situations that come out of one real-life situation; choose one and then save the others for future reference in the presentation.

Articulation sentence:
The real-life situation we have chosen is …

Subject vocabulary

analysis detailed examination

General vocabulary

airtime time given on TV/radio

- **Use convincing arguments that investigate different perspectives**
  This means students should decide how a question can be seen from different perspectives. Each perspective should be addressed in the presentation.

  Articulation sentence:
  The real-life situation can be seen from different perspectives. For example …

- **Relate the analysis to the real-life situation and to other real-life situations**
  This means students should take the main points/outcomes of analysis that have been raised by the presentation and say why they are important to their original real-life situation. And to others.

  Articulation sentence:
  The outcomes of our presentation have been … These can be related back to our real-life situation because … They also relate to other real-life situations because …

How to plan the presentation

Students should move through the process of choosing a real-life situation and knowledge questions by following Figure 13.1. The dotted line represents the division between the real world and the academic world of TOK.

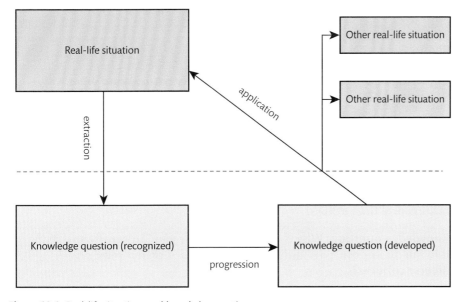

Figure 13.1 *Real-life situations and knowledge questions.*

A summary of the main requirements for the TOK presentation

- Presentations must be delivered in a language accessible to all members of the class.
- The maximum group size is three. Approximately 10 minutes per presenter.
- The presentation should take place towards the end of the course, and teachers should provide class time and advice during the development of the presentation.
- Students may use multimedia, costumes, or props to support their presentations.
- While pre-recorded inserts within a presentation are permissible, the presentation itself must be a **live** experience and not a recording of the presentation.
- Under no circumstances should the presentation be simply an essay read aloud to the class.
- Students should identify and explore a knowledge question raised by a local or global real-life situation.
- The knowledge question should be general enough to apply to other real-life situations.
- Students should identify and explore further knowledge questions, and then state how they are connected to further real-life situations.
- If students incorporate the thoughts and ideas of others into the presentation, this must be acknowledged.

Example 1

Real-life situation

Usain Bolt is a world-renowned athlete who relies on an extreme and enhanced diet. His food is prepared by a **nutritionist**. As a consequence, his performance is **enhanced**. Despite the enhancement qualities of this diet, this training method is considered natural, and thus both **moral** and legal by the athletic governing bodies.

Central knowledge question

Knowledge question: How do we know what is 'natural' and what is 'unnatural'?

Further knowledge questions

Knowledge question: To what extent can diet be considered chemical enhancement?

Knowledge question: Why are some scientific applications considered more moral than others?

Knowledge question: Why is the notion of 'fair play' culturally specific? Is it 'fair' to impose a definitive cultural standard of 'fair play' on diverse cultures?

Knowledge question: To what extent is the use of chemical enhancers for students in exams an example of unfair play?

Further real-life situations

- Other athletes who have altered their biology through external means (e.g. athletes who train at high altitude to achieve a higher red blood cell count)

Example 2

Real-life situation

Female genital mutilation (FGM) is a procedure that **intentionally alters** or causes injury to the female genital organs for non-medical reasons. The practice of FGM has been illegal in the UK since 1985. It is also illegal to arrange for a girl to be taken abroad for FGM. If caught, offenders face a large fine and a prison sentence of up to 14 years. Furthermore, doctors are required to report suspected cases of FGM to the authorities.

Therefore, UK law prohibits FGM. However, FGM is a practice considered normal and culturally enriching by a small number of cultural groups and communities who live in the UK. By making FGM **illegal**, the UK is forcing subcultural groups to abide by the beliefs of a dominant cultural group.

Central knowledge question

Knowledge question: To what extent can cultural values be placed on a hierarchy?

Further knowledge questions

Knowledge question: To what extent can multiculturalism be successful if some values held by some people are seen as better than others?

Knowledge question: Is it possible to accept all cultural practices as equal under the basis of multiculturalism? If not, what does this mean for the concept of multiculturalism?

Knowledge question: To what extent should the wider society have to pay for the consequences of cultural values they do not believe in?

Further real-life situations

- The burqa ban in France
- The ban on female drivers in Saudi Arabia
- Forced or arranged marriages between close relatives, which can lead to babies born with disabilities

Example 3

Real-life situation

The photograph *Immersion (Piss Christ)* by American artist Andres Serrano (2011) is part of Serrano's series showing religious objects **submerged** in fluids such as blood, milk, and urine. *Immersion* is a picture of a Christ on a cross immersed in blood and urine.

Central knowledge question

Knowledge question: To what extent can 'offensive' actions be a valid part of the cultural process?

Further knowledge questions

Knowledge question: To what extent should art be allowed to challenge the collective morality (the cultural norm)?

Knowledge question: To what extent can a group of people impose their perception of morality on another group?

Further real-life situations

● American church groups who **picket** funerals of US soldiers **killed in action**

● In Germany the state has made it illegal to to deny **the Holocaust**

Example 4

Real-life situation

Any animal that has been claimed by a peer-reviewed researcher to be able to understand and express language. Examples include Alex, the parrot; Nim Chimpsky, the chimpanzee; Kanzi, the bonobo.

Central knowledge question

Knowledge question: To what extent is language uniquely human?

Further knowledge questions

Knowledge question: What is language?

Knowledge question: What is the difference between language and communication?

Knowledge question: If artificial intelligence or animals can be said to understand and express language, does this alter human moral obligations towards them?

Further real-life situations

● **Artificial intelligence** that understands and expresses language either now or in the future

Example 5

Real-life situation

In October 2012, a group of scientists in Italy were found guilty of failing to give adequate warning about an **impending** earthquake to the people of L'Aquila in 2009. They were sentenced to 6 years in prison.

Central knowledge question

Knowledge question: In the sciences, to what extent can we predict with confidence?

Further knowledge questions

Knowledge question: To what extent are scientists responsible for sharing scientific knowledge?

Knowledge question: To what extent can scientists be held accountable for failures in scientific method?

Knowledge question: To what extent should confidence levels in scientific results be influenced by morality?

Knowledge question: To what extent should scientists be detached from the ethical values of the communities they work within?

Further real-life situations

- Trials of life-saving drugs that do not meet scientific **thresholds** of causation
- Scientists who work outside religious orthodoxies and are punished

Presentation DOs

Suggestions for what you should be doing for your presentation.

- Do keep the knowledge questions simple enough to answer in the time you have available.
- Do make sure you can find research from appropriate sources before you decide on a question.
- Do make sure everyone in the group knows their exact role in the research and presentation process.
- Do have lots of knowledge questions that are linked to the main knowledge question **lined up** ready to answer.
- Do see the further knowledge questions and further real-life examples as their own sections that have to be addressed but using less time.
- Do make sure you practise the presentation many times before you present in front of your teacher.
- Do get **study buddies**; other TOK students whom you can present to away from school and who can give you advice.
- Do **return the favour** and be a study buddy for other groups.
- Do see the presentation as a clear process moving from a real-life situation to a knowledge question to further knowledge questions and then to other real-life situations.
- Do work within groups.
- Do use **note cards** to keep focused.
- Do cite and reference academic ideas the same way as you would in an essay.

Presentation DON'Ts

Suggestions for what you should *not* be doing for your presentation.

- Don't try and to change the world. Keep within the limits of your time.
- Don't spend more than 4 minutes in a 20-minute presentation on describing your real-life situation.
- Don't spend more than 6 minutes in a 30-minute presentation on describing your real-life situation.
- Don't **overuse** quotations.
- Don't overuse pre-recorded videos.
- Don't overuse props or drama.
- Don't write a big idea without a correct citation. You are not expected to define big ideas yourself. You are expected to find definitions from academics who have already defined them.
- Don't see the presentation as one block of time you have to fill in. Take each knowledge question and plan the time you will spend on each. For example, each knowledge question can be addressed in 3 or 4 minutes.
- Don't use the same academic more than three or four times to explain an idea. If you are doing this, you need to do more research.
- Don't start sentences with phrases such as 'Most people ...' . They are not considered academic.

Subject vocabulary

study buddies other individuals studying the same subject who can act as support, and give encouragement and new ideas

note cards small pieces of paper with short sentences written on them to help prompt the speaker

General vocabulary

lined up prepared and in order

return the favour help someone who has helped you

Synonyms

overuse .... use too much

Index